Dr. Eric Kaplan is one of the most highly endorsed authors of all time!

"Six Time Bestselling Author" and **"Four-time # 1 Bestselling Author"** now presents his latest book **"CAN'T STOP ME"**. **Dr. Kaplan** and his books have been highly acclaimed and endorsed by such people as President Donald Trump, Jack Canfield, Tom McMillen, Brian Tracy, Marla Maples, Kathy Coover, Norman Vincent Peale, Mark Victor Hansen, Earl Mindell, Harold Kushner, Mike Kryzyzewski, Johnny Damon, Lee Haney, Duane Clemmons, Ken Blanchard, Patch Adams, Les Brown, Wally "Famous" Amos, Rudy Ruettiger, Hall of Famers: Gary Carter, Barry Larkin, Billy Cunningham, Richie Guerin *and many, many more!*

Here are just a few of the many endorsements for Dr. Kaplan's books here is just a small sampling of this acclaimed author. Throughout his journey of life exemplified in his books shows how faith, dedication and perseverance, his CANT STOP ME ATTITUDE. Enclosed is a montage of his endorsements, too numerous to show all.

TESTIMONIALS

Wow, Can't Stop Me is an incredible inspirational book by one the greatest minds in Health Care, Dr. Eric Kaplan. This book and its messages will be true for all of time.

As a pro athlete I sought out the best in training, nutrition, and healing and Dr. Kaplan was always the first one I would call. His life experience and formal training as a doctor made him a trusted resource for guidance throughout my career. He exposed me to non-invasive, drug free, state of the art healing that repaired me and prepared me for a career in sports wellness after 10 years in the NFL. A life-long friend, mentor, and practitioner, his lessons of life are shared in his book. Dr. Kaplan has laid out a pivotal framework for the uninspired and uninitiated to see their potential and realize the power we have within us. Tap into EK's powerful and positive energy reserve and fill up for a future not limited by negative self-image, thoughts and actions. His book sacks the competition, literally. It's a must read and I'll share it with my players and friends.

—Duane Clemons, Vikings, Defensive Captain of Kansas City Chiefs & Cincinnati Bengals, 1996-2006

This book is destined to save lives, change lives, and inspire anyone because of its impact, inspiration, and insight.

—Les Brown, best-selling author of Live Life to the Fullest

Dr. Kaplan's book clearly represents the strength it takes to survive and succeed. He is living proof that it starts with a Dream. His story and message show that if you visualize your Dream and make a commitment anything is possible. Their comeback story is what makes life exciting. This book will teach anyone to never underestimate the power of a Dream. It will change your life as the Kaplans changed theirs.

—Rudy Ruettiger, whose life story was the basis of the 1993 TRISTAR blockbuster film, Rudy

Dr. Kaplan is an incredible motivator and always brings out the best in you. This book is relatable and an inspiration to so many that may have had a similar journey.

YOU ARE A ROCKSTAR!!

—Jenn Noon Athletic director, Fairleigh Dickinson University

Dr. Kaplan's secrets to success are big time, yet easy to understand, implement and follow! I'm very fortunate to be able to call Dr. Kaplan a friend.

—Jeff Slanovec Head Basketball Coach, Fairleigh Dickinson University, Madison, NJ

Dr Kaplan's book is more than highly motivational. It shows you how to simply and elegantly remove mental toxins, naturally. It's mandatory reading for anyone who wants to live a healthy, happy life.

—*Beth Greer, Best-Selling author Super Natural Home and Environmental Health Consultant*

Two is better than one if two can act as one. Obviously, the Kaplans acted as one in their courageous fight to overcome obstacles that seemed impossible. I am so excited that they are sharing this story with us. It is inspiring.

—*Mike Krzyzewski, Head Coach, Basketball, Duke University*

Dr Kaplan is without a doubt, a virtual force of nature. Like an unstoppable storm that renews those in its path instead of destruction. Dr Kaplan is an inspiration to all who are fortunate to know him as he gives without end, leaving a legacy and goal for us to follow!

—*Dr G. Forrest Edwards, DC, DABCO*

"In a job as stressful as mine, a guide such as Dr. Kaplan's is a lifesaver."

—*Roger Brinbaum, Former President, Twentieth Century Fox Film Corporation, CEO MGM studios*

Dr. Kaplan has the tools to take ordinary and turn it to EXTRA-ordinary! I can't thank him enough!!

—*Dr. Darrell Swolensky Henderon, NV*

Your story will motivate and inspire others. I wish you and your wife every success.

—*Wally "Famous" Amos*

Dr Kaplan is one of the best. On top of his game. Love to learn from him. Has made me a better Doctor and our clinical outcomes have improved tremendously since working with him.

—*Dr. Troy M. Dreiling, D.C. Disc Centers of America - Vancouver; Advisory Board Member of International Disc Education Association*

Dr. Kaplan is the gift that keeps on giving, a true inspiration. This book could be his best yet. A must read.

—*Dr. Brigitte Rozenberg*

Few people have lived such an extraordinary life as Dr. Eric Kaplan. Accomplished doctor, sought-after speaker, next-level business developer, respected teacher and prolific author, he has written multiple inspirational best sellers. His newest book is his BEST! His exceptional humor and wisdom are deftly woven into the anecdotal glimpses of his life story. I learned some amazing things about Dr. Kaplan, people in general and especially about myself as I read his latest book. You will too!"

—*Dr. Mark Kestner*

"This is a one-of-a-kind book by one-of-a-kind man".

—*Dr. Idan Snapir DDS*

Thanks Dr. Kaplan for another phenomenal book that I couldn't put down.

—*Dr. Alan Rosenthal*
Thousand Oaks, CA

True success is not about the money you make but the person you become. A must read, will help anyone.

—*Dr. David Cifra*
Sarasota, FL

This book inspires you to confront your problems and draw on your inner resources to overcome even the greatest of life's obstacles.

—*Brian Tracy, Best-selling author of*
more than 40 books, including Crunch Point

Dr. Kaplan has personally helped hundreds of thousands of people to be their best and live their best life. Now through mentoring a select group of doctors, he will touch millions of lives as we help our patients to live their best lives. I am truly blessed to be a part of Dr. Kaplan's legacy.

—*Dr. Christopher Pearsall D.C. C.C.E.P.*
Winter Springs, FL

Dr Kaplan has taught me just that over the years that you can't stop me from being successful. As he taught, I am on fire and I just keep getting better and better and I do not look back.

—*Dr Mark D. Losagio, Lehigh Valley PA*

Dr. Kaplan is without a doubt one of the most innovative leaders in the chiropractic profession. We are all lucky to have him"

—*Dr. Todd Walters*
DCOA Foley, AL

Dr Kaplan is not only a brilliant physician who wrote a brilliant book, but he is a brilliant CEO in the world of business as well. Wherever he speaks across the globe, I make it a point to attend, and I devour anything that he writes. This amazing book will change your life as it has changed mine. Dr Kaplan inspires me every day of my life as he has for the last 25 years that I've known him personally and professionally.

—*Dr. Richard Lohr, Disc Centers of America, Decatur, IL*

This book is a classic, I love sharing the philosophies of life with my family. A must-read to anyone who wants to grow. I'm excited to share this book with patients and friends. Thank you, Dr. Kaplan, for a fun and entertaining read.

—*Dr. Reza Nikpour*
Annandale, VA

Throughout the once in a life-time pandemic, our practice grew over 30% because of a made-up mind, not allowing the negative to influence what I knew was right. I was surrounded by like-thinking masterminds and collectively we all benefitted. The take-away: Seek wisdom from others! Learn and earn together, as no man is an island!

—*G. Forrest Edwards, DC, DABCO*
Hoover, AL

As an author, teacher and businesswomen, I will incorporate your lessons into daily ideas for living. I found your book uplifting and motivating. Your book is a gift that keeps on giving.

—*Catherine MacDonald, #1 Amazon Best-selling author of The Way*

Dr. Kaplan's story depicts how the power of love, faith, and family can triumph in the face of adversity. Faced with what many considered certain expiration of life as we know it, Dr. Kaplan and his family banded together and used the power of love and faith to turn an almost certain tragedy into success. I am inspired by their story.

—*Barry Larkin, Cincinnati Reds, Hall Of Famer*

Dr. Kaplan's book is more than highly motivational. It is a must-read for anyone who wants to live a healthier, happier lifestyle.

—*Billy Cunningham, Hall of Fame Basketball Player and Coach*

Enjoyed the book, I highly recommend it.

—*Kevin Loughery, NBA Veteran, Former Coach Miami Heat*

An excellent book for the man on the run.

—*Norbert Schlei, Former Assistant U.S. Attorney General*
(Kennedy and Johnson Administration)

Wonderfully written with an understanding of a person's health and personal needs. A book you must read.

—*Richie Guerin, Former NBA Coach of the Year,*
General Manager Atlanta Hawks

Wow. This book is a simple, straightforward answer to the question, "How do I make myself and everyone around me better?" It is a must-share with all the people who work for me and are important to me. Thank you, Dr. Kaplan, for your dedication and commitment helping others achieve success and a happy, rewarding life.

—*Michael Putman, DC, CFMP,*

I am forever grateful that I met Dr. Kaplan when I did. I was burnt out and could only focus on quitting. Thank you, Dr. Kaplan, for your honesty when I needed it and your ability to translate your successes into the lives of many others in our profession. I wrote a goal a long time ago that described the life you are living. Thanks for being my real-life inspiration!

—*Dr. Charlie Schuster*
Charleston, IL

Dr. Kaplan has proven himself as a physician, leader, coach, teacher, motivator, speaker and author! This book is a must read for anyone to improve their personal self, relationships and life by looking introspectively for a positive outcome.

—*Dr. Lawrence B. Ashkinazy*
Coral Springs, FL

I would like to personally thank Dr. Kaplan for his guidance and direction over the past few years. He has helped me take my practice to a new level thereby treating more patients than I ever thought possible. You're the man Dr. K!

—*Dr. John Zilliox*
Niagara Falls...Step by Step

It has been said, "The road to success is always under construction." Dr Kaplan's book provides the empirical formulas to success, not only in business, but in life!

—*Dr Ted Wedell, Kirkland, WA*

Dr. Kaplan's books are so motivational, I read them over and over. Imagine the power of "1 Minute."

—*Dr. James Dietrick, DC, CCEP*

Dr. Kaplan, D.C. is truly one of a kind Doctor. A True inspiration to Chiropractors everywhere. I have known him for only 4 years, but it has changed my life and my practice and allowed me to be a better Doctor and to help more people. Thanks.

—*Dr. Dan Weymouth*
San Leandro, CA

Life is not easy, nor should it be. However, having a super-bowl play book from an elite coach. Not only crushes the competition. It takes you as a doctor to another level.

Thank You Dr. Kaplan.

—*Dr. Partite*
Cream Ridge, NJ

Anyone who wants to lead a happier, more successful life needs to read Dr. Kaplan's new book. I will give it to my staff. It will empower any reader.

—*Dr. Raymond Bates*

Dr. Kaplan has taught me to even if you think you are succeeding in practice to never become comfortable, always look to learn more, offer more to your patients and become better, become the best.

—*Dr. Peter Peduzzi*
Wexford, PA

I enjoy reading about others personal hardships and struggles, and garner how they succeeded. In Dr. Kaplan's case it almost seems his personal hardships and struggles were a recipe for failure, from the outside. I was touched learning about his father and mother. It is apparent that Dr. Kaplan was greatly loved. Knowing part of his beginnings sets the foundation for the advice and suggestions he has on becoming the best you. All the hardships and struggles, Dr. Kaplan looked at them and said, "you can't stop me!" Enjoy the book.

—*Gilbert E. A. Rodriguez, LMSSBB*
Elmira, NY

After reading this book, YOU CAN'T STOP ME! This book gives you the strength to succeed!

—*Dr. Kimberly Trainor, D.C.*

There's always a purpose of why someone comes into your life and stay in your life. Dr. Erik Kaplan has and continues to inspire me to be a better doctor and better human being. His passion for life and chiropractic is contagious. I continue to learn from him every day. I only hope to make him proud of me!

If you're looking for a path to higher levels of success this book is it!

—*Bryan Dufrene, D.C., DABCO*

Dr. Kaplan, it is rewarding and special to be part of something great – to be part of a group of doctors who are giving back – who are making a difference – who are about giving people their lives back and allowing our patients to live their lives again. Thank you all for you do for this group of doctors – the family of Disc Centers of America.

—*Dr. Rex W. Roffler, D.C.*
Winter Park, FL

I was 64 years old, 38 years in practice with a highly successful practice. Dr. Kaplan took an existent great practice and 3 years later, made it even greater and more successful. Now at 67 years of age, I had my greatest year in practice in the "COVID YEAR" and my practice is STILL GROWING and has become a "dream come true" IT IS TRULY EXTRAORDINARY!

—*Dr. John Sandoz*
Mount Laurel, NJ

It is my sincere prayer your book will be a help and blessing to many people.

—*Norman Vincent Peale*

"This book is unique in its common-sense approach to health. It is an exceptional guide to anyone interested in health, sports, fitness, weight loss preventative health plan of action."

—*Tom McMillen, Co-Chairman of President's*
Council on Physical Fitness, Congressman, 11-year NBA Veteran

As a cosmetic dentist and Mrs. America 2005, I have seen firsthand the measures some take in trying to achieve what they consider beauty. In this amazing true-life story, the Kaplans' message helps exemplify true beauty, inner beauty. Their courage should never be forgotten.

—*Dr. Chiann Fan Gibson, DMD*

The Kaplans' story will provide chicken soup for anyone's spirit or soul. Their book Dying to be Young shows miracles can take place with hard work and the right attitude. Their story demonstrates that you can transform your life into exactly what you want it to be, regardless of your situation, by simply shifting your mindset and creating a renewed reality.

—*Jack Canfield, Co-Author, Chicken Soup for*
the Unsinkable Soul® in America

It's an honor to endorse your book. Thanks for all you do while making the world a healthier place.

—*Lee Haney, Eight-time Mr. Olympia, Author,*
Former Chairman President's Council of Sports and Physical Fitness

Awaken the Wellness Within will change the way you think about healthcare and wellness. Finally, a practical book full of solutions for what is making us sick. Thank you, Dr. Kaplan.

—*Dr. Fab Mancini, International best-selling author, speaker, and media personality*
BE FABulous, Dr. Fab
Dr. Fabrizio Mancini
America's #1 "Healthy Living" Media Expert, World Renowned Chiropractor,
International Best-Selling Author & Speaker and President Emeritus of Parker University.

Awaken the Wellness Within is an insightful resource for how we become ill and how we can awaken our inner natural power to become well.

—Dr. John Demartini, International Best-Selling Author of Count
Your Blessings: The Healing Power of Gratitude and Love

Dr. Kaplan picks up where Dr. Deepak Chopra left off.

—Dr. Leo R. Boisvert, DC

Dr. Kaplan has done it again—he motivates, inspires and entertains the reader throughout the entire book. This book is simply awesome. It's loaded with good values and lessons that every person should instill in their lives.

—Jaki Baskow, CEO Baskow and Associates

GAME OVER!!! Again Dr. Kaplan has peeled back all the layers and allows both doctors and patients to understand the root cause of disease. Dr. Kaplan has created the "plug & play" RETURN-TO-HEALTH game plan that empowers both doctors and patients alike with the tools necessary to reach the HIGHEST levels of health and wellness possible.

The real "MAGIC" is how Dr. Kaplan COMMUNICATES, CONCISELY, CONGRUENTLY, COMPLETELY and CHIROPRACTICALLY the CELLULAR message of health, (The 6 C's). Then again that is Dr. Kaplan's GENIUS. His ability to deliver a message that resonates through every CELL in your body. Awaken the Wellness Within is Dr. Kaplan's CROWNING ACHIEVEMENT and a gift beyond measure for the readers fortunate enough to get their hands on this book that UNLOCKS the door to one's own health and life potential!

—Dr. Perry Bard, DC
CEO Concierge Coaches

Dr. Kaplan's gripping story about coming back from the brink of death after a botched Botox treatment proves once and for all that beauty is an inside job. As Kaplan shows, there isn't a scalpel, pill, lotion or injection that can make us as radiant as an open, loving heart.

—Ken Blanchard, co-author of bestsellers,
The One Minute Manager® and Leading at a Higher Level

I have known Dr. Kaplan as a friend, the family chiropractor, an incredible motivator, and now as an author who has lived to share his purposeful message. Imagine making one choice that could send you to a place of unimaginable suffering. That's what happened to my friend Eric and his dear wife Bonnie. They could have given up, but chose to turn inward and found a power and insight so far beyond the physical self. Their courageous story teaches us to be grateful in all that God has given and to draw wisdom from all of our challenges. Anyone who reads this book will be blessed and know that yes, we are responsible for our choices, but there is so much love and guidance available to us if we just ask and listen. Living, loving, being, and accepting the moment and ourselves is the greatest gift!! Thank you, Eric, for stepping so deeply into the divine space and bringing back such wisdom to share. If anyone would live to uplift others, I knew it would be you!

—*Marla Maples*

…I have always been against cosmetic procedures and have considered them malpractice since I became an MD. Good luck on your crusade to change the way the world thinks about cosmetic procedures, especially Botox. Please give your life to peace, justice, and care.

—*Patch Adams, MD, Author*

Bonnie and Eric Kaplan's story is a true story of hope…and faith…and true unconditional love. Dr. Kaplan is an inspiration to everyone. He is my inspiration. The 5 Minute Motivator offers a practical, unique approach to experience greater success and happiness. This book will help you appreciate the blessings in your life.

—*Marci Shimoff, New York Times Best-Selling author of*
Love for No Reason and Happy for No Reason

This wonderful book shows you how to become a totally positive person every day and accomplish more than you ever thought possible "5 Minutes" at a time.

—*Brian Tracy, Professional Speaker, Bestselling Author of more than*
40 books, Business/Life Coach, Sales Trainer, CEO of Brian Tracy International™

For decades we've searched for a "magic bullet." Dr. Kaplan succinctly explains that the "magic" is within us all.

—*Dr. Jason Helton*
Lubock, Texas

The 5 Minute Motivator is a slam dunk for anyone who wants to reboot their life. Dr Kaplan's prescriptions are time honored—the power of the mind to change our lives. As the Bible and Dr Kaplan teach us, "What you sow in your thoughts, will determine what you reap in life". This book is a must read.

—*Tom McMillen, Former Congressman and Chairman of*
Presidents Council on Sports and Physical Fitness and 11-year NBA veteran

Dr. Eric Kaplan's, The 5 Minute Motivator is the complete guide for positive transformation! Brilliantly simple and simply brilliant. I encourage you make this book your daily helping of positivity and watch your life transform into the beautiful destiny you were meant to live.

—*Peggy McColl, New York Times Best-Selling Author of*
Your Destiny Switch

The 5 Minute Motivator lays out a simple and powerful program for achieving your goals and dreams and triumphing over the inevitable setbacks and challenges we all experience.

—*Pamela Yellen, Author of the New York Times Best-Seller*
Bank On Yourself: The Life-Changing Secret to Growing

I love Dr. Eric Kaplan's new book, The 5 Minute Motivator, for its simplicity and yet profound impact on one's life. It is truly an inspirational book for many Ping Li, Best-Selling Author of Awakening:

Fulfilling Your Soul's Purpose on Earth

A powerful guide to living life well, The 5 Minute Motivator proves that time invested in our truest purpose is indeed time well-spent.

—*Christine Louise Hohlbaum, Best-Selling author of*
The Power of Slow: 101 Ways to Save Time in Our 24/7 World

Dr. Kaplan Talks the Talk and Walks the Walk, literally. After being 100% paralyzed and making a miraculous recovery, he understands what it takes to win. His will and positive mental attitude are displayed in the pages of his new book, The 5 Minute Motivator. As a professional athlete, I understand the inner winner we all must reach for to succeed in life. Dr. Kaplan's book Awakens the Winner in us all. This book is a must read. I highly recommend it,

—*Mark McNulty, PGA Tour Professional, winner of 58 events,*
including 5 Majors, Senior PGA Championship, Senior British Open
Championship, US Senior Open, Senior Players Championship

Dr. Kaplan's book provides not only the empirical formula to winning and success, but he provides you with a map, "5 Minutes" at a time. His skills as a teacher, educator, and motivator are second to none. This book is a must read for anyone looking to reach their full potential.

—*Tom Ness, Golf Professional, Author Golf Digest, Recognized by*
Golf Digest as one of the Top 50 golf instructors in the United States

Dr. Kaplan has written another life-changing book. The 5 Minute Motivator is a powerful and comprehensive guide to success and happiness that anyone at any age can experience. His book will help you build the life of love and happiness "300 Seconds" at a time. Thank you. Eric, for this important, life-changing book. "If you want to experience inner fulfillment on a whole new level, read this book."

—*Dr. Stuart Hoffman, Amazon #1 Best-Selling author of*
I AM a Lovable ME!

It is said that 'a people without a vision perish.' In The 5 Minute Motivator, Dr. Eric Kaplan takes you on an incredible journey where he unveils your inner gifts and unravels hidden mysteries to enable you to think with a winning mind and experience the dreams you've long desired.

—*Ken Lang, Author of Walking Among the Dead*

As a firm believer in the power of believing in oneself, I was overjoyed to read a success story in which a small amount of time set aside every day, as little as 5 minutes, can command worlds of success. As proud as I am to endorse this book, I am even more gratified to know that its message will help and inspire others.

—*Michelle Franklin, Award-winning fantasy and romance author*
Creator of The Haanta Series

Dr. Kaplan's new book, The 5 Minute Motivator will help you gain a renewed and vivid appreciation of life, minute by minute. The book offers a "tool kit" that will infuse your brain with a new sense of aliveness and possibility.

—*Anat Baniel, Clinical Psychologist and Best-Selling Author*
of Move Into Life and Kids Beyond Limits

Dr Kaplan's book, The 5 Minute Motivator inspires anyone and everyone to be better—"5 Minutes" at a time. His words elegantly and spiritually compel the reader to look at the blessings of living, laughing, loving, and learning. A fun and powerful read.

—*Anna Maria Prezio, Author of #1 Best-Selling book*
Confessions of a Feng Shui Ghost-Buster

The 5 Minute Motivator might be an understatement. This is a 5-minute life changer! While each snippet requires only 5 minutes to read, they contain a day's worth of digestion. There is so much power in each story and the quotations are inspiring and thoughtful. A great way to start each day that all rolls into an abundant life! How cool is that!

—*Carl Bozeman, Amazon Best-Selling author of*
On Being God – Beyond Your Life's Purpose

What does it take to engage all your senses in a journey to discover your richest, most fulfilling life? According to author Dr. Eric Kaplan, it only takes 5 minutes! The deceptively simple premise—and sheer genius—of The 5-Minute Motivator is that miracles can happen by thinking and focusing differently for only 5 minutes a day. Using this inspiring book as your daily guide to those transformative moments will become a habit that you will never want to break.

—*Dr. Christine Ranck, Amazon #1 Best-Selling*
Co-Author of Ignite the Genius Within

As a professional golfer I understand what it takes to win—on and off the golf course. Dr. Kaplan has written another life-changing book that can show you the way to health and happiness. He provides the reader with a powerful and comprehensive program that anyone can employ in their life regardless of their occupation. If you want to experience happiness and success at a whole new level, read this book. It will be the best "5 Minutes" you will ever invest in yourself.

—*Dana Quigley, PGA Golf Professional, winner of 29 events,*
2005 Champions Tour, Player of The Year 2005

The 5 Minute Motivator offers advice to help the reader construct a life of success and happiness.

—*Tony Hsieh, NY Times Best-Selling author of*
Delivering Happiness and CEO of Zappos.com, Inc.

Dr Kaplan's book proves that in life you should never, ever, Give Up On Love. His book is more than highly motivational, it is inspirational. In an interval of only "5 Minutes" he helps the reader remove mental barriers that exist in life, in a natural and positive manner. I would consider this book essential reading for anyone who wants to live a healthy, happier, and more loving life. It is simple to understand and elegantly written. This book can help transform anyone, enabling them to reach their potential and fulfill their dreams.

—*Tim Carroll, Best-Selling Author of Don't Ever Give Up On Love*

In the game of life, there is no playbook to winning better than Dr. Kaplan's new book, The 5 Minute Motivator. This book will take you on an adventure to success, 300 seconds at a time, I will share this book my staff, my friends, and my family. I know it will change and enhance their lives as much as it has mine.

—*Carlos Becerra, CEO North America Medical*

Dr. Eric Kaplan's, The 5 Minute Motivator shows us that the fulfillment which we so eagerly seek is actually just a few steps away. Through incredibly simple exercises, Dr. Kaplan helps us realize that we can achieve what we dream, inspire others to do the same, and that abundance already exists in each of our lives. It's up to us to recognize it. Pick up this book whenever you have a few spare minutes and allow it to replenish your positivity and reactivate your drive for life.

—*Dr. Carmen Harra, Clinical psychologist, intuitive counselor,*
and best-selling author of Everyday Karma and Wholeliness

Kaplan promises. Kaplan delivers. I have written, co-authored, and ghostwritten more than 40 published books, many of them on motivation and management, and I wish I could claim some credit for participation in Dr. Kaplan's latest project. He covers all the bases of achieving and maintaining genuine success—mental, physical, emotional, spiritual, and practical. His book is as uplifting as it is informative.

—*Dan Baldwin, Author of The Caldera Series and*
Sales Prospecting for Dummies by Tom Hopkins

The 5 Minute Motivator is a must read for any leader. Just setting aside 5 minutes per day for personal growth can be life-altering. Many pearls of wisdom are jammed-packed in this book with most of them told in parable stories which are memorable. Well worth the price of admission, I highly recommend that you also take a ride on this book adventure.

—Sam Santiago, PMP, Amazon Best-Selling Author of
The Official Book of Innovation

Awaken the Wellness Within is a revolutionary approach to healthcare. Exposing ObamaCare and providing a personal solution is the essence of this powerful book. This book is not only a must-read, it is a must for every person's personal health library. I will share this model with my patients so they can take a practical approach to health. Thank you, Dr. Kaplan.

—Dr. Glenn Zuck
Orthopedic Surgeon, Former Sports Fellow
Philadelphia Eagles/Flyers

Thank you, Dr. Kaplan for having the inspiration to bring forth a new paradigm in health care. Our entire health care culture will evolve to the next level when they embrace your words of wisdom.

Finally, someone has the insight and courage to reveal the truth about sickness and disease!

Endless gratitude,

—Dr. James Cronin, DC

Awaken the Wellness Within is another fine example of the easy-to-implement, new, and contemporary concepts for understanding wellness and healthcare shared by best-selling author Dr. Kaplan. A must-read for anyone who is looking to polish their communication abilities in this new era!

—Dr. Rob Jackson
Co-Author of You Can Expect a Miracle: With Chiropractic
CEO Back Talk Systems Inc.

WOW. This is 21st century medical wisdom shared by an internationally renowned physician to his readers, just as a wise teacher would speak lovingly and personally to his students. Dr. Kaplan is a pioneer in a new paradigm of medicine that all physicians of all specialties will see as revolutionary now but as "why didn't I accept that" within a decade

—Steven M. Rosman, DC, PhD, Rabbi, MS, Dipl. Ac. (NCCAOM),
LMHC (New York), Author, Director of Rosman Whole Person
Healthcare, Wellness Clinic, in Sarasota, Florida

Dr. Kaplan's new book Awaken the Wellness Within is a modern approach to healthcare. If your goal is to be healthy and you want to find the secrets to being healthy, Dr. Kaplan has exposed the truth about "inner Healing" and has template a modern, natural way to health and well-being.

—*Salvatore D. LaRusso DC, F.I.C.A.(Hon.)*
Former Chair, I.B.C.E.
Former Director, N.B.C.E.

Too often people search for the answers to their health problems in the wrong places. Awaken the Wellness Within is the right place and is a valuable resource for discovering health solutions that begin at the very core of all our health issues. Dr. Kaplan's newest best-selling book teaches us to assume responsibility for our own well-being, to understand that the answers we hunger for lie within ourselves and he explains how we can...Awaken the Wellness Within. A book not to be missed!

—*Dr. Michael Axelrod, DDS*

Awaken the Wellness Within is surely destined to be a blockbuster that revolutionizes the health game. Dr. Kaplan finally puts into perspective precisely why health is not a game of chance, but rather a choice. From this day forward you no longer need to be confused about health. Through Dr. Kaplan's stories and useful techniques, you'll know how to unlock your innate healing potential. You've taken the first step. Now read and apply the wisdom, just like I am doing to improve my understanding of cellular health and take control of my health.

—*Patrick K. Porter, Ph.D.*
Author and Inventor of Brain Tap Technology

Thank you! Thank you! Thank you! For years I've looked for different and better ways to help my clients reach their full health potential. I love the way Awaken the Wellness Within weaves together stories that are practical and inspiring. The bottom line every reader will walk away with is: The body will heal itself. It is our basic nature. The body is inherently healthy and self-healing and always strives to maintain or reestablish optimal healthy conditions. This is a book I can recommend to all my clients, family and friends. Dr. Kaplan has done it *again!*

— *Dr. Cynthia J. Porter, Ph.D.*
Best-Selling Author/Speaker/Coach

Dr. Eric Kaplan has done it again! With Awaken the Wellness Within, he has done a masterful job of demonstrating the healing power of the human body, as well as how you can take control of your health and well-being. A must-read for anyone that is truly interested in learning and enjoying the benefits of a natural approach to health.

—*Dr. Daniel T. Drubin*
Best-Selling Author of Busting Your Rut and Letting Go of Your Bananas

Awaken the Wellness Within is an insightful resource for how we become ill and how we can awaken our inner natural power to become well.

—*Dr. John Demartini – International Best-Selling Author of*
Count Your Blessings—The Healing Power of Gratitude and Love

Innovators are often ridiculed for looking at the world in a different way. I don't believe Dr. Kaplan will be ridiculed for this newest work, but he will influence millions of people to start taking control of their own health in a better way with his unique insight and perspective on cellular vitalism.

—*Dr. Jeffrey L Dickhut*

In simplicity there is elegance and in Awaken the Wellness Within, Dr. Kaplan takes a revolutionary and powerful new path toward dispelling old myths and actually enabling the reader to know how the body heals itself! Brilliant!

—*Dr. Larry Markson*
Author of Talking to Yourself is Not Crazy
Facilitator of The Cabin Experience

The doctor who revolutionized my practice and improved the level of care I can provide my patients does it again! Dr. Kaplan's books are required reading for every doctor committed to unlocking their full potential and giving their patients the best care!! A must read.

—*Dr. Edward Buonadonna B.S., D.C.,F.I.A.M.A.*

Oral Health has a wide-ranging impact on our overall health and well-being. Dr. Kaplan's book will change the way we all look at the process of health and healthcare. Bravo, Dr. Kaplan.

—*Dr. Roy Hart*

Awaken the Wellness Within is a revolutionary book that will change the way we view healthcare forever. Thank you, Dr. Kaplan.

—*Dr. Eric Nepute*
CEO Nepute Wellness Centers

A must-read book for anyone thinking of losing weight and keeping it off.

—*Dr. Earl L. Mindell*

CAN'T STOP ME:
GOING FROM ORDINARY
TO EXTRAORDINARY

DR. ERIC KAPLAN D.C., FIAMA

ISBN:

Hardcover: 978-1-64184-732-2
Paperback: 978-1-64184-733-9
Ebook: 978-1-64184-734-6

Jetlaunch Publishers

*D*edication

First and foremost, I'd like to thank all my friends, family, all my mentors, all my coaches and teachers whose patience and support put me in this position.

I would like to especially want to thank all my doctors at Disc Centers of America for their ongoing support and love. Daily these special group of doctors both motivate and empower me. I would like to thank my friend and manager of Trump National in Jupiter Florida Tony Servideo for graciously allowing me to educate my doctors on this illustrious property. With special thanks to Nancy Dean, Event Coordinator superior, head golf professional John Ebmeyer, Chef Chris Corvelle whose meatballs are legendary and addicting. I would like to give thanks to the entire Trump staff and family for being to being so gracious to me, to my family and our family of doctors.

Special thanks to my two special son's Dr's Jason & Michael Kaplan and their lovely wives Dr. Stephanie Kaplan and Jessica Kaplan. Most importantly my wife of 41 years Bonnie Kaplan. This saint of a woman allows me to go into my office for hours on end and never asks for anything. I am totally blessed by her love.

I especially want to thank my friend, my partner, my muse, my brother from another mother, Dr. Perry Bard. Dr. Bard teaches "Success Leaves Clues." Well, he has now been in my life 34 years. I owe him my love and gratitude - he was my gift from God. And a very special thanks to Dr. Bard's amazing wife, Laura. Thank you for allowing him to work so hard, and for being a part of my family.

I'd like to thank the President of Life University Dr. Rob Scott, Dr. Gilles Lamarche VP, and the entire board of Life University, for honoring me and choosing me for their Prestigious Presidents Circle. I will wear my new blazer with honor.

I want to thank Fairleigh Dickinson University which Bonnie and I both attended and are alumni. This wonderful University on a majestic campus in Madison New Jersey gave us the fundamentals to succeed. With special thanks to basketball coach Jeff Slanovic and athletic director extraordinaire Jenn Noon, for first nominating me for the prestigious Pinnacle Award the school's highest honor. Thank you, President Dr. Christopher Capuano &

staff, for choosing me. Out of 130,000 plus alumni only 0.02% have ever achieved this honor, I am more than grateful and honored. My picture now proudly sits on the University wall. It is truly the Pinnacle; I am thankful and greatly honored.

The PINNACLE Award

Recipients of The PINNACLE is chosen by past inductees, based on the following criteria: success or distinction in one's chosen field of endeavor, significant contributions to society and humanity through public or humanitarian service and outstanding service to the University or reflection of the unique character of FDU in one's life. Chosen out of 130,000+ former alumni or less than 0.02%, The **Pinnacle Award is the highest and most selective honor the University bestows on a graduating student**. Annually one former alumnus will be recognized who has demonstrated ongoing academic excellence, public service and commitment to both career and community at large, as well as to the University is honored. Winners will address fellow winners, dignitaries, business leaders, Board members, Officers and Directors as well as the assembled audience at FDU in a special gala ceremony. Their Pinnacle pictures will hang on University Wall of Honor.

Fairleigh Dickinson University

2019 Distinguished
Alumnus Pinnacle Award

Eric Kaplan, DC, FIAMA, BS'74

Chief Executive Officer, Disc Centers of America and Concierge Coaches

From a young age, you understood the value of hard work. You set high ambitions for yourself and would not stop until your dreams were realized. You attended FDU on a basketball scholarship in the early 1970s — and you quickly excelled both on and off the court. As a young student, you had a clear vision about your future and a strong sense of mission.

Today, it's safe to say that you have lived up to that vision and have achieved significant success as a nationally known chiropractor, lecturer, author and business consultant. Upon earning your medical degree, you began your career as a chiropractor owning and operating six clinics. As a doctor, you were always more than just a health care provider. You not only delivered the highest standard of care, but you also gave each patient the tools necessary to get the most out of his or her life.

As the years went on, you treated some very well-known names in sports and entertainment — including members of New York's Major League Baseball teams and the Miss Universe Pageant, to name just a few. Eventually, you transitioned into the corporate world. Your entrepreneurial abilities, combined with your excellent leadership and communication skills, led you to become President of the premier weight loss company, NutriSystem. You later founded Discforce, Inc., one of the nation's leaders in non-invasive treatments for herniated discs.

Today, you are CEO of Concierge Coaches, a physician consulting group boasting membership of hundreds of doctors across the country. Through one-on-one coaching, you guide these doctors and help them to build their practices with non-invasive patient care. As a result, thousands of patients are now able to avoid dangerous narcotics, risky injections and often unnecessary surgeries.

You are a five-time, award-winning author with three #1 bestsellers. You have spoken at hundreds of conferences, and have made numerous radio and television appearances, from Dr. Oz and Good Morning America, to CNN and many more. You generously share your wisdom and experience to educate and inform others about their health and wellbeing. It's no surprise you are the most followed chiropractor in the world on Twitter, with 105,000 followers!

You have always held your formative years at FDU close to your heart. You continue to share your passion and love for your University with so many others, often speaking about your FDU experience in your lectures and keynote addresses.

Your family has always been a grounding force in your life. You and your wife, Bonnie, have been there for each other through the good times and the tough times. Your love for one another is truly inspiring. Your two sons, Michael and Jason, and your granddaughter bring you so much joy, love and pride.

You are a shining example to others that perseverance and hard work pay off. Anyone who meets you is forever changed for the better. With immense admiration for your wide range of achievements, we are privileged to award you with our highest alumni honor, THE PINNACLE.

June 7, 2019

Karin Hamilton
Executive Director, Alumni Relations

Richard Reiss
Senior Vice President, University Advancement

Memory

"A person dies two times; once when they stop breathing, and once when we stop thinking of them."

I will always remember these great teachers, friends and family

My Grandparents Bertha "Red" & Mitchel Kaplan, Joe & Birdie Adler.

My mother Elsie Kaplan

My father Mike Kaplan

My brother Steve Kaplan

My Aunt Gloria Punyon

My Uncle Herbert Punyon

My professor Dr. Donald Gutstein

My Aunt Diane and Uncle Buddy Adler

Aunt Vivian Daniels, Uncle Mark Levine

My son's father-in-law Bob Adler

COUSINS

Doris & Milton Garfunkel

Norman and Natalie Roth

Judge Louis Brenner, Judge Marty Brenner, Dr. Dick Brenner

Honey Kramer, Ruth and Phil Zuck

All of the above and so many more played a big part of my life, THANK YOU

Acknowledgments

6 Time Bestselling Titles by Dr. Kaplan:

1. "5 Minute Motivator," #1
2. "Lifestyle of the Fit & Famous," National
3. "Dying To Be Young," #1
4. "5 Minutes To Wellness," #3
5. "Awaken The Wellness Within," #1
6. "The 1 Minute Motivator" #1

*C*ontents

oreword

If there was ever three words in the English language that describe Dr Eric Kaplan, it would be the words "CAN'T STOP ME".

This is a story about commitment, persistence, passion, challenges, hunger, drive, determination, adversity, victory and love.

CAN'T STOP ME is part of Dr Eric Kaplan 's genetic code, as it encapsulates his "One of a Kind" desire to win the game of life. I've watched him do this year after year in spite of the many obstacles that were placed in front of him. I watched him literally see 250 patients in one day and hug and love them all. This is a man dedicated to helping others. This is a man of family. This is a man who leads by example and never looks back.

However, his victories are not geared towards him personally. His victories have been best encapsulated by his ability to make everyone around him better.

His magnetic and attractive personality reminds you that the moment you meet him, he is unlike anyone you have ever met before.

I was so blessed. 34 years ago, when I walked into his office as a young associate doctor knowing one thing. I knew that I needed to learn how to fulfill my potential. Call it the "Moon and the Stars", Kismet, or Serendipity, but that day when I first met him, I knew that the greatest single thing I can do personally and professionally was to make sure that he was by my side for the life journey.

Dr. Kaplan has written some of the bestselling masterpieces of all time, however, CAN'T STOP ME is my absolute favorite book. The reason that this is my favorite book is simple.

What Dr. Eric Kaplan does in CAN'T STOP ME is he gives you a "behind-the curtain, inside look" as to what makes him ultra-successful and as a result, has made everyone around him a better version of themselves. He does this daily to each and every person he touches.

The facts are the facts. Success is not easy. However what Dr. Kaplan does in his infinite genius in CAN'T STOP ME is he gives you his "special sauce" in a way that very few if any could ever do. If you want to be the best, if you want to go from Good to Great, this book provides the empirical formula to success. His success library is unequaled and after reading this book you will know the secrets to success. If there is "One Thing" you will learn from this book is the power of perseverance.

A gifted and natural leader, Dr Eric Kaplan is a master storyteller. His ability to inject humor into Life's challenges is the rocket fuel of success. He is a master at painting a picture and utilizing metaphors and analogies, so you can grasp the BIG IDEA. Throughout his book he shares not only motivational stories that he shares as a lecturer all over the world, but personal stories that will touch your heart.

CAN'T STOP ME gives you a look inside as to how Dr. Kaplan lights up every room he walks in and when he walks out nobody is ever the same, in the most positive, uplifting and enlightened way.

He is a leader by example and is the ultimate role model as a husband, father, grandfather, friend and partner.

You learn in CAN'T STOP ME that at the core Dr. Kaplan is the ultimate giver. In this book he gives you his heart and soul. In this book, he shares some of the most intimate details of his and his wife's life. Bonnie Kaplan his wife of 41 years was raised in an orphanage by the State of New Jersey. Like Dr. Kaplan she is a warrior, this dynamic duo will make you understand the power of commitment, the values of love and family.

Dr. Kaplan gives out of abundance and understands that this journey is best fulfilled when we can fulfill our own human potential. He is a lover of life, and he talks the talk and walks the walk. His CAN'T STOP ME attitude shows the reader that the secrets to winning at the game of life is an inside job. In his latest book he gives you the keys to unlock your own success.

CAN'T STOP ME is your personal road map to success because it simply gives you the understanding that there are some things in life worth fighting for. Dr. Kaplan gives you the tools to be able to win the heavyweight championship of life.

I have often referred to Dr. Kaplan as our own version of the movie character "Rocky". The difference is his life was never fiction. It has always been non-fiction because the truth is everybody gets knocked down at some point. The key is getting up and moving forward. He did this throughout his life. The question is do you have what it takes to get back up and to win?

Dr. Kaplan teaches how you can get back up and to eventually have your hand raised in victory in any personal or professional challenges you are engaged in.

Dr. Kaplan has proven that Life is a game and if you play to win by looking deeper inside yourself and inside your soul, you have what it takes to come out victorious and you too can win the game of life.

In CAN'T STOP ME you now hold the playbook written by the BEST coach in the world.

Guard this sacred trust wisely and you too can never be stopped.
Win The Day!!!

Dr. Perry Bard
ACCLAIMED AUTHOR, ENTREPRENEUR, COACH, BUSINESS LEADER, LECTURER, COACH
BEST SELLING AUTHOR -DR. SUCCESS SPOTLIGHT
HOST, FOUNDER DR. SUCCESS RADIO SHOW, CEO DISC CENTERS OF AMERICA
CEO NEUROMED
CEO NEURODOC
FOUNDER PALM BEACH MASSAGE

CHAPTER 1

Home is Where Your Journey Begins

"If you want to live a happy life, tie it to a goal,
not to people or things."

—Albert Einstein

Life is about living, loving, laughing and learning, not just whining, worrying, and working. The one thing I promise you about life, is you will not get out of it alive. Live, love, laugh, learn, enjoy each moment of life; that is the gift, which is why it's called the PRESENT. So, unwrap your gift and enjoy it. Average is the best of the worst and the worst of the best. I just never wanted or accepted being average.

I am writing this book to inspire you; I want you to know how great you are, and I need everyone to realize their true potential. No one is ordinary, and this book is about being extraordinary.

I believe now, at 69 years young, I am nothing less than exceptional, and I have achieved everything I have ever wanted and more. I am the best version of me I could be. But I want you and everyone else to achieve greatness as well. Success is an inside job. No one can make you a success but yourself. I am nothing more than an ordinary person with extraordinary dreams and goals.

Success was not my birthright. I was actually a premature baby, and many still wonder if, to this day, I ever really matured. But I've learned that you can be better no matter who you are; you can have more. Your appetite for health, wealth, and happiness can be fulfilled if you are willing to do **'Whatever It Takes'** and take on a **'Can't Stop Me'** attitude.

I will start from the beginning of everything, where, and how it all happened. My father was a tough man, and he fought in World War II. He was a Sergeant in the Rangers and served under General Patton. He has experienced and seen things that I can only imagine. They were terrible and traumatizing. He rarely discussed the war, and it clearly left him with scars. During his tenure in the Army, he earned two purple hearts and a silver star for his efforts and work in the Army.

However, after the war, he couldn't find any opportunities. As a war veteran, he worked in a factory, which was not the most desirable job. He made girls' dresses. He started out as a cutter and ended up the foreman of the factory. He was always a leader, and he led by example. He worked two jobs my entire childhood. We didn't get to spend much time together. As a youth, I was always in bed when dad came home, and I'd always lay awake to see him. He'd enter my room and say, *"How was your day? How was school today?"*

I'd say, *"Good."*

He would say, *"Good boy, make me proud, son, now go to sleep,"* and kiss me on the forehead. Yes, I rarely saw my dad. We never had many conversations, but I knew he loved me, and I wanted to make him proud.

His life was not easy, and daily he was up and out of the house before my brother and I. He'd down a glass of orange juice and be off to work. His days were long, the factory in the day, and he sold men's clothing at night. Even with two jobs, he could hardly pay his bills. But despite his life and struggles, all he ever wanted in his life was for his two sons to do better than he ever did. He did not like the life he had to lead, and he wanted us to have more. He wanted us to do more and be presented with more opportunities to have a better life.

My father never received a college education, and he did not have the best opportunities because of that. But despite this, he had a '**Can't Stop Me**' attitude. So even without a formal education, he did the most and made the best of everything. He went to the school of hard knocks; he was street smart and knew how to motivate people quietly. He was always a leader. He looked you directly in the eye, and you knew from that gaze not to cross him. As a result of these qualities, he became the Vice President of the International Ladies Garment Workers Union and also became the President of our Temple, the largest in Jersey City.

Because of his union connections and community service, he was later chosen by Dr. Paul Jordan, the Mayor of Jersey City, to become a mayor's aide. His hard work, perseverance, and dedication, lead Mayor Dr. Paul Jordan to choose my father to be the Director of labor for the entire Board of Education. How ironic. If somebody wanted a teaching job, even a career as a janitor in any school, it went through my father. He did not let his lack of education stop him. He just realized he had to work harder than the next man. My father taught me many lessons in my life, but his '**Can't Stop Me**' attitude was the greatest lesson of them all.

But as someone who continuously worked two jobs just to provide for his family, he wanted better for us. My mother was a unique lady. She came from money. Her father, Joseph Adler, was at one time one of the wealthiest men in Jersey City, NJ. So, she grew up with privilege. But my grandfather was a gambler. He loved the ponies and gambled away all of his money and his business away. By the time I knew him, he was a shell of the man he was. As a result, my mother and father had to help pay his bills. My father resented that, but with his love for my mother and his commitment to family, he paid his share of my grandparent's bills with two other uncles, siblings of my mother.

My mother also worked (not by choice) as a secretary for the board of education. So, with all this, my parents and my father, specifically, realized the value of an education. He knew that if we were to have a better life, we had to seek an education. No matter the situation, he always emphasized the importance of studying and school; he did it out of wanting the best for us. Even when I was an athlete in school, I remember my father saying, "*Enough about sports, let's talk about school.*"

His attitude may seem harsh and strict, but it came from a place of caring and genuine concern for our well-being. He knew the importance of education because he did not have this opportunity. Let's face it. It's hard to start near the bottom. I went to public schools, which actually was a blessing. My father told my brother and me, "*Look, what are you going to be when you grow up and what price are you willing to pay?*"

According to him, we only had two choices, we either went to college and got educated, or we would go to the Army. It was that simple. He felt, either way, it would turn his boys into men.

My father also always said that you either become a lawyer or a doctor or own your own business. According to my father, the key to success was to be your own boss, and you had to have your own business. This was because he was an employee all his life, and he hated it. He wanted us to do everything he never did. Which was a little constricting in terms of choices, but that was what we grew up hearing—either become a lawyer or a doctor. I think this came from my mother's side, the German side. It was filled with lawyers and judges and one famous surgeon Dr. Richard Brenner. His father Uncle Louis Brenner and later his brother Marty Brenner were both judges. I grew up saying, Judge or Doctor. My parents saw their successes and wanted that for us.

I remember my older brother, Steven said to my father that he did not want to go to college; it was not something he envisioned himself doing. But my father made it clear that he only had two options to choose from, go to school or enlist in the Army. He made it clear that he would not allow him to stay in this house forever. If my brother wanted to make it big and wanted to be successful, he knew the right choice. So, he went to and later graduated from Saint Peters College in Jersey City and became a successful accountant.

But all these limited choices our father wanted us to pursue did make life a little difficult for me. I was not particularly great in school or academics; as a matter of fact, I was less than average, or so the teachers thought. Upon going to Snyder High School in Jersey City, they told my mom I did not score well enough to be in college preparatory. They recommended trade training. She had to meet with the principal and told him in no certain terms, "**He's *going to college, now do your job and prepare him*.**"

Initially, while I was in college, I had no idea what I wanted to do. I went to college to play basketball; that was my initial passion. It was only after my major knee surgery did I decide I wanted to become a doctor. When I met with my advisor, I was told that my grades probably were not good enough to get into professional school. I remember that meeting to this day. I heard my advisor, but as usual, I did not listen.

As discussed, my father was a very disciplined man, and he had to be, he did serve in the Army, after all. But it was his '**can't stop me**' attitude that I have learned from has influenced my life, and he inspires me with everything he achieved just because he worked hard. To this very day, I miss my dad. His discipline and hard work were extraordinary, and thankfully, I have learned these great traits from him. I remember calling him and telling him that my advisor said I could probably never go to professional or medical school; he said four words, "*Work harder, study more*."

He always told me, "*Do not tell me what you cannot do, tell me what you can do, tell me what you are willing to do, and tell me if you are ready to pay the price*."

Many people develop their personalities from their homes and the people they grow up with. I have. Honesty, ethics, commitment, sacrifice, discipline, and a '**Whatever It Takes**' attitude are all critical contributors to my success today. And I learned all of these from my parents, coaches, and many of my teachers. My father was the most disciplined man I knew; he was an army man. He sacrificed years of his life in the Army and bypassed college as he worked away at multiple jobs with a fierce commitment for us. He would say, *"You can't go back, so move forward."*

I had a father who was willing to sacrifice everything for his children, and I will always remember that about him. I remember once when we had a basketball game against Long Island University; after the game, my father went into his pockets and gave me about ten or twenty dollars. So, I could take a few teammates out for a bite to eat. But that was a lot of money back then, I was so happy about this, and he knew it would make me happy. But I remember my mother saying to him, *"Mike, you cannot give him that. That's all the money you have for lunch all week."*

And he replied saying, *"Don't worry, I'll make do."*

It was things like these that my father did for our family and me that stuck with me. He gave me all the money he had for his own food because I had played a good game. And even when I tried returning the money, he refused to take it back, saying he would make do. I never really realized until I was much older all the sacrifices my parents made for us.

He was a great man, my mom was a great woman, and if I'm successful today, I have learned from both of them. And all these sacrifices made me realize how I could have been a better son to them. They did so much for me. My mother was a tough woman as well, a typical Jewish mother. A lot of guilt, hard to please. I may have fought with her, even some days hated her, but I know her intent was for my betterment.

She always in her way supported me, pushed me, guilted me, and deep down believed in me. And we had a unique relationship. She loved my dad, respected my dad, but like us, she pushed him. To better her life, his life, our lives. This led to a lot of fighting in our home. She always threatened to leave my dad and once even did for a few days, but she came home.

"Only because of you and your brother I returned" she'd say.

Oh, the guilt.

I did not always consider myself a smart man early in my life in Jersey City, and I was utterly ignorant about how success happens. My father was successful as a father, my mother was successful as a mother, but neither was very successful in business. I often found a look of desperation on my father's face when he opened up the bills and threw them in the garbage.

Then, like any curious young man, I looked at those bills that he did not have the money to pay.

This hurt my father because he wanted to provide for his family. That was his number one purpose, his number one goal. However, he wanted a better life for both of his sons. He regretted his four years in the war versus going to college. The one quality I got from my father, though, was his '**Can't Stop Me**' attitude. He worked two jobs, and he did whatever it took to put food on the table. Often, in my early years, I remember the landlord talked to my father about his being late of his rent, In the summer the factory was slow, and they would lay him off for weeks at end. He'd sit in a chair, the empty look in his eyes on those days I will never forget. My father may have struggled, but he promised he would take care of it and always did.

Let me share this story with you, it's not mine, but one I've come to love and understand.

One day a father came home from work late again, tired and irritated, to find his 7-year-old son waiting for him at the door.

"Daddy, may I ask you a question?"

"Yeah, sure, what is it?" replied the father.

"Daddy, how much money do you make an hour?"

"That's none of your business. What makes you ask such a thing?" the father said angrily.

"I just want to know. Please tell me, how much do you make an hour?" pleaded the little boy.

"If you must know, I make $ 20 an hour."

"Oh," the little boy replied, head bowed. Looking up, he said,

"Daddy, may I borrow $ 10, please?"

The father was furious.

"If the only reason you wanted to know how much money I make is just so you can borrow some to buy a silly toy or some other nonsense, then you march yourself straight to your room and go to bed. Think about why you're being so selfish. I work long, hard hours every day and don't have time for such childish games."

The little boy quietly went to his room and shut the door. The man sat down and started to get even madder about the little boy's questioning. How dare he ask such questions only to get some money? After an hour or so, the man calmed down and started to think he may have been a little hard on his son. Maybe there was something he really needed to buy with that $ 10 and he didn't ask for money very often. The man went to the door of the little boy's room and opened the door.

"*Are you asleep, son?*" he asked.

"*No, Daddy, I'm awake,*" replied the boy.

"*I've been thinking; maybe I was too hard on you earlier,*" the man said.

"*It's been a long day and I took my aggravation out on you. Here's that $ 10 you asked for.*"

The little boy sat straight up, beaming. "*Oh, thank you, Daddy,*" he yelled.

Then, reaching under his pillow, he pulled out some more crumpled bills. The man, seeing that the boy already had money, started to get angry again. The little boy slowly counted out his money, then looked up at the man.

"*Why did you want more money if you already had some?*" the father grumbled.

"*Because I didn't have enough, but now I do,*" the little boy replied.

"*Daddy, I have $ 20 now. Can I buy an hour of your time?*"

I love this story, because this is my story. My father loved me very much, but rarely had time for me. Only later in life did I realize that here was a man who worked two jobs, six days a week.

For the lucky ones, our parents and our childhood give us our core values and beliefs. These are the things we were taught and shown as a child. Most people are the way they are because they were raised and follow a particular religion. That is all they have ever known. Our early years play a significant role in our life.

Let me get this straight. My home life was not always a happy home. Neither of my parents liked their jobs and hated to be hounded by bill collectors. They tried to keep up with the Jones's, but the Jones's always had more. My mother always wanted a home in the suburbs as her siblings had. They fought continuously and mostly about money. Being raised in Jersey City was not ideal. No carpools, no school buses, no school lunches. You walked or took the bus. Throughout my life, neither of my parents ever drove me to a practice or a game. They were both working.

However, you do not have to be from the right home, with the right parents, to make the right choices. Take my wife and her life; it is the perfect example. Bonnie Kaplan, my wife of 41 years, had no known parents. The state of New Jersey raised her in an orphanage. As one of the older children, her life was always cooking, cleaning, and serving the younger ones in the state-run facility. My wife, however, like so many, wanted a better life for herself.

She never gave up or gave in to her situation. She wanted more out of life. Her youth was full of helping orphans adapt, adjust and survive. The lessons she learned from helping children inspired her, motivated her. My wife thus decided at a young age that she wanted to be a teacher. She never thought only rich kids could go to college. She had no parents to pay for her education. She earned scholarships and took out student loans. She worked all during college; she sewed, cleaned, and did what she had to. She set a goal and was willing to do '**whatever it takes**' to achieve it.

Bonnie became an avid reader, and when not tending to the children or her chores, she would lose herself in books. John F Kennedy said, *"All great leaders are readers, but not all readers are leaders."* My point here is regardless of who you are, regardless of your upbringing, regardless of your education, you can succeed if you put your mind to it. If you develop '**A CAN'T STOP ME ATTITUDE.**'

With purpose comes desire, discipline, and the '**Whatever It Takes**' attitude. In life, you can reach any level you put your mind to. Life is a marathon, and you must always keep your focus on the finish line and never give up when you are tired or feel defeated. The great ones in history, like Sir Winston Churchill, were famous for giving a speech. He recited only three words. He stood up, and he said these three words, *"**Never Give Up.**"* If you can master these three words, you can master your destiny.

"Success is not the key to happiness. Happiness is the key to success. If you love what you are doing, you will be successful."

—Albert Schweitzer

CHAPTER 2

Success Is An Inside Job

*"Success is not final; failure is not fatal: It is the
courage to continue that counts."*

—Winston S. Churchill

There are a few phrases that I live my life by, '**Can't Stop Me,** '**Whatever
It Takes,'** and '**The Road to Success is Always Under Construction.'**
Most successful people have had long and winding roads on their journey,
but you get what you want in life. I think the famous phrase by Winston
Churchill, **NEVER GIVE UP,** is the key to obtaining your desired destiny.

Many factors influence personality, including genetics, environment,
schooling, coaches, parenting, and other societal variables. Perhaps most
important, though, is the ongoing interaction of all these influences that
continue to shape a personality over time.

Personality involves inborn traits and cognitive and behavioral patterns
that influence how people think and act. Temperament is a vital part of the
character that is determined by genetically inherited traits. But inherently,
we were all built to survive, to thrive, and to succeed. Imagine the human
heart beats 72 times per minute, a hundred thousand times per day, over
37 million times per year, and never takes a minute off. The human body
was made for perfection, and it is proof you can overcome anything, that
the greatest miracle of life is life itself.

*"Over time, our personality helps develop our character.
Character is a part of personality influenced by experience that
continues to grow and change throughout life. While personality
continues to change over time and respond to life's influences
and experiences, much of it is determined by inborn traits and
early childhood experiences. The great news is you can always
change. A man's mind may be likened to a garden, which may
be intelligently cultivated or allowed to run wild, but it must,
and will, bring forth whether cultivated or neglected. If no*

useful seeds are put into it, then an abundance of useless weed
seeds will fall therein and will continue to produce their kind."

—James Allen, As a Man Thinketh

You have most likely, at some point in your life, heard someone say that people are a *"product of their environment."* This means their personality has been greatly influenced by the three things we just looked at. They were born with particular traits. Their living situation and any impacting situations they experienced all helped create who they are.

Being a product of your environment can be good or bad. You can grow up in a violent environment. It is not always good. Your environment consists of more than just your parents or your family. It also includes the area and era you grew up in, how you think, and your peers. Having a weak environment at home can lead to venturing out to seek an identity.

Not having the proper guidance can even lead you down the wrong path. You cannot choose the environment you grow up in, but most likely, you are the way you are because of it. However, with goals and dreams, you can alter your life and your destiny.

We as people build an impression of ourselves by reflecting on how our loved ones and others around us treat us. We tend to believe that we are a product of our environment and that nothing can be changed if it had been bad. However, James Allen states about our mindset,

"As he thinks, so he is; as he continues to think, so he remains."

So think BIG.

Self-image is a product of learning. Early childhood influences, such as parents, teachers, and caregivers, significantly impact our self-image. They are mirrors reflecting to us an image of ourselves. Our experiences with others, such as teachers, friends, and family, add to the image in the mirror. Relationships reinforce what we think and feel about ourselves. The image we see in the mirror may be an accurate or distorted view of who we really are.

Based on this view, we develop either a positive or negative self-image. The strengths and weaknesses we have adopted affect how we act today. With a positive self-image, we can recognize and own our potential while being realistic about our liabilities and limitations. With a negative self-image, we focus on our faults and weaknesses, distorting failure and imperfections.

Self-image is important because how we think about ourselves affects how we feel about ourselves and how we interact with others and the world around us. A positive self-image can boost our physical, mental, social, emotional, and spiritual well-being. On the other hand, a negative self-image can decrease our satisfaction and ability to function in these areas.

There is a connection between one's self-esteem and performance. People who feel good about themselves produce good results. We believe that other people's wrong opinions of us are who we are; they affect us. They can paralyze and stop your progress.

Even if you have a "**can't stop me**" attitude, sometimes you have to stop yourself. You see, there are good habits and bad habits. First off, you need to know the difference. Secondly you must convert bad habits into good ones.

Who would've thought I used to smoke cigarettes? This was a habit I picked up in college. Heck, my mother was a chain smoker, my father smoked, my brother smoked. If genetics and geography come into play, I was destined to smoke. My Uncle Herb Punyon was the only one in the family that said you need to quit. Yet, I felt it was cool, made me look tougher. I was hooked mentally and physically.

It was not until during my first year in Chiropractic School I was invited to try out for the United States Maccabi team. A team is chosen from the best Jewish basketball players in the country and all over the world. Basically, it is the Jewish Olympics. My older son Michael eventually played and stared for the team from Florida. Funny how life goes full circle.

Personally, I was honored to be invited. However, I was on this day trying to bring my game back to its old level, I realized how out of shape I really was. Running up and down the court with 100 of the best players from the United States was humbling. I played well and passed the test but knew I could not continue to smoke.

It was on that day I knew I had to quit smoking; it took me a few years to accomplish that task. I continued to try to quit smoking over the years and failed miserably every time. But I realized once I became a doctor, successful doctors were not smokers. I made up my mind (set a goal) that once I got into practice I would quit smoking. I can now say that I have not had a cigarette since 1978, 43 years.

My wife never saw me with a cigarette in my hands. I learned things don't make you cool; you make things cool. The sadness of the story is my mother ended up dying of pneumonia, my father ended up having a pacemaker and then quadruple bypass, and my brother died of lung cancer. Sometimes we have to drop habits to be successful and there are many other habits that we have to drop besides smoking. Some of these habits may seem harmless, but Bad habits can be broken according to Maxwell Maltz, who wrote the book "Psychocybernetics", says it takes 21 consecutive days of doing something to break a habit, so let's start our 21 days now.

Everyone has bad habits they want to break, but instead of scorning yourself for being helpless to break them, use the fundamentals of forming habits to your advantage. Habits, good or bad, follow a typical three-step pattern. By breaking down the cycle of a bad habit, you can identify what triggers the routine and begin to address what really needs to change. This way you can establish a pattern for new and healthier habits. Engaging in habit changes for self-improvement is key to vitality and well-being at all ages. Summoning motivation for long-term goals gets harder when we move beyond the family- and career-building stages of life.

Motivation and confidence

One common reason people do not succeed in making lasting change is that they don't first create a solid foundation. You need to make sure the habit change is important and you have confidence that you can achieve it. This might sound simple, but often people take on changes that are important to others but not to themselves, or they feel down deep that the task is too daunting. Before you can focus on changing a bad habit, you need to measure both motivation and confidence.

The three Rs

Once you have chosen your habit and measured your readiness, identify the three Rs:

Regret: *a trigger initiating the behavior, why I quit smoking.*

Routine: *the behavior or action you take, change your routine.*

Reward: *the benefit from the behavior or action. Heath Happiness.*

Review reminder and routine

To break the bad habit, just drop it. This may sound like the simple solution, and it is. When you drop something, it often breaks. First, stop eating the junk food. But, of course, this is never easy, because the real issue is the habit, not the food itself. Understand the reminder and routine. Your first step is to shine a light on what happens with the current reminder and routine. In this example, at 8 p.m. you visit the kitchen for snack foods and then get comfortable on the couch. With me and smoking, after a meal, a cup of coffee, or during a break at class, it became a routine that I would smoke a cigarette with the feeling, but sometimes routine can trigger the regret.

Now ask yourself, why do you smoke, eat junk food? Make a list of short words or phrases that describe your feelings before you begin the routine. Hunger? Boredom? Habit? The desire for pleasure, even though pleasure can lead to pain. To REGRET.

Find your triggers. Research has found that habit triggers typically fit into five categories: location, time, emotional state, other people, and surroundings. Boost your motivation. Next, make a list of different types of rewards you also enjoy. The goal is not to 'punish' yourself for seeking pleasure, but to choose rewards that make you feel good while investing in your new healthier habit. These may include taking a walk, meditating, or calling a friend, or snacks that are good for your brain and body like whole fruit, low-fat plain yogurt, or a cup of hot tea. I started chewing a piece of gum, or having a lifesaver, every time I wanted a cigarette. My ultimate reward was improvement in my own self-image. I am not proud that I smoked or any other bad habits I have had, but conquering each bad habit with the reward that you can change, you can defeat anything, is a great tool to have in your arsenal.

Make a plan

Once you have examined your routine, the reminder that triggers your behavior, and the reward for your habit, you can figure out which factors you can shift and thus break the cycle. It may take some time, and you may have to experiment with different rewards or triggers to find the right ones, but soon you can shift your bad habit into a good one. Once you know how to choose the habit you want to change, and break down the cycle of how habits work, you are empowered to make lasting change. Regret a bad habit, break the routine, and reward yourself. Remember nobody can stop you, but you. Turn bad habits into good habits and good things will happen in your life.

My partner, my muse Dr. Perry Bard's favorite word is yes. He hates the word NO. Winners say yes to every task. Example, if a project, partnership or opportunity doesn't resonate with you and does not feel aligned with your values and your goals, you need to be comfortable about setting boundaries. Learn how to say no with kindness right from the start because, as you become more successful, more people will compete for your time and attention. Not setting healthy boundaries will end up in overwhelm and burnout. It's OK to say no, but do it under your terms.

The people who impact us can leave deep, lasting impressions on a young mind at an early age. What messages did they leave you with? What bad or good habits did you obtain?

By careful introspection, you can now examine the validity of such judgment. Is it wise to still carry their opinions, or can you now move on? Too many of us fall into the trap of making wrong career choices based on others' opinions, and we end up focusing on improving weaknesses, which can never measure up to the power of just working with our strengths. Every day, if you live up to who you naturally are, you will be one of the few who follow an authentic life. By flowing with your strengths, you gain greater work satisfaction and become invincible in your character.

Even I have been affected by how others treated me, the mean things people ever said about me have stuck with me. Yes, I have gotten over all the adversities and have come out on the other side better than ever. I have proved everyone wrong, but you never forget the things people say about you and how they treated you. These things heal, but they still show.

As a high school kid and college kid, I had terrible acne, which did terrible things to my self-image. I was so insecure at this time I never even went to my senior High School prom. But winners win and whiners wine, so I started getting into nutrition because of this and tried to figure out how to fix this. But being teased for my acne and not looking perfect like some other kids affected me deeply. Even being told I was not good enough to get into professional school affected me but did not stop me.

Early on, the world told me I did not look good, and I was not good enough to be a high school basketball player, I was not good enough to play college basketball, I was not good enough to be a doctor, something my father and mother so deeply desired for me. I worried I could not live up to those expectations, so I felt terrible about who I was. I did not do well in my early years or high school, and I did not do great in my SAT's. My self-image was tied to these external factors and people. That is why I smoked cigarettes. However, I dreamt of a better life. I saw myself through a different looking glass. I rewarded myself for not smoking.

When your self-impression is tied to what other people think of you, how do you feel when others approve of you and your decisions? You feel great. But when other people disapprove of you, you feel like crap.

You end up becoming a slave to what other people want running around trying to please everyone with every decision. Never really tuning into your own needs. Not just that, you think terribly of yourself and who you are because of someone else's biased opinions.

This people-pleasing turns into you squashing your desires. By contorting and molding yourself to fit the idea of what other people think you should be, you stop showing your real personality. You stop feeling like you can be yourself. And you stop trusting your judgment because you assume that other people know better. Early on I smoked cause when other people's opinions are more important than your own, you live life on their terms and not yours. And yet, you are the one who will be left with regret for not having lived a life truly authentic to who you are. Other people will not be in your life forever; they and their opinions will be long gone. And you will be left wondering why you gave them so much power over you.

Any time you allow someone to negatively influence the way you think, feel, or behave, you give them power over your life. It will rob you of the mental strength you need to reach your most tremendous potential. Other people stunt your growth.

Some people will not like you, and some people will not approve of your choices. But you do not have to let their opinions affect how you feel about yourself. Feeling bad about yourself based on what someone says or how that person thinks about you gives that person too much power over you.

If you are reading this, I wish you knew how much I believe in you. I hope you could read my mind and know that I actually feel this way about you. Even if you do not consider yourself super intelligent, talented, or worthy enough for others, know that I believe in you. If you just stop thinking of what other people think of you and realize your own worth, you can reach your full potential, and that would blow your mind.

If somehow, the entire world reached its full potential on an individual-by-individual basis, we actually could create a utopia. And maybe that will never happen, but here's the next best thing you can do.

We all have a choice; we can choose to accept our circumstances, and we can choose to believe something blindly because this is just what others have taught us, or we can choose to do the total opposite. We can choose to question everything and change our values and beliefs if they do not serve us for good. Regardless of your situation or upbringing, you should never limit your life and what you can do; by placing a limit on your life, you give yourself a reason not even to try.

Those who believe their life has no limit will take chances, try new things, and push themselves, enabling them to achieve great things inevitably. Do not spend years trying to behave appropriately so that other people will accept you; do not even waste a second doing this. You do this because underneath, you feel like your true self is unworthy and undeserving. But once you realize this and unravel this truth, you recognize that you are just as worthy and deserving as anyone else, and you should start being yourself—your true self.

None of this means that you do not care about people or anyone but you. We are humans and we need connection and support. But seek out your kind for mutual support and growth. Being around people who share your visions and goals is tremendously more helpful than trying to change those who have the opposite agenda. Somewhere out there, some people can identify with you and appreciate you for who you are.

Do not waste time trying to hang on to bad habits or those who expect you to conform to their wishes and wants. Cultivate authenticity, and you will always find those you are meant to be with.

Other people's negative opinions are likely reflecting their own limiting beliefs about life. Develop the skill to recognize and ignore these. Put on your blinders and stop looking at what everyone else is doing. Seriously, everyone's journey is different, and so no one's life will look the same. Often when we get lost in worrying about what everyone else thinks, it's because we exist in a state of perpetual comparison. We look at what everyone else is doing and believe that we fail unless we do it similarly.

You need to develop positive self-esteem and self-image. And these are things that only we can give to ourselves. We can only grant ourselves self-esteem. No one else can provide it to us, and no one else can believe in us enough to fill this gap. That is just not how it works, and it has to come from within. And this is part of the issue, that we tend to over-value other people's opinions over ourselves.

When you overvalue what other people think of you, it is because you're looking for someone else to make you feel good. You are looking for someone else to give you self-esteem, but only you can create a better impression of yourself for yourself. The most successful way to stop caring so much about what other people think is to start feeling great about yourself regardless of their opinion. Your life is not about impressing them. It is about impressing yourself, doing your best, and knowing that you are doing the most that you can.

You would care a lot less about what others think about you if you knew how little time others actually spend thinking about you. It is true: Everyone has enough to occupy their mind, and everyone has their own insecurities. If you are worried about how you come across someone, keep in mind that they are probably worried about the same.

Get to know yourself instead of others. What do you really like? What do you really want? Are you making choices about your career, relationships, and pastimes because you want them or because they will impress someone else? Allow yourself to try new things and wonder what you would pursue or enjoy if you were not so worried about being judged.

Before anything else, you need to love yourself. When you constantly worry about what others think of you, it can sometimes make you realize that you do not spend much time on your thoughts. Try and practice self-care to show self-love, which can be done through many things; whatever brings you joy can work; just try and self-love yourself every day. This can take a while, but once you learn to love and accept yourself, you can start to stop worrying so much as you will accept yourself for who you are and will not need anyone else's approval.

Everything in life involves making a choice. Choose to believe that regardless of how you begin life, the way you live and the person you become is determined by you. Choose to seek out new opportunities and surround yourself with good people. Break bad habits, develop healthy habits. Anything and everything are possible if you want it enough and believe in yourself. I am a prime example of this.

Nobody, and I mean nobody, ever thought I would be a doctor. I was laughed at and mocked for how terrible I was in grade school, and I was told I could not be much. And it affected me but not for long because what they believed didn't matter. The only thing that matters was what I wanted and what I thought about myself. Sometimes it simply comes down to desire. I desired a better life, I desired being special. Once I stopped listening to others and focused on my desires, I started achieving little successes.

However, once I got to college and then professional school, I realized I had to work harder than the average person. I could not give 80%, and I had to give 110%. I could not listen to my naysayers, and I had a listen to that inner voice within me that said, "**Never Give Up**," "**Do Whatever it Takes.**"

I was not born a student, but I became a student, and even today, I teach the doctors that I work with throughout the United States that the enemy of great is good; it's not good enough to just be good when greatness may be around the corner. The road to success is always under construction, that's your job to build the life of your dreams, to remember the only person that can stop you is you.

When I was in the third grade, I had a teacher named Mrs. Duncan; she was very abusive and often smacked me because I could not sit still. Heck, breakfast in the Kaplan house was a bowl of Sugar Frosted Flakes, and the sugar rush led to constant explosions that were going on in my brain. Mrs. Duncan would always call me out in front of the class and would say that I'm a "*no-good person.*"

She made me sit next to this one girl named Anita, she was the quietest girl in the class, but I had her talking in no time. This made my teacher go crazy; how could I get the quietest girl in the whole class to talk to me?

I recall raising my hand to be excused to use the men's lavatory, but my third-grade teacher, Miss Duncan, refused to recognize me. So, I stood up and raised my hand. She glared and said, "*Sit down.*"

I really had to go to the bathroom, which I didn't want to do, so I stood up and raised my hand again.

"*Sit down!*" she yelled, but I didn't move.

"*Sit down, or I'll send you to the principal's office,*" she said again as I stood there.

I knew I was in trouble at that point, and not just with the teacher. The way our school was set up, adjacent to every class was a coat room where we would hang our coats and put our lunch there. It was almost like a mini locker room, away from the class. Well, I went to the coat room, but I had to go to the bathroom, so on my own accord, I decided that there was no way I would pee in my pants. Disregarding her instruction, I walked to the bathroom, but I coincidentally was walking to the bathroom when she came to check on me, and I had disappeared. Finally, she found me in the hall, walking back from the bathroom. She grabbed my shirt and hit me on my bottom.

"How dare you disobey me!" she yelled.

When I returned she told me to go and see the principal right away.

They kept me in the principal's office for the rest of the day, telling me that I couldn't return to the classroom until my parents came in to see him. That day, I came home and told my father about the whole event. Except for that morning, I don't recall my father ever showing up at my school, skipping his work. I don't think he ever came to my school before, and I don't think he had to again.

"Mrs. Duncan" he said.

"Excuse me, did you not allow my son to go to the bathroom?"

"He was being disruptive" she said.

"That was not the question. Did you not allow my son to go to the men's room?

"Sir, he was being disruptive"

"That was not the question. Did you not allow my son to go to the men's room?"

"Sir he was being disruptive" she again repeated.

"Mam. Let's get one thing straight here and now. If my son has to go to the bathroom, you will allow him. Because I am the last person you'd ever want to see again."

The principal now chimed in, *"Well, rules are rules,"* the principal stated.

"Sir, my son had to go to the bathroom, to the point where he was going to pee his pants. Unfortunately, the teacher left him no option," he told the principal flatly.

Holding back his temper but with a strong stare he said, *"We have rules in our house, too. If my son had peed in his trousers, his classmates and friends would have laughed at him, and he would not have been permitted back into my house. Now put my son back in class, have the instructor treat my kid with respect, and I hope never to see you again,"* my father stated, giving the principal a stern look and a sharp tone.

The principal stood frozen; you did not want to make this man mad. He never had to come back to the school and Mrs. Duncan stopped picking on me.

By defying Mrs. Duncan on that day, I stood up for myself for the first time in my life against an adult. I did what I had to do, and to me, it was the best decision I could have ever made. Making your own decisions is part of building your own self. Don't let anyone control your destiny.

The mind is the most powerful weapon in the world and what you think is what you become. My failures were never failures if I chose to think of them differently. I thought of them as steppingstones to my eventual success. But this is all because I took control of my thoughts and did not let other's opinions about my life interfere. All I want from you is to "**never to give up**" and "**do whatever it takes**" to get what you want.

We must be conscious of the expectations and standards of others around us. However, we must cultivate the strength to act despite such standards and expectations when we believe it is necessary. We must develop the ability to act by ourselves and for ourselves.

"Life imposes things on you that you can't control, but you still have the choice of how you're going to live through this."

—Celine Dion

CHAPTER 3

How to Rise Over Adversities

*"It's Not Whether You Get Knocked Down,
It's Whether You Get Up."*

—Vince Lombardi

Success, my friends, is an inside job. I see being successful as a desire that resides somewhere in all of us. It does not matter whether it's a child, a youth, middle-aged, or old aged person; at each stage of our wide life span, is our inbuilt desire to be successful and proceed forward consistently towards more massive success.

The mindset or the necessary mentality of competing with others is an innate instinct. It can frequently be noticed during all phases of our life, including schools, colleges, coaching, work fields, including organizations, offices, etc., to name a few. Compared to our efforts towards the desire and effort to succeed, we often expect much more and want success to knock on our doors very soon. If it does not happen, we usually get frustrated, which may result in us giving up. If we quit, it may take us deeper inside the darkness of inferiority and even depression. It is better to fight, to lose than to quit. I never quit; let me share a story of when I could have surrendered, could have stopped, but I did not.

When I was nine years old, I tried out for Biddy Basketball. I was one of 80 children who were trying out for the team. In those days, there were no trophies just for participation and no certificates. I remember this as if it was just yesterday, and I was standing there in excitement and anticipation of being chosen, hoping to be selected. I was just a kid; I thought I would be picked.

My brother, who was four years older than me, and my cousin Steven Garfunkel were also trying out, and they were two of the better players. Name after name was called as I waited for mine. Yet, my name never came; out of 80 boys, I was the last boy standing and the last kid chosen.

I cannot tell you exactly how I felt at that moment, it was too much to even describe in words, and as I write this with a tear in my eye, I can still remember the shame, the absolute disappointment, and the look of sympathy in my father's eyes. I remember hearing laughing, and they were all laughing at me. I might have been only nine at the time, but it was the worst day of my life; at least I felt like it then.

My father tried to make me feel better and shared some words of wisdom, he said,

"Son, you are only nine, you will grow, but you need to practice more and show them that they are all wrong."

I cried myself to sleep that night, vowing to be the best of them all one day. I took my father's advice to heart and promised to achieve greatness. I just needed to practice and work hard to achieve my goals, and I would never have to relive this shame ever again. Shame and embarrassment were my motivator, not my enemy.

Nobody is great without work, and I could not be either. Hard work is always the guideline of outstanding achievements. Nothing extraordinary comes without it. Getting organized is hard work. Setting goals, making plans to achieve your goals, and staying on track is hard work.

But if you work hard, there is little chance that you will ever fail. Practicing and hard work is a slow process, and you may rise slowly, but you are sure to rise. There is only one way to the top: '**Hard Work**.'

The only thing that separates talented individuals from successful ones is a lot of hard work, and that is precisely what I intended to be, successful and the best of them all. And as Henry Ford says, *"The harder you work, the luckier you get"* — the more successful you get.

Hard work is one of the essential things in life as it helps us be more confident. If you work hard, you will achieve all your goals and fulfill all your dreams. Working hard with full determination always pushes us one step ahead in life and surpasses our limitations.

Being chosen last that day for the Biddy Basketball team made me feel terrible, but it gave me the push I needed to work hard and practice; if I wanted to be chosen first and be the best, I had to be the best. From that day on I always had a ball in my hand. I was laughed at as I dribbled my way to school. I was laughed at when I dribbled home. The key to laughter is who gets the last laugh.

The more efficient you are with your practice, the more focused you are on your goal, the more quickly you will learn and the faster you will excel. When it comes to learning new skills, and in my case, basketball, it is easy to get discouraged with our progress, but it is essential to realize that learning skills can take time – and that is okay. The most important thing is that you stick with it and keep progressing towards your goals.

Although I tried, I didn't score one basket the first year, not one. My dad said,

"There's always next year, don't give up."

"But dad," I said,

"I'm not big enough."

He said,

"The difference between a little shot and a big shot is that a little shot keeps shooting."

And so I did; I went to the community center every day. And when the center was closed I went to the park or anyone's back yard who had a hoop. I made up my mind that I was going to be the best.

Focusing on what you want to learn and improve upon is the best way to practice effectively. By focusing on your goals during your practice, you will be much more effective with your time, and you will learn a lot faster. What I mean to say is that I practiced, I worked hard, and I grew; I discovered an entire sport because I wanted to; I found a whole sport because I wanted to. The following year I was picked in the first half; at eleven years old, I was chosen in the top 10. At about age twelve, I went on to be the leading scorer in the league. I became a captain and was selected for the All-Star team, and I was the top scorer. I was also recruited to play for St. Aloysius. I was recruited by Eddie Ford, the same Eddie Ford who scoured the schools for talent. He later helped Duke and Coach K get Bobby Hurley Jr. his uncle Brian Hurley was the top point guard in the city. He was clearly better than me at age 12. From him, I developed another goal, beat Brian Hurley.

I knew then that I wanted to play high school basketball, and private schools recruited me, but the competition was in the public schools. So, I went to Snyder High School. In his book **"The Miracle of St. Anthony"** (a must-read for any basketball junkie), Bob Hurley Sr., told his kids at St. Anthony's if they did not study, he'd send them to Snyder High School with the thugs. A suburban kid would be scared as hell if he or she spent one day in a Jersey City public school or even on the streets of Jersey City because they would be introduced to an environment they never knew existed. This was not the lifestyle that we necessarily wanted; this was the lifestyle that our parents could afford, and we had to make the best of it.

From my early childhood into young adulthood, being brought up in Jersey City was not easy. Because of drugs, fights, mugging, the pool and showers at my high school were only open to teams and only after practice. Fights, muggings and drugs were a major issue and the showers were off limits. After gym class, you simply toweled off and went to class. I wanted out, and I wanted to live in the suburbs like my cousins; I dreamt about it; I longed for it and knew not only did I need to play high school basketball, but I also needed to get a scholarship to get out of Jersey City.

Every child faced many difficulties being brought up in Jersey City. You never had to be the one to start the trouble, and no, do not worry about that, because trouble would have its way of finding you. As elementary school kids and high school kids, the playground games and fights were epic. Daily we would have to fight to protect ourselves or make sure that we weren't being bullied.

My friend Neal Chapnick was a tough kid; he enjoyed fighting and always had my back. In high school, who would think we would have to worry about someone having a knife, maybe even punching you in the face and scaring you into giving up your personal belongings? Daily people would ask you for your lunch money. You never gave it, or they'd know you were weak. These were the things we would eventually have to deal with, come face to face with, and we were just kids.

Imagine going from the last boy chosen to become the leading scorer in the league. Being known in the leagues and at the parks in Jersey City helped you develop a reputation. My name was on the radar for all private and public schools, one school that recruited me was Newark Academy. They just had their leading scorer named Steve Kaplan (no relation) go onto Annapolis. What a school Newark Academy was, what a campus. However, when I tested, I did not test well. They wanted me to repeat 8th grade and do a preparatory year, and even then, they didn't know if I'd academically qualify. The naysayers are always there. Like dragons espousing fire, you take the heat, and you slay the dragon, you move on.

So, it was off to Snyder High School, one of the most challenging schools with some of the most talented players in all of Jersey City. In High School, I quickly moved up from the freshman team and played for Junior

Varsity as a freshman. This team was one of the most talented teams I'd ever played on. Practices were intense. Each practice was like a game, and you played to survive. This was a great experience, and I was no longer the best on the best team in Jersey City. I was just happy to be on the team. My goal was to be a starter as a sophomore, to one day lead the team in scoring.

Eventually I accomplished both. Sports taught me to believe in myself, to set goals.

"Goal setters are goal getters."

This team was talented and well-coached by Eddie Butler. Coach Butler believed in me; he saw my desire not only to be good but to win. And win we did. We were unstoppable. Although we didn't go undefeated, I don't remember losing a game. Our leading scorer was a kid named Henry Frey, he didn't look like a player, but he could score on anyone. I was proud of how this kid from the projects took me under his wing. As a freshman, I learned the power of winning, the power of teamwork. I was not the best player that year, but I played on the best team. This taught me the lesson of teamwork. I went on to play in the county championship game against Hoboken at the Jersey City Armory in front of 5000 to 6000 people. That was the best day of my life I had so far.

I remember my whole family being there. I remember looking up at the crowd's vastness, playing in the same arena that St. Peter's College played their home games. Although you heard the cheering of thousands of people, nothing meant more to me than the look of pride in my father's eyes. My father believed in me, he pushed me, consulted and consoled me, and he knew now, at that moment, that I was not just an ordinary boy, a regular player. Imagine in a few short years I went from the bottom, being laughed at, to now playing in front of thousands of screaming people. WOW

After my freshman year, I knew what I wanted to do, needed to do. I wanted to be the captain of the Junior Varsity and the leading scorer. Not a simple task, but going from ordinary to extraordinary takes extra. I worked twice as hard every day, and my summer was spent on the courts, playing, practicing, and preparing every minute of every day. I played under the sun and at night under the lights. I only went home to eat and then back to the courts. I went on to not only be the captain, but I also became the team's leading scorer of the Junior Varsity as a sophomore and even sat some varsity games on the best team in Jersey City. That summer, I met and worked with legendary coach Bobby Knight. Most coaches worked in camps in those days, and he worked at Five Star Basketball Camp. Five Star was the premier basketball camp with the best players in the country. Founded in 1966, Five Star was the brainchild of two New York City basketball junkies Howard Garfinkel and Will Klein, and both shared a common passion and purpose: To create a top-notch teaching camp and help kids improve their games.

Five-Star was filled with Future Hall of Famers, Hubie Brown, and Chuck Daly taught and lectured at that very first session. Bob Knight invented 'teaching stations' as the camp's lead instructor two years later. Who would have thought Coach Knight would have taken a liking to me. Daily, dozens of legendary coaches, including John Calipari, Rick Pitino, Mike Malone, and Frank Vogel, all launched their careers on Five Star courts. I was lucky to have two legends, two former NBA players from South Carolina, as my coaches. Bobby Cremons of Georgia Tech coaching fame and John Roache of New York City and New Jersey Net fame.

No, my parents did not have the money to send me there, but my mother got me a job working in the kitchen and as a waiter; not the best job, but one of the best experiences of my basketball life.

Playing at Five Star working daily with coach Knight was intense. He was then a new young coach at Army. He focused on defense, so I became a stopper. I came back my junior year as twice the player I was my sophomore year and became the 6th man on the best team in the city.

I guess from the time I was nine years old, I loved nothing on this earth as much as I loved the sport of basketball. I loved to fast break, play defense, I loved to run and gun. I was even given the nickname "Green Light" as I never saw a shot I did not like in high school, college, or at any gym or schoolyard I played at.

I spent two summers with the legendary Basketball coach Bobby Knight, plus, a day with him and my dad at West Point. His practices were mesmerizing. He is the one coach who revolutionized the game of basketball. No players intentionally picked up offensive fouls before Coach Knight. He mastered the art of defense; his success speaks louder than words. He is the second-winningest coach in the history of college basketball, and the first was one of his players Coach Mike Kryzewski. Knight was a no-nonsense man but truly a master motivator and teacher.

People have read a lot of stories about Coach Knight. I loved "**SEASON ON THE BRINK**" by John Feinstein. This # 1 sports bestseller chronicled a year with Coach Knight. He was intense; look at his disciples around the game, most notably Coach K from Duke. His influence on me was germane, and he knew how to make you better, stronger, and smarter. He was a professor of the game. With Coach Knight, you were always in class.

He taught me to play defense, pick up an offensive foul, and break up a full-court press. I loved the game as much as anyone who has ever lived and played the game, black or white, male or female. Like most former players, I would consider selling my soul just to play college ball again. It was a drug to me, and I was more than obsessed, I was addicted.

As a senior starter, I was now getting recruited by many Universities and accepted a scholarship to play college basketball at Fairleigh Dickinson University. Today, my picture hangs proudly on their walls. How quickly things changed, I went from last to first, from ordinary to extraordinary. All because I never gave up. I never stopped believing in myself. And because I developed the mantra, "**You Can't Stop Me**."

I went from an underachiever to an overachiever. My life has been a wild journey going from ordinary to extraordinary. Today I consider myself to have many talents. However, I do not believe they were innately given. Like Robert Redford, who starred in the movie "**The Natural**," I consider myself to be the opposite, the "**Un-natural**". I was a skinny, often sickly youth; I missed many school days and watched a lot of television. Television taught me how to dream. I watched "The Donna Reed Show", "My Three Sons", "Leave it To Beaver" all with good family messages all taking place in the suburbs. Then there was my Aunt Gloria and Uncle Herb Punyon. She was my mother's youngest sister and she lived in the suburbs of Teanck NJ. With my cousins Ellen and Amy, we often spent Sundays at their house, I'd play catch in the yard with my Uncle Herb while my exhausted father slept in front of the television. This was the life, imagine a backyard where you could play catch. Dinner was either Chinese or pizza, this was the life. I started dreaming every night of a better life of living in the suburbs. I didn't count sheep to go to sleep; I fantasized, dreamed of my future. I wanted it all and was willing to pay the price.

Although I was not naturally the most athletic, what I lacked in talent I made up for in passion and desire. Every day of practice was a game, I kept pushing myself knowing that basketball was a way out of Jersey City. After college basketball I even had offers to play professionally in Israel.

For all the success I have achieved, I believe basketball was the common denominator; basketball is a big part of my life; I think that is where I got that "**Can't stop me**" attitude from. I learned in basketball at a young age it did not matter that I was the smallest person on the court; I thought I had the biggest heart and could compete with anybody. I proved this to be true, in school, in sports, business, and life.

I realized I might have been small and skinny and considered not the most innately talented, but I made up for it. Talent is an inborn quality that gives you a shortcut to achieve what you want. But talent is futile unless you try hard to develop it. You cannot just sit around and expect a good result. Just because you have talent does not mean you can go on the court and be the team's Star. Hard work definitely beats talent when talent fails to work hard.

Whereas hard work is more important than talent and talent will only carry one so far. If one is not willing to put in the work to cultivate their talent, then the skill itself is virtually useless. Hard work, perseverance, and practice will beat out pure talent any day. You cannot truly become great at anything without motivation. Here is where the hard work comes into play. Anyone can have an idea, vision, or dream, but it takes hard work to make it a reality. That is how I became the best at basketball, talent or not.

There was a time in my life when I walked through the world known to myself and others as an athlete. It was part of my own definition of who I was and certainly the part I most respected. When I was a young man, I was not well built or ready for the rough-and-tumble of the game played in Jersey City, New Jersey.

From a young age, basketball provided an outlet for a repressed short, and rambunctious boy to express himself in public. Playing basketball transformed me. Once I put on that uniform, I was no longer the short, skinny acne-ridden kid. Basketball allowed me to introduce myself to anyone who had never met me or heard me speak out loud. It was through basketball I received praise, praise without uttering a single word. This was a far cry from my teachers at PS 17 that told my family I would never be college material.

I lost myself in the beauty of sport and made my family proud while passing through the silent eye of the storm that was my childhood. I cannot explain what the sport of basketball meant to me, and I always miss it. With my love of basketball and the love of being special, I believe it provided me with the goal, the dream, to be a doctor. It was because of basketball that

I had discipline, and this discipline helped me with professional school as I was not the best student that entered my class.

I was a far cry from being an All-American player, but I played with many of the best players in the country over the years and always held my own. Basketball gave me glimpses into the kind of man I was capable of becoming and how extraordinary I could be. I delighted in the pure physicality of that ceaseless, ever-moving sport. When I found myself driving the lane amongst even 7-foot players, the pure adrenaline of the crowds humming and screaming my name ignited a passion so deep that I still dream of the crowds. Basketball was my first passion, my chosen game, the love of my life, and I was the happiest boy who ever lived. Even at sixty-nine years old, I think of the many great players I played and the many coaches who saw something in this short, skinny white kid.

I was a kid who fell in love with the smell of the gym and the shape of a basketball. One skill I brought to the game was my ability to handle a basketball, and if you tried to stop me, I would dribble around and eventually get past you. No matter how big, how tall, I would go past you. I guess I learned the "**Can't Stop Me**" attitude at a young age.

Basketball forced me to deal head-on with my inadequacies and terrors with no room or tolerance for evasion. Though it was a long process, I learned to honor myself for what I accomplished in a sport where I was occasionally overmatched but never out of my league. I never once approached the greatness I so desired, but I was always tough, a winner and in the game throughout my career. Because I think in many ways I grew up a complete stranger to who I was, or who I could be. I first caught a glimpse of a determined young man who developed the ability to compete at a higher college level. Sometimes I look in the mirror and do not recognize this intense person who stares back at me.

In my early years, basketball was the only thing that granted me a complete and sublime unity and oneness with the world. I found joy beyond the realm of speech or language, and I lost myself in the pure, dazzling majesty of my sweet, swift game.

Basketball was not the only challenge I had to overcome because I also had difficulty studying while I was growing up. I didn't have just ADD, I had ADDDDDD. I did not do well in school early in life or in high school, and I did not do great in my SAT's. This, too, affected me terribly, but again only temporarily.

The first time I took my college boards, I do not think I hit even 700. Some Colleges that recruited me for basketball knew that I had to increase these scores to get entrance into these universities. So, I took more SAT review courses, read more SAT books, and took the SATs about five times, but to this day, I still am not confident if I could score well on the ACT or the SATs. The lesson here, **No test determines your potential.**

Imagine I did better in math than I did in English. I eventually got my score to just below 1000, 511, and 467. No, I never broke 1000. That was the initial target of respectability in those days. I still remember these scores precisely to this very day, and they are etched into my mind. Why? Because I had tried so hard and had taken a guess on so many questions. But in his best-selling book "**Outliers,**" Malcolm Gladwell confirmed that people with the highest IQ are not necessarily the most successful in life.

I may not have had the highest IQ, but I managed to improve my grades. To succeed, I had to be disciplined, hard-working and focused. A lot of it I learned from basketball; most of those principles applied here. Discipline is the best driver for a student. Discipline goes hand in hand with hard work. In addition to this, I had to have focus. The focus will make you want to work extra hard to achieve your goals.

Hard work will get you much farther than high IQ, usually. It's also a lot more rewarding to know your work brought you everything you have and that every challenge you faced was overcome with effort.

High IQ can often give you an advantage or a head start, but steady concentration, repetition, though, and a genuine interest in the subject can get you just as far. The biggest misconception with having a high IQ or having a good SAT score is that the score measures how smart you are, but it does not.

Through various measurements, it arrives at a value. At most, these scores and numbers predict your ability to learn. I even believe many schools no longer utilize this benchmark.

Maybe you are naturally smart at academics or math, but it has to be accompanied by a lot of hard work. A high IQ may make it easier for you to learn and comprehend those facts that make you smart, but that is about it. Many people are brilliant but in limited areas. Maybe a subject does not interest you, so you do not apply yourself and do not learn. It does not mean that you have any less of an IQ or that you are not smart. You can succeed at anything you want as long as you are interested in it. This lack of inborn talent or IQ can very easily be overcome by working for what you want.

At a young age, I set my first goal, not even knowing then what a goal was. My first goal was to defy all the doctors, teachers and coaches that said I was not smart enough, tall enough, gifted enough.

Well, guess what? I did; I defied them all. Through hard work, I excelled at sports, school, and extracurricular activities throughout my childhood, high school, and at Fairleigh Dickinson University. I even went on to be class President. Later, I got accepted to professional school and excelled at professional school at New York Chiropractic College and was honored at graduation as one of the outstanding interns. And as of now, I have written six books, over 20 manuals and am considered one of the leading professionals in my profession. I have written six bestsellers, of which four hit number one on Amazon's bestseller list.

Anything is possible if you just learn to rise over your adversities. You will not always be great at everything from the start, but if you want something enough, you can be. Have that "**Can't stop me**" attitude and do your best, keep practicing, and you will be the best.

COACH KAPLAN'S CORNER

Rules to Live Your Life By:

10 Golden Nuggets to Daily Empowerment.

These mantras have become my way of life, and I am happy to share them with you:

1. Let Go of the Past. Before any of us can create a better future, we must let go of the pains in our past. Failing once does not mean we will fail forever. Even if we fall flat on our face, we are still moving forward. We need to get up and brush ourselves off. Learn from the past, but don't hold on to it or let it stand as an obstacle between you and your future. I had to let go of my past or I would have to remain diseased. I am no longer mad at myself for what happened. I learned from my mistake and have come to cherish my life.

2. Success Stays Forever. Just as important as learning from and overcoming past failure is recalling past success. Hold on to everything good in your life. Memories are magic, and memories create miracles. No matter who you are, you have succeeded at something in your past. Don't forget those moments. You have earned those memories. They are your right of passage. Use them. Replay them to remind you that you can achieve your goals. Bonnie and I successfully beat botulism by holding on to all that was good in our lives and remembering the good things about our past. It was my past memories and past victories that gave me my greatest success.

3. Visualizing is Realizing. Fairy tales can come true, and they can happen to you. Whatever you visualize, you have the power to realize. Close your eyes and see yourself as who and where you want to be. You can create a better life. Look to your inner eye to see and create the future of your dreams. I never saw myself in a wheelchair. I never saw myself as the world saw me until Primetime live. Even then, I saw myself in the future as a healthy person. Yes, you can realize what you visualize. I am living proof.

4. Be a Dreamer. We need dreams and desires to inspire us to take action and gain achievement. Dreams are powerful affirmations. Let them guide your physical body and remind you that your goals are within your reach. If you don't get excited about what you have planned for the future, you will never find the inspiration or the power you need to change your life. I dreamed every day of getting better. It was my imagination that helped guide me to a new reality. Dreams are real. They are superconscious powers from other states of reality. Harness your dreams, and you will harness a superpower that rests within your soul. While paralyzed, it was my dreams that gave me life, restored my hope.

5. Work to Change. No matter how bad you want something to happen, change will never result from thinking alone—you must take action. Work is a four-letter word, but so is love, and so is hope. Hope, work and love will help you change. The world is swimming in dreamers, but only those who act on their desires and only those willing to change can achieve truly remarkable results. As Winston Churchill once said, "**Never give up.**" Work is a way of life. My wife and I worked hard to regain our ability to walk, talk, eat, and breathe, but it was worth the price.

6. Maintain Healthy Habits. There are good habits and bad habits. Know the difference. The best way to break a bad habit is to drop it. Healthy habits will help you realize your goals and dreams. Remember, there is no right way to do the wrong thing. Being healthy in mind and body is a full-time job. You must eat healthfully and exercise. Eating, exercising and breathing is a gift of life. Develop habits that can save your life, enhance your life. These habits may one day save your life. The fact that Bonnie and I exercised regularly and didn't smoke cigarettes probably saved our lives. Instead of a coffee break, take a family break and call and give thanks to your family.

7. Life Is A Team Sport. Achieving a goal or dream requires a team effort. One of the surest ways to overcome setbacks in life is to have the support and guidance of a partner. Share your dreams and goals with your family, friends and community. There will be times when you feel like giving up or feeling like things are too much to handle. Remember, you are not alone in this universe. Ask for help! I was never alone in my journey to health. I was guided by angels from life and the afterlife. The universe works in harmony. Each person is like a cell. We are all interconnected, as is the microcosmos.

8. Get Excited About Your Future Today. You are on your way to getting everything you have ever wanted! Now is the time to get excited and inspired about what your future holds. Imagine living your ideal life, then make it happen. Enjoy the moment as if this day would be your last. In my case, one day, I was healthy, and the next, I was totally paralyzed without warning. Such is life. Don't regret what you can't do or what you should have done. Enjoy your future as if it were here today.

9. Plan Your Life and Live Your Plan. Goal setting is important. You must focus on your tomorrow by planning today. Set aside at least ten minutes each night to review your day and plan for the next one. Utilize this time to set goals, affirm what is good in your life, to visualize your future as you want it to be. You can see the future today. A goal without a plan is nothing more than a wish. I first visualized this book while I was in the throes of recovery. I set a goal and then made a plan. Plan your life, work your plan. Don't wish for a result; work for it, plan for it.

10. Be the Best You Can Be. At the end of each day, look in the mirror and ask yourself, *"Was I the best me I could be today?"*

The mirror never lies. Each day we must work, plan, visualize, dream, appreciate, exercise, eat responsibly, give thanks, give love, and give hope. What we think about comes about. We must cherish the past and anticipate the future. Our lives are merely a reflection in the mirror. We must carry this reflection with us every day. I am a better person. I am a more patient, more loving person. I may not be Super-Eric or a superhero, but I know I am the best "me" I can possibly be.

You Learn More From
Failure Than From Success.
Don't Let It Stop You.
Failure Builds Character."

—Unknown

CHAPTER 4

Choosing the Right Path

*"If you're walking down the right path and you're willing
to keep walking, eventually you'll make progress."*

—Barack Obama

Many of us grow up not knowing what we want to do with our lives. It can take years to figure it out, and some never do. Many of us change jobs, careers, move to a different location, and even different relationships, searching for our purpose and destination.

To achieve success in finding our way, we need to know ourselves. You need to ask yourself what you want to do? Think about your strengths, your weaknesses, and most importantly, your passions. It may take a day, a week, a month, or even longer, but when you answer your question, your unique destination becomes clear. Your direction will not fall in your lap, so do not waste another moment; create an inner compass and find it yourself.

Life is for the living, and dreaming creates reality. What if Edison didn't see the light, Morse didn't hear the code, or Graham didn't hear the bell? What if the Wright brothers were wrong? What if Galileo wasn't a night owl? What if Columbus didn't like to sail? What if Einstein didn't like math or didn't have the time?

By converting your dreams into goals and your goals into plans, you can design your life to come to you the way you want it. You can live your life on purpose instead of by chance. Allow yourself the freedom to grow and develop the habit of saying yes to your own potential. Take the time to think of all the reasons why you can, and why you will excel at something wonderful, because there will always be plenty of people around you to tell you why you can't. It takes just inner strength to dig into your subconscious spirit—to your soul—and transform your being. You must have a positive thought for every day—an inner core, an inner saying, a mantra. A lack of opportunity is driven by a lack of vision. Go for the opportunity!

Cherish your visions; cherish your ideals; cherish the music that stirs in your heart, the beauty that forms in your mind, the loveliness that drapes your purest thoughts, and if you but remain true to them, your world will at last be built.

—James Allen

You already know that early on as a child, I was never considered smart or academic; I was always told what I could not do and that I would never even get into a four-year college. But I did what everyone said I could not; I have even been honored by the University that I graduated from and am now recognized as one of the most outstanding graduates in the University's history. Out of 130,000 plus graduates from Fairleigh Dickinson University, from their business school, nursing school, dental school, from both the undergraduate and graduate programs, only 0.02% receive the Pinnacle Award from the University, its highest honor and I am the first Varsity Basketball player in the school's history to receive this award. My picture now hangs proudly on the University wall.

Considering that I was mocked by teachers in grammar school and did not even graduate in the top half of my high school class, this shows how hard work and perseverance pay off. You do not have to be tall, dark, and handsome with a 150 IQ to succeed. I do not have any of those things; I never have, but what I have is my mantra. I just live by one mantra "**YOU CAN'T STOP ME.**"

I have owned and operated seven clinics and ran a public company, including Nutrisystem, the Weight Loss Company. With former Congressman Thomas McMillan, I helped quadruple the stock of the company as well. And currently, I am the CEO of Concierge Coaches and Disc Centers of America, the nation's largest group of non-surgical treatment Centers for disc injuries with over 160 clinics nationwide. We demand excellence. We teach them the enemy of great is good. Nobody wants to go to an average doctor. They want to go to the best. Dr. Bard and I push the doctors to reach their potential to be the best. We are saving thousands of patients from having back surgery. This, I believe, was my ultimate goal: to be able to change the world one disc, one patient at a time.

Who would have thought all of this could be possible? I did; once I got past everything people told me I could not do and focused on what I wanted to do, I achieved everything I ever wanted and more.

Life was never easy for me; not only was I never considered the smartest, but I also had a long history of illnesses when I was a kid. I was a premature baby and riddled with all sorts of illnesses in my childhood. I was a small, skinny child with big ears that other kids loved to make fun of.

My parents were told that I had rheumatic fever and had to take insane and vast amounts of penicillin daily. This left me with a mild heart murmur and an overly protective mother. I was shuffled from one doctor to the next throughout my childhood and early adulthood. During annual school physicals, a mild heart murmur was frequently picked up. I always had to get clearance before playing sports. I even had to get clearance to participate in gym class. At one doctor's office, I willingly got on the floor and did 50 push-ups to show him that nothing was wrong with my heart. As a matter of fact, the one thing that made me so competitive was the fact that I had heart, a burning desire beyond the typical person. Rudy Ruetteger had nothing on me, and I still cry when I watch the movie "Rudy".

During my journey, I actually got to speak with him, which was a great honor for me, he even endorsed my book. Rudy had heart, desire, and the" **CAN'T STOP ME**" attitude that I did, that we all need to have. During our call, this was something we realized we shared and had in common.

With basketball at a young age, it did not matter to me that I was small or frail, that I had frequent visits to the doctors; what matters is that I knew I had a big heart and that I could compete, as long as I knew that I could compete with anyone. I have proved this to be accurate, in school, in sports, in business, and in my life.

As months and years passed, different doctors had a different take on what was wrong with me. Each one eventually labeled me with a different diagnosis every time. They settled on Rheumatic Fever. And while my doctors diligently tried to fix me with drugs and potions, privately, I vowed to myself to keep moving forward and to never look back. It later turns out after a visit at the Mayo Clinic, they determined that I did not have Rheumatic Fever, yet I had to take penicillin daily during my youth. I attribute this to my acne during my adult life.

I think it was my many early health issues and eventually the knee surgery that made me decide that I wanted to be a doctor. Yet my advisor at Fairleigh Dickinson University told me to change my major. He said, "*I was not doctor material*". Apparently, I just was not gifted enough as a student. Gifted? What the heck does that mean. Once you take on a "**whatever it takes attitude**," once you take on a "**YOU CAN'T STOP ME**" attitude, there is nothing you cannot do. There is nobody that can stop you but yourself. You on your own have to turn your life from ordinary to extraordinary, and it all begins with setting goals.

Life has taught me firsthand what it is like to have my dignity stripped from me, what it is to feel invisible and not have a voice, what it means to continually wonder if tomorrow will be any better than today, what it is like to live in constant limbo, not knowing the status of my future or if I would even have one. I was viciously chewed up and spit out by early education and the health care system that never promised to help or heal me.

I had been told that I could not play basketball because of my health, nor was there any hope of improving my murmur. My mom and dad got me clearance to play. Physically I was behind because of my guarded childhood. But I persevered and learned to substitute hustle for talent and showed every player, every teammate, every coach that I wanted it all more than my opponent. I would never let anyone defeat or humiliate me just because nature denied me a few gifts. What I had was heart, fiery competitiveness, and the burning desire to be excellent in every aspect of my life.

I desired greatness for myself and longed to be the best point guard who ever played the game. I wanted to be the best at everything, not just basketball; I wanted to do everything I was told I could not, it was my life, and I could do whatever I wanted.

To achieve all this, I set goals and improved my work ethic, and my work ethic is credible, and you can count on me with anything. When given an assignment, I carry it out to completion, my five senses all light up in concentration. I learned these skills because of the hardships I faced throughout life. My goal, even as an intern as a professional, was to excel more than anyone, to be the best; I am so appreciative that Dr. Donald Gutstein, unlike many other people in my life, saw me for who I was. He saw me as someone who had so much potential and pushed me beyond my limits. He was an amazing man, a true teacher; I loved him and still miss him. He turned boys into men and men into doctors.

I remember him visiting me at the hospital, the Shepherd Center in Atlanta, Georgia, I was poisoned by botulinum toxin injections, we will talk more about that later. I was still on a ventilator when I first met him, and he looked at me, and he said,

"*Schmuck, what did you do? You were never that good looking anyway.*"

"*Son, a great doctor, never worries about how they look, they only worry about their patients, think of yourself less and your patients more, being a doctor is more than your destiny, it is your duty.*"

I enjoyed my visit with Dr. Gutstein on that day, and many days afterward, I realized what a little success could do; many people become more concerned with appearance and material things than with their purpose in life. He knew I wanted to be the best and pushed me as an intern daily. He read people, he knew I had a "**CAN'T STOP ME**" attitude; having a "**CAN'T STOP ME**" attitude will always be challenged, but when people say, "*only the strong will survive,*" they are not talking about Arnold Schwarzenegger strong, we are talking mentally strong.

My wife has survived Colon Cancer, and Sloan Kettering told us to get our affairs in order and gave her six months to a year to live. I scoured the Internet to find alternative treatments. I thank our Oncologist, Dr. Henry Shapiro, for working with us. We introduced many products from abroad, constant chiropractic care, daily supplements. I talk about this in detail, in the second printing of my book, "Lifestyles of the Fit and Famous," where President Donald Trump, sits on the cover. To this day, Dr. Shapiro still calls my wife his miracle patient.

Bonnie also has that "**CAN'T STOP ME**" attitude. Wow, first cancer and couple that with the fact that later in life she overcame botulism where she was 100% paralyzed; like me she had to learn to walk again, talk again, swallow again, and breathe on her own again. If you want to know a true survivor, a person with a **can't stop me** attitude, it is this phenomenal woman.

How did we make it? She never gave up, and I am blessed to have this woman in my life for over 41 years. She is a survivor, and there was nothing that was going to stop her from reaching her dreams; as an educator, as a principal, as a mother, as a wife, as a grandmother, she motivates me daily. Maybe it takes someone with a "**can't stop me attitude**" to understand what that really means so that they can share in that experience.

Most good things in life require commitment, hard work, and a positive outlook. The secret is doing hard work and a good attitude. Our thoughts do carry actions, which correspond to outcomes. Our secret was we never would accept a life of disability; we had the will to live free—free of disability, free to love again, to be happy again, and to look good again.

Each and every day, my wife and I only look to attract what is good, what is natural in the universe. We recognize our health has been compromised, but our spiritual awakening also has us give thanks to life every day. When I was paralyzed, I knew there had to be a reason; I had to find the reason why God spared us. Maybe it was to alert the world that there was a better way, a healthier way, and a way to keep going.

You only get one life. It is your job to live it to its maximum; I start every lecture with "life is for living, laughing, loving, and learning. Not just whining, worrying, and working". No one can stop you but you.

I cannot even remember the first time someone told me that "*you couldn't, you won't make it, you're not good enough, tall enough, smart enough*". They did not know that there was a monster inside of me, a living, breathing animal, that said, "**YOU CAN'T STOP ME**," the sky is not the limit. The sky is only what you can see with the common eye.

My point is to let you know that there is that same monster deep inside of you. We each have two dogs inside our head, the red dog, we call the Devil dog and a white dog, the angel, or a good dog. Remember this, "*the dog you feed the most becomes your dominant dog*". Attitude is everything. Your conscious, feed your subconscious, **FEED THE WHITE DOG**. Starve the Red dog.

Life is all about many paths. There are no two people in this world whose journeys are the same. What people must realize is that all paths are different. Each lead someone in a different direction; ultimately, one can lead you to your purpose in life.

Each thought, moment, decision, and experience lead us to a new path in our journey. Choosing the "right" path is a difficult subject to discuss; after all, who is to say that a path is right for one person, but wrong for another? It is all about your thoughts, where you are in your journey. You will be able to determine how and when to seek opportunities ultimately. These decisions will all inevitably take you on a whole new path in your life.

Character development takes work and discipline. The key is letting each and every experience shape and mold us as we experience them. We must discipline ourselves to always be moving toward our goal and never allowing negative circumstances to destroy us but make us stronger. This is what true success is about!

The world needs men and women. . . *who cannot be bought; whose word is their bond; who put character above wealth; who possess opinions and a strong will; who are larger than their vocations; who do not hesitate to take risks; who will not lose their individuality in a crowd; who will be as honest in small affairs as in greater; who will make no compromise with wrong; whose ambitions are not confined to their own selfish desires; who will not say they do it "because everybody else does it;" who are true to their friends through good and bad, in adversity as well as in prosperity.*

who do not believe that shrewdness, cunning, and hardheadedness are the best qualities for winning success.

who are not ashamed or afraid to stand for the truth when it is unpopular;

who can say "no" with emphasis, although all the rest of the world says "yes?"

—Author Unknown

Once, a psychology professor walked around his classroom full of students holding a glass of water with his arm straightened out to the side. He asked his students, *"How heavy is this glass of water?"*

The students started to shout out guesses–ranging anywhere from 4 ounces to one pound. The professor replied, *"The absolute weight of this glass isn't what matters while I'm holding it. Rather, it's the amount of time that I hold onto it that makes an impact.*

If I hold it for, say, two minutes, it doesn't feel like much of a burden. If I hold it for an hour, its weight may become more apparent as my muscles begin to tire. If I hold it for an entire day–or week–my muscles will cramp and I'll likely feel numb or paralyzed with pain, **making me feel miserable and unable to think about anything aside from the pain that I'm in. In all of these cases, the actual weight of the glass will remain the same, but the longer I clench onto it, the heavier it feels to me and the more burdensome it is to hold."** The class understood and shook their heads in agreement.

The professor continued to say, *"**This glass of water represents the worries and stresses that you carry around with you every day. If you think about them for a few minutes and then put them aside, it's not a*** *heavy burden to bear. If you think about them a little longer, you will start to feel the impacts of the stress.* **If you carry your worries with you all day, you will become incapacitated, prohibiting you from doing anything else until you let them go."**

"Class put down your worries and stressors. Don't give them your entire attention while your life is passing you by."

I tell you this story for a simple reason we need to let go of things that are out of our control. Don't carry your worries around with you everywhere you go, as they will do nothing but bring you down. Put your *"glass down"* each night and move on from anything that is unnecessarily stressing you out. Don't carry this extra weight into the next day.

Life is like a journey down a long winding road. It is not always straight, and you come across bumps on the road. When you reach a bump in your life, you need to decide to choose the right path that you should travel on. The right path enables individuals to meet their needs increase. Yes, it is true the bumps on the path can set you back, but when you are faced with significant decisions, make the one that is best for you.

The bottom line is that no matter what others may tell you to do, it has to be your own choice and decisions to act on it at the end of the day. The last thing you want is for someone to make up your own mind for you and to be in control of your destiny and choices. You have to be comfortable with the choice and path you are on.

I am my own person with a unique and specific set of obstacles that impact my life; my thinking and my beliefs are based on my life. However, because I have refused to follow the path that others have taken or tried to choose for me, I have been called stubborn. Just because I claim to know better what is best for me.

I focused on what is essential for me, I have been called many things, but I accept these names gladly since it is a small price to pay for my freedom and choice for myself. However, it is invigorating and empowering to know that I control my life and succeed at the end of the day.

At the end of the journey, the choices I have made in my life have taken me at times to a very prosperous place. This is the place where I experience the fulfillment of knowing that I arrived there because I chose to. Now the choice is yours. What do you want in life? What price are you willing to pay? Are you willing to do whatever it takes? Life, my friends, is about choices; choose to be the best you can be.

"To See What Is Right And Not Do It Is A Lack Of Courage."

—Confucius

CHAPTER 5

You Can't Stop Me, But I Can Stop You

*"The Best Way to Get Started Is To Quit
Talking And Begin Doing."*

—Walt Disney

One day, the devil decided to have a garage sale. In this sale he wanted to include his magnificent set of tools, such as fear, anxiety, depression, procrastination, negativity, hostility, and jealousy. As one of his demons helped him lay out these items for his sale, he noticed off in the corner an old wedge that boasted the most expensive price tag of all. The demon asked the devil why such an old, rusted wedge was displayed proudly with the most expensive of his tools. The devil responded, ***"This is my most valuable tool, the Wedge of Discouragement. When I use this wedge, I am able to pry my way into the subconscious of men and women. Once discouragement sets in, all of the other tools automatically do their work."***

Do not let anyone steal your dreams or visions. Be a liver (of life) not a gallbladder. Life is a combination lock; a lock filled with numbers. We must turn these numbers in the right sequence, in the right direction, to unlock the treasures within. We all know our combination; we just don't always follow the right direction or move in the right sequence. Success, health, and happiness are not miracles. The only real miracle is life. Success does not depend on luck; it counts on effort. It does not matter who you are, as long as you follow the combination to success.

Applying this metaphor to everyday life, you could say.

That there is a combination of thoughts and actions that will enable you to accomplish whatever you want through your super-consciousness. We have the ability to unlock the potential that lies in each of us. You will find the combination if you search for it. Health, wealth, happiness, success, and peace of mind are inherent within each of us. If you do the right things, in the right manner, at the right time, you will get the right results. Successful people do what unsuccessful people dare not to do—or do not even want to do. Yet every success we have is based on some degree of failure.

We were not born walking and talking. The first time we walked, we fell. The first words we uttered, we stuttered. The first time we read, added, multiplied, divided, shot a basket, or swung a bat or a golf club, we met with some degree of failure. Yet, we persisted. Remember how awkward your first date was? I'll bet it wasn't your last date. Life is a culmination of learning experiences based entirely on obstacles and failures. Remember, it's the rocks in the stream that give the river its music.

There was once a little boy who armed himself with a bat and ball and went out to play. He began by throwing the ball up in the air and trying to hit it as it came down. However, with every toss came a strike. Time and time again he threw the ball in the air attempting to hit it. After an hour of futility, the boy picked up the ball and said,

"Boy, am I a good pitcher."

Now is the time for achievement. Never before in the history of the world have more people had so many accomplishments.

Dennis Whatley said,

"Failure is only a temporary change in direction to set you straight for your next success."

No matter what don't ever let anyone steal your dreams. I shared with you my love of basketball, my meeting of Coach Bobby Knight, but let me share my story of when we first met. I first met Coach Bobby night at Five Star Basketball Camp, and it was there he first noticed me. After my game, I remember it was when I had played against a New York City all-star team that he approached me and asked me how I thought I had played.

"Good," I responded.

"How many points did you score?" Coach Knight asked.

"Eighteen," I responded.

Then came the tough question that I did not expect.

"How many points did the kid from New York City score?"

"I don't know," I replied.

And then the coach drilled me.

"And that my son is the problem, he scored 20 points. If you would've played better defense, you might've won the game. But you're too lazy to play defense."

He said, "*Son, you are short, you are white and Jewish, there are not many people in the NBA that have those credentials. And actually, the way you're going, you only have a one-dimensional game; you'll probably never play college basketball.*"

I was literally heartbroken, and I felt tears forming in my eyes, and the shame and fear paralyzed me. At that moment, I hated Coach Bobby Knight, and I hated everything he stood for, I just wanted to go and hide in a corner.

But after all that, the Coach Knight that very few people know about or hear about appeared. Coach then looked in directly in the eyes and intensely stated,

"*Yet, son I saw something in you, and I think if you dedicated yourself to defense, you would be able to double your game and double your chances of taking your game to the next level. It takes heart and desire to play defense, and I think you have both. If you want to learn how to really play defense meet me on the courts tomorrow morning at 7 am.*"

"*But Coach,*" I responded.

"*Revelry isn't till 7 o'clock, how would I get up?*"

"*That's your problem,*" Coach barked back.

"*Just get your butt there,*" and he walked away.

Well, I was there at 7 am the next morning, along with another young man he invited. He invited a third who showed up late at 7:15.

"*What do you want,*" he said.

"*You told me to be here at 7 am, well here I am.*"

"*What time is it?*" Coach asked.

"*I don't know, about 7:15,*" the boy replied.

"*Go back to your bunk.*"

"*Seven means 7, I have no time for kids that are not dedicated.*"

Well, we stood in amazement; I was happy I was on time and knew never to cross this man. From that day forward and every day for the next week, he worked with us for an hour each morning before breakfast on the art of playing defense. He later would come by and watch you in a game. Trust me, you worked your tail off not to disappoint him. When he was around your game, your energy went up a gear.

The defense he taught us comes from the inside out, and defense is driven by desire; defense is the ability to beat your opponent, to get where they want to go before them. To outwork them, out-think them. To prove that you are the stronger, tougher and more disciplined, and dedicated opponent. The lesson I learned was that "**You can't stop me**," but I surely can stop you.

Because of his help and coaching, I went on to be one of the best defenders on my high school team. This led to playing time and being noticed by colleges. I had a strong junior and senior year and did great in the summer leagues. Coach Knight even invited my father and I to West Point. We sat through an exciting practice, like nothing I've ever seen. Coach told my father I like your son, but I don't see him as a starter here. I think he could be a good role player and get a great education.

When I got in the car I said to my dad, *"I want to go to West Point"*

"Like Hell," he said, *"He's not going to start you and then they'll ship you to Vietnam"*

"No son no, I didn't work my whole life for you to go into the army when I couldn't wait to out of it, NO"

And that was that, the ride home was very quiet, but I got the message loud and clear.

However, thanks to hard work and the lessons taught me by coach Knight, I was heavily recruited by Fairleigh Dickinson University and Coach Paul Lizzo. Coach Lizzo loved defense; he was an old school coach whose teams focused on defense. He went on to coach in the NBA with the Philadelphia 76'rs.

Thanks to Coach Knight I became a stopper, and it did not matter how big anyone was, you would have a hard time getting past me. This lesson I had learned that I could stop others but not let them stop me helped me immensely; I was unstoppable.

Coach Bobby Knight taught me about discipline and desire. The fact is that when the ball hit the floor, it was mine, and it was too bad for you if you got in my way. I led every team in offensive fouls, and Coach Knight taught me to sacrifice my body for the good of the team. Teams always liked to put the bigger men on the floor, I might have been short, but in my heart, I was the best there was. I took every day, every practice seriously; my goal was to not only outplay but to outwork my opponent. In one game against Sienna College, they had a 6'4-point guard, and every time he tried to dribble past me, I picked up an offensive foul on him; I picked up four in one game on this player in the first 10 minutes, and he was off to the bench. He picked up his fifth, trying to trip me when I dribbled past him. I smiled at him on the bench, and I guess that was the hot dog in me. But more importantly, I wanted him to know I owned him.

Here was this taller, more notarized player who thought he'd dominate me now sitting on the bench after fouling out, watching this short kid lead his team to victory. I loved every moment of it. Coach Lizzo just smiled. It was moments like that that made me realize how good I was, and I would never have done so without Coach Bobby Knight's help.

He taught me the most valuable lesson; he made me realize that even though I was not precisely gifted in certain aspects, you could still be great. You just had to work hard, and you worked hard to acquire all the necessary skills to succeed. People may not have always liked his ways, his directness, but I did and am forever grateful.

I would never have improved my skills and worked harder to become so good if I had never listened to Coach Knights' criticism on my performance. It hurt to hear at first, but it was necessary. It is usually up to us to decide on the areas where we could use some self-improvement.

And while this self-reflection process is essential, we can sometimes be bad judges of our own abilities; we usually assume we know much more than we actually do. So why not look to our relationships as a source of feedback about where we can improve?

Feedback is crucial for our development. Research has shown that when we seek feedback and use it as an opportunity for growth, we are more likely to improve over time. How much faster would that process be if we went and asked for feedback instead of waiting for it to come? Imagine your partner's reaction if you were to ask for feedback on what you could have done differently after a big fight, or how blown away your teenager would be if you asked how you could be a better parent this school year.

Our positive relationships represent a safe space for us to work on ourselves with support from people who care about us. But sometimes, we have to make the first move and ask for that support. My basketball growth was swift and fast because of Coach Bobby Knight's feedback even when I had not asked for it, but I am so glad it was given to me. It changed me for the better.

Yes, I was not naturally gifted in certain aspects because I was not tall, I was skinny, and I was often sick, but I worked hard to achieve it. What I did have was a burning desire to get better athletically every single day to be professional in my work ethic and to be better than everyone; I wanted to prove to Coach Knight, and Coach Lizzo that I could live up to their expectations of me. They believed in me, and that meant the world. So, I had to work hard; I could not let either of them down.

Yes, talent does count for a lot. Still, it is that burning desire, that special quality that a certain type of athlete possesses, that pushes them towards success every single day. It can only be traced back to their work ethic and their willingness to succeed athletically. This is what I had.

A good work ethic of working hard can change an average athlete into an extraordinary athlete. No one can last very long if they try to get by on talent without developing a work ethic. Unfortunately, some of us do not understand that success is not just a matter of hard work. It is a matter of hard work but over a significant period of time and having the right attitude, having a "**CAN'T STOP ME**" attitude. Hard work is just like it sounds, it is hard, but the rewards are enormous. To sustain your motivation and patience through the ups and downs, you need to be mentally strong and determined.

If you want to accomplish your long-term goals, you need to maintain your intensity, drive, and positive attitude over the long haul. With hard work and perseverance over time, you give yourself the best chance to reach that desired goal.

Hard work is the most critical key to success. Achievements without hard work are impossible. You cannot sit idle and expect to gain anything, and you will achieve nothing if you just sit and wait for a better opportunity to come. The person who is working hard is able to gain success and happiness in life. Nothing is easy to be achieved in life without doing any hard work. Hard work is a price that we pay for success in life.

We all have our own opinion of what it takes to be successful, but I firmly believe success takes hard work and patience from all that I have been through. I often tell the story of how my father believed in me more than I believed in myself. During professional school, I was confronted with so many classes and such a demanding workload, I called my father, and I said,

"I don't know if I can do this; it's just too hard."

He replied, *"Stop whining son you can do whatever you put your mind to do if you're willing to pay the price."*

This was the first of many calls, always the same answer. *"Shut up, study harder."*

Everyone can work hard, not everyone will be born gifted and willing to do hard work. The difference between someone mediocre and someone who has achieved greatness is the determination and drive they put into what they do. Through hard work, even the mediocre can achieve success.

There are never any shortcuts to success, but hard work complimented with the desire to achieve, determination, and always being motivated to reach your goal makes success possible and that much better. The thing with hard work is that, yes, it may be tough, but it is much better than the alternative. If you do not put in the work, success is much harder to achieve.

As someone who was initially far below average physically, athletically, academically, the fact is I had to scratch and claw just to reach mediocrity. But by that point, I had put so much effort in that I figured, *"Why not just go all the way?"* So, I improved my skills as a basketball player and as a student and eventually as a doctor, the average is "the best of the worst, the worst of the best" I did not want to be average. Now I am blessed I succeeded in making an excellent living doing what I loved most, but I was far from an overnight sensation.

Success is just not an overnight type of deal. It takes months, years, and in some cases even decades to become great at something. The biggest thing about becoming successful is that you have to be willing to put in the effort. You have to be willing to understand that there is no quick fix. To become successful is a process.

It is essential to take time to learn and practice. And do not ever stop learning. There is never a point to which you are too successful or know too much. There is always more to learn and become great at. It will take a lot of time to become successful, so fall in love with the process and be patient.

Wake up with the drive every day to want to become successful, knowing you are getting just a little bit closer to becoming better at what you want. The two most important qualities are to work hard and be patient. Everyone can succeed, but only those who are willing and determined to reach it actually achieve it.

A few years down the line, you could be regretting the opportunity that you passed up, all because you were not willing to put in the hard work when it mattered the most. In the end, it comes down to two things. Do you want to endure the pain of hard work? Or do you want to endure the pain of regret for not giving it your all when you had the chance? I wanted to be a great basketball player, and so I was willing to put in the work, to wake up at 7 am every day and practice. And I do not regret a single moment.

Coach Bobby Knight taught me a fundamental life lesson, that I could be whoever I wanted to be and that I could stop anyone I wanted. He believed in me, and that led me to believe in myself. Hard work is a fundamental part of life if you want to be successful in any field. There is no getting away from this. He was one of the many mentors in my life. My Father, My Uncle Herbert Punyon, Dr. Henry Keyishian, Coach Paul Lizzo, Dr. Donald Gutstein. All of these great mentors were tough, were disciplined and expected the most from me. I never wanted to let any of them down, but mostly myself.

Friends, it's your job, your duty to pay the price. Success does not come easily, or cheaply, but the time you invest in yourself will come back to you tenfold. Don't ever tell me what I can't do; tell me what I need to do, and I will do it. If you follow that advice, nothing will be able to stop you.

A man's favorite donkey falls into a deep precipice. He can't pull it out no matter how hard he tries. He therefore decides to bury it alive. Soil is poured onto the donkey from above.

The donkey feels the load, shakes it off, and steps on it. More soil is poured.

It shakes it off and steps up. The more the load was poured, the higher it rose. By noon, the donkey was grazing in green pastures.

In life dirt may be dumped upon us. However, after much shaking off (of problems) And stepping up (learning from them), One will graze in GREEN PASTURES.

Work is not always fun, but it is necessary; I needed to be good at basketball, I needed to become a good student, I was not a natural, but I became extraordinary in my life because I put in the effort. The alternative was simply not acceptable if I wanted to lead the life I desired. So if someone throws dirt on you, just keep climbing.

"The road to success is always under construction"

"I Think Goals Should Never Be Easy, They Should Force You To Work, Even If They Are Uncomfortable At The Time."

—Michael Phelps

CHAPTER 6

The Comeback Kid

*"The oak fought the wind and was broken, the
willow bent when it must and survived."*

—Robert Jordan, The Fires of Heaven

We as humans live in difficult times, and even the most successful among us can be overwhelmed by issues such as money, marriage, parenting, disease, stress, or any of the other adversities we all face from time to time. Few things put a leader to the test more than rebounding from a disaster, whether it's caused by a natural disaster, disease, malfeasance, blunders, or an unjust boss or in New York's case, Governor. True leaders, on the other hand, do not give in. They are energized by defeat and return to the fight with more passion and ferocity.

Our story is a real story, it is a story of love, compassion, dedication and commitment. I rarely talk about our poisoning with Botulinum Toxin. This was originally developed as a bioweapon, and it almost killed me. In my bestselling book DYING TO BE YOUNG, published by nationally acclaimed publisher Pegasus Books, I share our story. I fought hard to come back from being 100% paralyzed. I didn't want to be remembered as the Botox Boy. Comebacks are a form of success. An inner success that gives you a great deal of confidence. If it wasn't for my "**CANT STOP ME**" attitude, I don't know if I would have made it.

What are the ramifications of these comebacks? It's possible to stage a comeback, no matter what your situation or background, where you're from, or the mistakes you've made, even when things seem hopeless. Realizing that it can be done is half the battle; the other half is figuring out what plan to use.

Coach Kaplan's 5 basic principles:

1. *Life is difficult. It always has been and always will be.*
2. *Everything "I am" to be is up to me.*

3. *You can learn anything you need to learn, become anyone you want to become, achieve anything you want to achieve.*
4. *Life has few limitations, and most of those are on the inside, not the outside.*
5. *The sky is not the limit; the sky is only as far as we can see. The universe is infinite, and so we have no limits.*

We all experience pain, misfortunes, problems, hurdles, stress, insults, and misery, but dig deep and find a way out of the black pit. Things do alter over time. You grow stronger, wiser, and ideally kinder as a result of your trials. You'll heal and grow, and quite often, something greater, more amazing, and unexpected will emerge from the agony. We all go through adversity. However, because of the attitude and decisions, some people can get through problems more easily than others. Their way of thinking pulls them onward. They don't let hardship rule their life, and they persevere in the face of adversity, even when everything seems to be coming apart around them. This is what my wife and I had to do when we were poisoned and became botulinum toxin-positive.

Imagine being on top of the world one day and the world being on top of you the next. My goal is to pour my heart out and try to write a chapter on a real situation. Botulism poisoning is usually lethal, but my wife and I defied the odds and are still alive to tell our experience today. Everything that we went through during our rehabilitation, emotionally, physically, and mentally, could only be described as hell on earth. Spiritually, what we learned could be nothing short of heaven.

Our tale isn't a tragedy, comedy, saga, or soap opera. It would be called *"One Life to Give"* if it were a soap opera. This chapter is about surviving and triumphing against adversity. Some of us, die and return, as I did. A large number of people have returned from COVID-19 and have described the experience in the same manner too. My heart goes out to everyone who has survived this horrible pandemic, as well as those who have died as a result of it.

It was through my meeting with death that life took on a new meaning for me. The event awakened my inner sight, allowing me to see what just a few people can: ***that life is for living, loving, laughing and learning, not just for whining, worrying and working.***

The purpose of this book is meant to be a guide to your inner eye, to help you see the gift of life and realize that your spirit is immortal. I want you to understand that you are not alone in this universe, no matter what you are going through. This is not about religion, even if God is present in my thoughts and acts.

Belief is a manifestation of faith, and religion has nothing to do with faith. On our planet, there are only two types of individuals. First, some believe the Universe has no order and that everything happens at random and for no apparent reason. Typically, these folks are enraged or lonely.

There are also people who believe that everything happens for a reason and that nature does not make mistakes. They recognize life's perfection and perceive every situation as a part of a broader picture. They believe the universe is in a state of equilibrium. I belong to the latter group. I comprehend that darkness follows the light, summer follows winter, and I believe that the cosmos is ordered in the same way that the sun rises and sets each day.

No one in the history of the world had ever been poisoned by phony Botox or injections of raw botulinum toxin before November 23, 2004. The dose we were given should have killed us. We possessed enough toxin to kill 2400 people each, according to the CDC. My children were warned that we would most likely spend the rest of our lives in wheelchairs and on ventilators if we survived. Our prognosis was bleak, to say the least.

Fortunately, it was not fatal, and virtue has prevailed over evil. Physically, intellectually, and spiritually, my body has been altered, and I am now stronger than ever. I've discovered that our mental attitude has a strong influence on our physical health. Yes, intelligence trumps brawn!

Our mind, spirit, and soul have more strength than any muscle in our body, and the more powerful our spirit grows, the more we empower our bodies to recover.

I sincerely hope that this book will encourage you to look beyond the ordinary and appreciate the tiny things in life—the power to blink, breathe, move, laugh, cry, and love and be loved.

Allow me to describe what it's like to be completely immobilized, what I thought, and how terrified I was. I will never forget this nightmare, but I know from it I can, you can overcome anything. I began *"DYING TO BE YOUNG,"* my # 1, best-selling book with the following scene, let me relive it for you.

The room was freezing. I was surrounded by commotion and sounds I didn't recognize.

"Is that a machine?"

"Where am I?"

"What's going on?"

People were swarming around me. Some people were in tears.

"They're crying like if someone had passed away... They're wailing for my return!"

"Am I dead?"

"Is this my funeral?"

My mind was racing. I thought, am I alive?

"God, what is happening to me?"

Hold on, that's my brother's voice…

"Eric, it's Steve. Can you hear me?"

I tried to speak, but my lips would not move, and I could not utter a sound.

"This can't be real, I said to myself. I must be dreaming. If this is a dream, I can just open my eyes and wake up."

"Open your eyes."

"I can't! I can't open my eyes!"

As I talked to myself, I simply couldn't comprehend what was going on.

"Why can't I wake up?"

"Am I alive?"

Oh God, speak to me. "I am helpless! I can't move! I must be dead! Wait…how can I think if I'm dead?"

"I can hear, so I can't be dead, right?"

Someone is touching me.

"I can feel, so I must be alive."

"Come on, Kaplan. Open your eyes!" I screamed within my head, but no one heard me. I cannot open my eyes.

"OH GOD, I CAN'T MOVE."

"Why can't I move?"

I'M ALIVE! I'M TRAPPED IN MY BODY! *"Help me!"*

"Somebody help me!"

"I can think, but I cannot talk. I must have died. Oh my God, I am not in heaven. I am in hell!"

My perplexity was heightened when I overheard a stranger say, *"Your parents are in bad shape. They may be like this for a year to eighteen months. It could be six months before they are even able to open their eyes."*

This man, who is he?

He's referring to my wife and me!

"Eighteen months like this? No way! Where is Bonnie? Is she okay?"

"How did this happen? I want answers! Oh, God, please let this be a dream. Help me wake up."

Alarms blared, and a machine began forcing air into and out of something—someone—ME! I'm sure I'm in a hospital.

"I must be in bad shape"

I remember riding to the hospital with my 19-year-old son, Jason. I remembered seeing my friend, Dr. Dennis Egitto after I arrived in the emergency room.

Form a picture in your mind right now of a world where you can't see, touch, or move because it's completely dark. You can hear, feel, and think, but you cannot communicate with the rest of the world. Consider yourself a prisoner, confined to a cold, dead container with no evidence of life. For weeks, which was my predicament while I battled in a mental coma with minimal physical progress. Some may mistake this for another Steven King novel. It was even worse for me. It was my life, and it was both real and hellish. My first thought when I realized I was in Hell was,

"How do I get the hell out of here?"

You can only imagine what it was like to be in a paralyzed state, if you've seen the movie Ground Hog Day, that was my life awaking each day with the same battles ahead of me. Each day seemed to be the same as the last. I dreamed and fought my internal demons while I slept and awakened. Moments, both joyful and unpleasant, characterized my life. My muscles refused to cooperate. I learned to appreciate my mind's originality while unable to move, speak, swallow, or open my eyes.

I had the desire to survive and fought the need to give in to my circumstances; yet fear and doubt were formidable foes. I was still terrified and perplexed. Because the days were noisy and I had visitors, I could tell the days from the nights. I could sense the terror of those who had come to show how much they loved me, even if I couldn't see them. I wished I could inform everyone that I was still alive. I ached to see their faces, but I couldn't wake up since I was in a nightmare.

The nights were dark, lonely, and frightening. I yearned for my son's, wife's, family's, and friends' touch. I became my own best buddy as a result of my loneliness. I may have lost physical strength, but as I turned inward to my underlying intelligence—to the force that produces life—I gained inner powers far superior to anything I had before. These abilities are present in all of us. We rarely know what we're made of until we're faced with a crisis. It makes us think about things like: Is there life after death? What exactly is death? Should we be afraid of death? Were we put on this earth for a specific reason?

I can now confidently and fearlessly answer those questions. We have been placed on this planet to learn, grow, and evolve.

"There are no mistakes in life; only lessons".

"We are all enrolled in the University of Life, and we will matriculate".

"We can learn from our lessons or perceive them as random events".

Picture in your heart the anguish of being completely paralyzed, unable to open your eyes, and reliant on machines to keep you alive. It wasn't something I imagined; it was something I experienced. I had to re-learn how to open my eyes, speak, move, and swallow again. I understand how easy it is to give up, but whatever your situation, don't give up, don't give in. I discovered the meaning of compassion and gratitude as a result of my near-death experience. It is for this reason I tell my clients you can overcome anything if you simply believe.

Today more than ever I appreciate the simple pleasures that most people take for granted: breathing, eating, seeing, tasting, smelling, walking, talking, laughing, and loving. We learn that nothing, not terrorism, natural calamities, or even death, can break our spirit at our lowest points. Although both the spirit and electricity are unseen, the spirit is more powerful. While devices kept me alive, this driving force kept me hopeful for better health. I would have died if it hadn't been for the machines. Also not being a smoker anymore saved me. My lungs were ready for the battle of the ventilator. Yes, good things can come from bad habits. I was scared to breath on my own again. But knowing I had the power to quit smoking allowed me to know I could defeat anything. After 10 weeks I got off the ventilator and began to reclaim my life.

People frequently inquire about what I took out from my encounter. GOD IS REAL, I discovered. I have Jewish ancestors and a smattering of

Italian ancestors, so guilt runs in my family. Early on in my life I had some doubts about religion and the physical existence of God.

I used to play basketball for St. Aloysius in Jersey City when I was a kid. My father's colleague and the President of St. Peter's College was Father Yanatelli. They'd often come to my games. I recall inquiring about God with him. He assured me that God is present in everything. I had no idea what he was talking about at the moment. After further study of the Kabbalah, with my friend Rabbi Joel Levine I was able to grasp his message. According to the Kabbalah,

"It's the rocks in the river that give it its music."

I've always been innately a believer, and faith is more than just words. Now more than ever. Look at what I overcame. Being paralyzed, being told you may never walk again, that you may live the rest of your life on a ventilator. That the prognosis for your wife is the same. Like always I wouldn't listen to the doctors, I dug deep into my soul, I implemented my **"CAN'T STOP ME"**, mindset to overcome what they said could not be done. Faith is important, but do you believe, really believe?

Words have different connotations for different people. Words paint pictures for us depending on what we've learned, what we've experienced as children, what we've learned in school, and what we believe. To say the same thing in different countries, different terms are used. Is one country correct and the other incorrect?

To a Christian, the word "Jesus" implies one thing, to a Jew, to a Catholic, and to a Muslim, it means another. Love, religion, power, paradise, and hell; all of these concepts that are interpreted differently by different people. While all faiths and cultures view God differently, the majority of people believe in an ultimate being or power. Despite the fact that we believe that God is a Universal Intelligence, we have waged wars trying to persuade others that we are correct and incorrect.

Words are a means of expressing our beliefs. Many times, our speech and language are the only things that distinguish us. Words aren't the same as reality. The mere mention of the word "water" is insufficient to satiate our thirst. For life, the meaning of spirit, or the belief in God, we must search beyond the words and into our hearts and souls.

I tell my tale to encourage anyone who is going through a difficult time. We must all learn to gaze inward and see life through the eyes of our inner eye. God is good, and God's presence may be found in everyone, regardless of their religious views, place of worship, heredity, or region. Our actions, however, speak louder than our words. Our actions have the potential to negate the goodness that exists inside us.

"I CAN, I WILL, I MUST!"

I kept repeating to God as I prayed for a miracle.

The fear of not speaking, communicating, moving your hands, or opening your eyes was the most terrifying experience of my life; my body was dead, but my mind was fully awake. The key was not giving up and not expecting a quick fix. Miracles often take time. I remember Father Yanatelli telling me as a youth *"**Gods delays, are not always God's denials.***

How do you overcome such misery, such tragedy? You look inside yourself to all of the teachings you have learned about life, ambition, determination, and success. All of the coaches, mentors, and instructors who you, you were not good enough, who told you couldn't do it, as well as all of the coaches, instructors, and mentors who pushed you and told you were special.

We tend to believe only what we see. Faith is the ability to believe in something you can't see. Although we cannot see electricity, we can sense its strength. Even if we can't "see" winter, the frigid temperatures signal the changing of seasons. Is it possible to see the wind?

No, but we can sense and see its influence. We believe in the laws of the Universe, but we are unable to see the power that rules it. The day will follow night, summer will follow winter, and the sun will follow rain, according to our beliefs. When our trees lose their leaves, we don't panic. Mother Nature, we believe, will restore them.

What is Mother Nature's name?

Do you have faith in her?

We all believe in something, whether or not we can see it or feel it.

What my wife and I went through I would not wish on anybody. I share this so you now know tragedy can be overcome.

Our life is celebrated and remembered by two dates: our birth and our death. However, it is the "**dash**" on your tombstone that represents the journey of your life. If you died tomorrow, what would people remember about you? Friends, it is what transpires between these two dates, that "*dash*", that defines who we are. We must spend our days preparing the world for future generations. We must live our lives as each day is our last and then we can give thanks for tomorrow. Life has no meaning if there is nothing afterward. The Laws of nature dictate that an acorn will become a tree, and that life will be followed by afterlife, or as you will learn later, your Legacy. It is part of the never-ending cycle of life.

Nothing is ever lost in life only transformed. Nature does not create anything in vain. There is not a person in the world who has never suffered at least once in his or her life. Does pain and suffering give meaning to life? Should we accept them as part of the adventure or learning process? There are no mistakes in life—only lessons. Suffering may help us realize our need to acknowledge our spirit, find purpose in life and to have faith in God. Your life matters and all that you are and all that you do will affect the lives of others. You make a difference.

We see the world thorough our human filters, and we don't always see it as it is. We perceive by our five senses: "*touch, smell, sight, hearing, and taste*", or by instruments that increase their range. Anything beyond the scope of our senses or our scientific explanation does not exist as far as many people are concerned. We cannot see God, so how do we know He or She exists? The spiritual world exists as surely as the physical world does. We cannot see our spirit or our soul, yet is it the essence of our life. We cannot see love, yet we know it is real.

Although many people thought I would be in a wheelchair for years and maybe forever, I never visualized myself in that situation. I only saw myself walking and running again. Yes, I had to learn to walk again, talk again, swallow, smile and breathe again. I tried never to see myself as I was, but rather how I wanted to be. This is the key, your imagination can create your reality.

We should not fear the future or the unknown. We must let go of the past. Why fear what we do not know and cannot see? Worrying about a situation is usually prolongs its resolution and makes it more painful. Life is best when you face it directly. Your efforts are far more effective when they don't have to push through layers of denial, avoidance and anxiety. Confront your fear and live in the moment. The key is to never panic, let me share a story of outthinking the competition, of succeeding in the moment.

Centuries ago, in a small Italian town, there was a business owner who was in a great amount of debt. His banker, who was an old, unattractive man, strongly desired the business owner's younger beautiful daughter.

*The banker decided to offer the businessman a deal to forgive the debt that he owed the bank completely. **However, there was a bit of a catch.***

In order for the businessman to become debt-free, he was to have his daughter marry the banker.

The businessman didn't want to concede to this agreement, but he had no other choice, as his debt was so extreme.

The banker said he would put two small stones into a bag—one of which was white, and the other black.

The daughter would then need to reach into the bag and blindly choose a stone. If she chose the black stone, the businessman's debt would be cleared, and the daughter would have to marry the banker. However, if she chose the white stone, the debt would be cleared, and the daughter would not have to marry him.

While standing in the stone-filled path in the businessman's yard, the banker reached down and chose two small stones, not realizing that the businessman's daughter was watching him. **She noticed that he picked up two black stones and put them in the bag.**

When it came time for the daughter to pick a stone out of the bag, she felt she had three choices:

1. **Refuse to do it.**
2. **Take out both stones and expose the banker's cheating.**
3. **Pick a stone, knowing it would be black, and sacrifice herself to get her father out of debt.**

She picked a stone from the bag, and immediately 'accidentally' dropped it into the abundance of stones where they were all standing.

She said to the banker, *"I'm sorry, I'm so clumsy! Oh well. Just look in the bag to see what color stone is in there now so you will know what color stone I picked."*

Of course, the remaining stone was black.

Because the banker didn't want his deceit to be exposed, he played along, acting as if the stone that the businessman's daughter dropped had to have been white. He cleared the businessman's debt and the daughter remained free from having to spend the rest of her life with the banker.

This story has a simple moral that I live my life by. While you may have to think outside of the box sometimes, it's always possible to conquer a difficult situation. You don't have to always give in to the options you're presented with. Challenge the status quo. Think creatively. Engage in productive nonconformity when possible. Don't be afraid to question the things that are expected to be true. In order to overcome challenges, you have to think in ways that you've never thought before.

Regardless of the situation, inside yourself you have all the answers. What is holding you back? There is no lack in the universe. The power of life is abundant. Push forward. Let go of the need to cling to any fleeting thing or circumstance. Toss out any memory that does not good serve your highest good. Only preserve memories that are worth reliving. Open your eyes and allow your spirit to make room for joy to grow. Do it today. It can be tempting to put tasks off until later, or to think that problems will just go away, or to wait for some magical occurrence to fulfill your desires. Yet, the truth is that fulfillment in life comes from putting all of yourself into the living of it.

When something must be said, stand up and say it. When something needs to be done, get busy and do it. So many people say,

"I should have done this",
"I should have done that".
"STOP SHOULD-ING ALL OVER YOURSELF".

From this day forward, NO more can'ts. NO more won'ts. NO more should's. Instead, say,

"I can. I will. I must!"

Go ahead and face that fear. Make an effort to move forward and live fully in the grand possibilities with which you're blessed. Face life boldly and you'll find it to be better than you ever imagined. It's all a matter of choice. Like my father told me, "You have free will. Choose wisely."

I close this chapter by reminding you to make a difference today.

COACH KAPLAN'S COMEBACK LESSONS

What You'll Need To Make The Ultimate Comeback

1. Self-Love

Anytime you experience a loss, the most important thing you can do is commit to pouring all your energy into loving yourself. Because the healthier the relationship is with yourself, the happier you will feel about your purpose in this world.

At any given moment of defeat, you can feel emotionally held hostage. However, taking action and doing something for yourself can inspire you to alter your emotional state. This can have you from feeling less than ideal to gaining back your internal power. And one of the best ways to take care of your emotions is by establishing a healthy daily regimen.

A growth mindset entails having a positive perspective on life, even when you have to jump through hoops. When you have self-doubt or self-deprecating thoughts, it becomes a mental game you are playing with yourself. Remember, the past is already gone, and the future has yet to arrive. So, say goodbye to the noisy conscious voice in your head and hello to your inner voice that holds your true power.

A daily regimen that benefits my optimal performance and love for me is healthy eating, exercising five to six days a week, positive self-talk, writing, cooking, detox diets and working strategically on my goals. While everyone is different, you'll need to discover what best suits you to ensure you're on track to nurturing your mind, body and spirit.

2. Confidence

Did you know confidence is silent yet the most powerful tool you have?

If you are a confident individual, then you know how to rock it without saying a word. It is probably the exact reason you attract your ideal clients or your ex-partner in the first place. Going through a loss can weigh on your self-esteem heavily. It can have you thinking things about yourself that are not true. You may think, *"I'm not lovable", "I'm not smart enough",* or *"I'm never going to be successful. I'm completely worthless."*

It's your responsibility to hold yourself accountable or hire a coach to help you overcome the thinking patterns that prevent you from valuing your capabilities for relationship success, both personally and professionally.

You have to tell yourself you are badass and don't let anyone tell you differently, including yourself! Combating weaknesses and insecurities begins with a daily practice of positive affirmations. Being able to rewire your brain by eliminating false beliefs and replacing them with healthy, truthful beliefs gives you the courage to honor who you are inside and out.

The energy you put out into the world is the same energy you'll receive in return. And the only kind of comeback we are making is a powerful yet positive one.

3. Grit

Determination is your best friend when it comes to conquering your goals. It's one of the easiest ways to get a jump start on your comeback regimen, yet don't be discouraged when you hit a lull. It happens to the best! Finding the courage to trust yourself and the process will be crucial, as each day is a new day to try again. Taking each day one step at a time helps you find the power of now because nothing great was achieved overnight. My healing took time, baby steps. Success takes time, take baby steps, but keep moving forward.

Live in the NOW=WON the moment!

Now spelled backwards is WON. Let your setback be the fuel you need to achieve new heights by increasing your performance and productivity. Prove to yourself why you are the most valuable person in your life and the best team player. Above all, rise each moment with grace, confidence, and kindness. Becoming numb to *"No"* will keep you pushing ahead. Because only you decide what you are capable of, not anyone else. You already have everything you need within you to push yourself to succeed.

4. Goals

When you're making a comeback, you will need to set goals. And, with goals comes strategy. It's like playing a game of chess; you are in it to win it. The best-kept secrets are kept to yourself. Allowing your success to be your noise is the best policy, instead of telling others your strategic plan. The ultimate comeback is all about the reveal of your results.

Maybe your goal is to land your next big client, or attract a romantic partner, or perhaps it's to become the best version of yourself. Ultimately, you win when you elevate your life solely for yourself. The more value you add to your life, the more desired, admired, and sought after.

In fact, many of my successes have been built in my most vulnerable times. Every business I have built has been launched after going through a painful setback. It has catapulted me into my own success and made me that much stronger. I am thankful for my losses, as they have given me the strength to grow. And as a coach, I often get asked, *"How are you such a badass? You make it look so easy."*

I often tell them, *"I live and breathe everything I want. I don't give up even when things get tough. I continue to pursue my goals because they are more powerful than the emotion I feel during an upward climb."*

5. Boundaries

Boundaries are about having integrity with yourself and others. This is how you show up every day according to your values and what makes you tick each day. If you get off on a beaten path, your values take precedence over the distractions leading you back to yourself. Having integrity is crucial to your success story because being consistent is key to getting results.

When you have boundaries in your life, you feel internally and externally powerful because your words and actions hold weight. You are able to trust yourself to cultivate the relationships you need while also saying, *"no"* to people or things that don't serve a purpose in your life.

Boundaries are the ultimate skill that you can't live without, and it keeps you accountable and mentally and emotionally healthy. Without boundaries, you may allow others' actions or words to dictate your journey, which leads to self-abandonment. This is the opposite of self-love.

The best way to identify your personal limitations is when others have disrespected you or used your personal core values. This will bring clarity and more certainty in your life, so you have a clear vision of what you need to thrive regardless of what challenges you face in your discovery process. When it comes to making the best decisions for your ultimate come back, it will require you to rise above the deep trenches and continue to track ahead even when you are tiresome.

And when one strategy doesn't work, then try another. Regardless of the pain, you experience and the obstacles you encounter, your opportunities will appear the minute your breakthrough keeps you stuck. Throughout the process, keep in mind your long-term goals need to outweigh your short-term emotions.

My wife and I returned from death. Most people don't realize how important feeding your brain is for any illness and especially for any recovery. Our brain is the control tower for our entire bodies, including our emotions, personalities and well-being. If we do not feed this wonderful power organ the right nutrients (gasoline) our bodies cannot respond at a top level. Would you put sugar water in your Ferrari or my car? No. Absolutely not. It would destroy the entire system. The car would be sluggish if it even worked at all. Well, why would you even think of putting it into yourself? Especially now with a pandemic on hand we must take care of ourselves and keep our immunity strong.

The bodies of many Americans are breaking down because of what they are putting into them: sugar, processed foods, alcohol and add to these the reality that our soils are depleted of most of the nutrients we need and include the pollution in the air we breathe. Cancer, diabetes, heart problems, just about any disease can be linked back to what we feed ourselves. It is sad that we will treat our cars better than our children and ourselves. Flavonoids (vegetables and fruits) Anthocyanins, (antioxidant pigments) and my favorite: Omega 3' s help us, as the saying goes, to live to fight another day. We need these daily to counteract autoimmune conditions, cancers, fatigue, and to help us prevent heart disease, depression and in my case, recovery. It is hard to get antioxidants and vitamins from our foods nowadays. Tons of fruit and vegetables come onto our country with no nutritional value left! They are sprayed with pesticides, dipped in wax, shot up with hormones and steroids. There is no cure for botulism. My wife and had to rely on our bodies and products from Mother Nature to heal both Bonnie and me. I went back to my roots as a doctor and considered the phrase, physician heal thyself. I needed to do everything and anything to make my body stronger to get my life back. The more I studied the more I learned. Imagine, the nutrients found in Omega three antioxidants and probiotics, have been shown to reduce build immunity as well as reduce premature brain aging and enhance our memory. When you understand this and you help others to understand it as well, helping them change their lives forever, you have the best job in the world, not to mention an incredible lifestyle change for yourself. Now that is living, anti-aging naturally: from the inside out, not from the outside in, which is how I got into this mess.

My story reflects these truths:

- No matter what your state of health, you can always get healthier.
- No matter what your state of wealth, you can always get wealthier.
- What you think about can actually come about.

- We live in a world abundant with resources. There is nothing in life that is not possible.
- The sky is not the limit; it is only as far as you can see.
- The universe, like each of our physical and economic potentials, is infinite.
- If you can see the invisible, you can do the impossible.

My encounters throughout my journey with so many great people, so many athletes, bestselling authors, doctors and friends. When one door closes another opens our ordeal led us to places like Big Canoe Georgia, the Shepherd Center, and chance encounters which ultimately led me to my favorite publisher, Chris O'Byrne and Red Willow & Jetlaunch Publishing. These people, these encounters reaffirm all I have learned. There are no mistakes in the universe, only lessons. In those lessons, there are ups and downs. You cannot have darkness without light. You cannot have right without wrong, male without female, joy without sorrow, winter without summer, hot without cold, day without night, health without disease. As surely as spring follows winter and day follows night, you can believe that health will follow disease and happiness will follow sorrow. If you learn anything in a situation, it renders the situation a vital learning experience no matter how bad or unfair it may have seemed. People have asked me over and over what I have learned from all I have been through. My answer is short and sweet: GOD IS REAL. And it took me 69 years to realize God loves me. How else could I have survived the unsurvivable, attained what so many told me was unattainable. Superman had kryptonite; the Kaplan's had Botox. Love, passion, friendship, determination, lead us from weakness to strength. We may all at some time face our own personal Kryptonite. In those times we need to dig down and utilize our own superpowers to create a super life. And when kryptonite appears in your life, repeat these three words **'Can't Stop ME'**, and move on.

"A genuine leader is not a searcher for consensus but a molder of consensus,"

–Martin Luther King

CHAPTER 7

If You Want to Lead the Band, You Have to Face the Music

"My barn having burned down, I can now see the moon."

—Mizuta Masahide, Samurai).

In the 1940s, there was a man who, at the age of 65, was living off of $99 social security checks in a small house, driving a beat-up car.

He decided **it was time to make a change**, so he thought about what he had to offer that other people may benefit from. His mind went to his fried chicken recipe, which his friends and family loved.

He left his home state of Kentucky and traveled throughout the country, trying to sell his recipe to restaurants. He even offered the recipe for free, asking for only a small chunk of the money that was earned. However, most of the restaurants declined his offer. In fact, **1,009**

But even after all of the rejections, he persisted. He believed in himself and his chicken recipe.

When he visited restaurant #1,010, he got a *YES*.

His name? **Colonel Hartland Sanders**.

There are a few lessons that you can take away from this story. First, it's never too late in life to find success. In a society that often celebrates young, successful people, it's easy to start to think you're never going to be successful after a certain age. **However, Colonel Sanders is an example that proves that argument wrong.** This story also demonstrates the power of persistence. You have to have confidence in yourself and believe in your work for other people to believe it also. Disregard anyone who tells you "No" and simply move on.

Most individuals are frightened of failing. Therefore, they strive to avoid doing anything that can cause them to fail. That's a pity. You may end up skipping experiences that have the potential to enrich your life by attempting to avoid failure. You are not a disappointment just because you failed at anything. It is critical to comprehend the true meaning of failure is to you so that you are not hampered by it.

Instead, you can learn to embrace it as a necessary part of the process of achieving your goals and becoming successful.

What is failure?

It just means you have not achieved the goals you have set for yourself in the specified time period.

What can you do after you fail?

You can extend your time frame for achievement. Maybe you need to re-evaluate your goal.

Is your goal appropriate for who you truly are?

You can't push yourself to be someone you're not. You are more likely to suffer and fail if you violate your own value system. As you pursue achievement, you cannot overlook your mental, physical, and spiritual connections.

If necessity is the mother of invention, then experience is the father of learning. Let us be livers of life, not gallbladders. Do not let life's bile interrupt your quest for success. The difference between a .300 hitter and a .200 hitter is only one hit every ten times at bat. But the difference in salary is probably a million dollars or more per year! It's my belief that any 200 hitter could possibly be a 300 hitter. He could increase his speed and spend more time in the batter's box. Remember—only one hit every ten times at bat.

Recognize that the key to success in life is within you. We must acquire the building blocks of our, spirit step by step, one block at a time. The first building block from which we may shape a positive mental attitude is the habit of moving within definitions of purpose (in planning our life and living our plan). We must move in the direction of our goals, of our dreams. If we don't know what we want from life, it's time we define just what it is will make our lives complete. Without a purpose, without comprehensive plans for the fulfillment of whatever goals we set, our mind is vulnerable to negative and lazy attitudes. Set the plan and be relentless in its pursuit.

Roger Bannister had a goal that for thousands of years no man had accomplished. His goal was to run a three-minute mile: one mile in less than four minutes. No one had ever run a mile in under four minutes. While Bannister's relentless pursuit of his dream contributed to his success in accomplishing his goal, the story does not end there.

For centuries, man was on this quest to run a mile in under four minutes. Doctors and scientists said it physically could not be done. But within one year after Roger Bannister accomplished the feat, three other runners also broke the four-minute barrier. You see, once people accept the intangible possibilities as realities, goals become easier to accomplish.

This story that I first read in the book, *"Think and Grow Rich"* by Napoleon Hill, concerns one *R.U. Darby who went West to make his fortune during the Gold Rush days. After weeks of labor, he was rewarded by the glitter of golden ore. Realizing the need for proper machinery, Darby went to his friends and family to raise money for the necessary equipment. Once he completed this task, he went back to the mines, now with proper equipment and a crew. The first car of golden ore was mined and shipped, and the return proved they had one of the richest mines in Colorado. Only a few more cars of ore were needed to clear of Darby's debts; then it would be pure profit.*

However, as in life, success is not always easy. When they went back into the mine they came up empty; the vein of gold had apparently disappeared. The miners desperately tried to pick up the vein again. After several failures over many months, they conceded their defeat. Darby was influenced by the opinions of the other miners that the vein was now long gone and it was time to move on. Being an honest and honorable man he sold all the machinery to pay the remainder of his debts.

The junk man however was curious of Darby's success, so upon acquiring the machinery and the mine, he hired an independent engineer for a second opinion. Well, you guessed it, the engineer advised the new owner that Darby had failed because the miners were not familiar with fault lines. The engineer then guided him to a spot just three feet from where Darby's men had stopped drilling and that is precisely where the gold was found. The junk man mined millions of dollars in gold ore because he knew enough to take one more step before giving up.

When robbed of their dreams, many a man would have quit and given up. But Darby's story has a happy ending, for he learned a lesson more valuable than gold. He never forgot that he lost a fortune because he stopped three feet too soon. As an insurance salesman, he vowed never to give up because he was told *"no"* by a prospective customer. Darby went on to become one of a select group who sold over a million dollars' worth of life insurance annually at a time when a million was a million and a difficult feat to attain. **He learned never to let anyone rob him of his dreams or to give up, regardless of the price.**

What robs so many of us from our dreams is often nothing more than negative thoughts. Negative thoughts are the robbers of success. Negative emotions are the robbers of the emotions of life. They are the cause of sickness and disease, the root of both underachievement and failure. They are carriers of all illness. They make the physically fit— physically ill, the happy—unhappy, the certain—uncertain, the strong— weak, the content—discontent, and the tall—small. Negative emotions are parasites. They steal the joy a person might feel from achievement. They are enemies of happiness. A positive attitude and mindset are the antidote for negative emotions. The elimination of negative emotions is the key for anyone who aspires to great success and achievement.

W. Clement Stone said,

"There is little difference among people, but that little difference makes a big difference. The little difference is attitude; the big difference is whether it's positive or negative."

Peace of mind is the pinnacle of human existence. Peace of mind can only exist in the absence of negative emotions. This concept is no different than the fact that you cannot smile and frown at the same time; you cannot host positive and negative simultaneously. On my quest for the secret of life, I realized that all of the problems of life, in one form or another, are rooted in negative emotion. It became clear to me that the elimination of negative emotions would make life wonderful, a world of peace. It's amazing that we sit in the sanctuaries of our homes or offices while we have a world at war, a world in crisis. The problems in the Middle East, Sarajevo, Afghanistan, Rwanda, Haiti, and other parts of the globe are rooted in generations of negative emotions. We know this unrest only as images on the television screen, not the cold, hard reality that confronts the people of those ravaged lands on a daily basis. They put their lives on the line for causes that must seem utterly hopeless. We remain in the comfort of our offices and our homes with far less significant problems, yet we act as if all the troubles of the world are ours. Wayne Dyer said that life consists of two types of people: eagles and ducks. Ducks quack incessantly about the slightest problem. *"Why me? Quack, quack. Life is not fair, quack, quack. I could have been a contender, quack, quack."*

Eagles, on the other hand, do not have time to quack, as they soar majestically through the heavens as an everlasting symbol of freedom. Each of us must decide:

"Am I a duck or an eagle?"

So many of us have the eyesight of an eagle, yet we are constrained by having the vision of a clam. We were not born with negative emotions; we acquired them. They changed the natural into the unnatural. Our life is a reflection of our attitudes. A new attitude will invariably create a new result.

People learn by doing, failing, overcoming challenges, and learning from their errors. Failure teaches you valuable lessons that you will never forget. It's a good approach to improve if you don't succeed at something. It's an important step in the success process.

The universal law states that everything you are today is the result of your habitual way of thinking. The law of correspondence states that your outer world is a physical manifestation of your inner world. Everything you are you have learned, and anything learned can be unlearned. You hold the key to the lock on your attitudes, habits, and emotions. The Bible states, *"You will be renewed by renewing your mind."*

In life we can be a *"Winner or a Loser"*, a *"Victor or a Victim,"* a *"Winner or a Whiner"*, a *"Hero or a Zero"*. *You choose to be a liver of life or simply a "Gallbladder."*

Victor language consists of phrases like, *"I can,"* and victim language consists of phrases like, *"I can't."* If you went to a doctor and he said, *"I'll try to help you,"* you might seriously consider getting a second opinion.

The word *"try"* is victim language, as in *"I can't," "I have to," "I'll try," "I wish," "I'm sorry," "don't blame me,"* or *"that's not my fault."*

By utilizing these words, you are fueling the red dog, allowing him to dominate and intimidate your subconscious. Make the decision now to be a victor, not a victim. When you remove victim language from your vocabulary, speak with definition and conviction.

Feed the white dog by saying, *"I will"* or *"I won't."* You control your destiny.

Say *"I want to,"* rather than *"I have to."*

And lastly, but most importantly, say, *"I can"* or *"I will"* instead of *"I can't"* or *"I wish."*

Be definite in thought and purpose or, as Yogi Berra once said, *"If you don't know where you're going, you'll probably end up someplace else."*

Be a can-do kind of person; be a dreamer and don't let anyone or anything rob you of your dreams, especially not yourself.

One of the main keys is just being happy with yourself. Stop worrying about what you don't have and start appreciating what you do have. Affirm your uniqueness regardless of your job, position, or station in life. It's your attitude, your love of life that is your greatest asset. Let me share a story with you.

One day an American investment banker was at the pier of a small coastal Mexican village when a small boat with just one fisherman docked one afternoon. Inside the small boat were several large yellow fin tunas. The American complimented the Mexican on the quality of his fish and asked how long it took to catch them.

The Mexican replied, *"Only a little while."*

The American then asked, *"Why didn't you stay out longer and catch more fish?"*

The Mexican said, *"Why, with this I have more than enough to support my family's needs."*

The American then asked, *"But what do you do during a normal day?"*

The Mexican fisherman said, *"I sleep late till about 10, have a little coffee with my wife, play with my children, then I go fish a little. Then I come home, clean my fish, and take siesta with my wife, Maria. When I awake, we stroll into the village each evening where I sip wine and play guitar with my amigos. I have a full and busy life."*

The American scoffed, *"I'm a Yale MBA and I'm positive I could change your life. You should spend more time fishing and with the proceeds buy a bigger boat: With the proceeds from the bigger boat you could buy several boats. Eventually you would have a fleet of fishing boats. Instead of selling your catch to a middleman you would sell directly to the processor; eventually opening your own cannery. You would control the product, processing and distribution. You will eventually need to leave this small coastal fishing village and move to Mexico City, then Florida and eventually New York where you will run your ever-expanding enterprise."*

The Mexican fisherman asked, *"But, how long will this all take?"*

To which the American replied, *"15 to 20 years." "But what then?"* asked the Mexican.

The American smiled, laughed and said that's the best part.

"When the time is right you would announce an IPO and sell your company stock to the public and become very rich, you would make millions."

"Millions?...Then what?"

The American said, *"Then you would retire. Move to a small coastal fishing village where you would sleep late, fish a little, play with your kids, take siesta with your wife, stroll to the village in the evenings where you could sip wine and play your guitar with your amigos."*

The Mexican smiled, shook his head and walked away.

Each and every one of us has so much, yet we always want so much more, forgetting that what we already have may be perfect. The knowledge of who we are, and what we will act as, is an antidote for any epidemic.

COACH KAPLAN'S CORNER

1. Realize You Are in the Moment.

You are in the middle of something great right now: Life. Life is great, and you are living. Once you realize you are experiencing a moment you'd like to have last forever, stop yourself for a moment and take a look. Life is for living, loving, laughing and learning, not just whining, worrying and working. Every day is a beautiful day. Take a wellness break instead of a coffee break. Close your eyes and travel within your subconscious to a favorite place, perhaps your family vacation or a perfect afternoon with your wife and children.

2. Take a Step Back and Reflect

If you are feeling stressed, take yourself away from the present situation. Take a short walk, a quick break or simply close your eyes. Once you are removed from the situation, think about the special places and people you have met and seen in the past. Picture how happy you were then, the details of the scene, and the others around you. Feel the emotions you felt, see and hear the faces and sounds. See yourself as if you are there now.

3. Make Your Reentry to Reality

Once you feel the happiness of the past moment, it's no longer in the past; it's right now! You can relive any moment right now by letting your mind take you there. Reflect on all that is good in your life. Your body will respond to your mind. Peace and happiness are just a health break away.

4. Enjoy Yourself Now

The moment or situation you are in now will eventually pass, so enjoy yourself to the fullest. Appreciate your body, mind, health, and wealth and realize that God's creation is perfect, and so are you. There is something good about everything if you will just look. Make happy moments happier, and you will make them last forever.

5. Give Thanks

To appreciate anything, you must give thanks for it. No matter how bad you think you have it, someone somewhere has it worse. Be grateful for all that you have and take nothing for granted. Tell yourself how lucky you are. Attitude makes a big difference. Thankful people are positive people. Taking a step back every now and then will help you appreciate life. I hope you don't have to step back as far as I did to start enjoying life.

Most successes and innovations in life are done by trial and error. Failure and setbacks can be painful or even devastating, but they can provide great lessons and steppingstones for success. Dealing with failures and setbacks can transform you as a human being as well as an entrepreneur.

Things that make you feel vulnerable can make you stronger. Your mistakes, setbacks and failures point the way to your success. They can expose your ignorance and blind spots if you're willing to look. They show you what you need to learn and where you need to go in order to achieve your goals and become successful. Failing with regularity is the quickest path to success.

Failing faster allows you to accelerate the process of making a comeback. You can learn faster why your idea didn't work, figure out something better, adjust your game plan and try your new method. Yes! You can bounce back after you fail.

Dealing With Failure?

You're not alone. Deal with it and move on.

At the end of life, or in life's greatest crisis, we have only three things: family, friends, and memories. These were my greatest support, and I am forever grateful for the doctors, nurses, medical staff, friends and family who cared for us and believed we would recover.

There is a story of a man who went to heaven and said to God,

"I know I was not the man that Abraham was, but I did not have his strength or his tools."

God responded, ***"All I wanted was for you to be the best you could be and meet your potential."***

Have you realized your full potential? Make each day a little bit better. At the end of the day, be able to look yourself in the mirror and ask if you were the best you could be today. Raise your expectations. Expect more from yourself than from others. Accept nothing less than your utmost best in all you do, and you'll have no trouble living the life of your dreams.

Before you can make any constructive changes, you must accept responsibility for your current situation. You are in charge of your destiny, and you are the only person who can ensure a better life for yourself. You will never enjoy the magnificent chances that life has to offer if you play the victim character and give up control and ownership of your life. These are the codes by which I live my days, and I am confident that they will serve me well.

All of the scientists and researchers who are attempting to extricate our world from COVID -19. Don't forget about the truck drivers, delivery men and ladies, grocers, and clerks who all helped one another. We are all cells in the same body, following the same blueprint, and our actions and reactions bind us together. The secret of life is people assisting people.

We are powerful spirit beings encased in a human body, eager to learn and progress. What would you do if you suddenly lost all control of your physical abilities? Would you believe in your body's ability to repair itself? You are linked to a force greater than yourself. Would you put your trust in that power if you were in a pinch? Regardless of your religion, if you believe in the order of the universe or in God, you are on the path to healing. And for those atheists who might read this book, believe me when I say that in your hour of need, you will pray for someone, anybody, to help you.

Mother Nature, Buddha, Jesus, Allah, Creator, Source, Angels, Spirit, or any other name you want to give it. But, regardless of whether we can see or feel them, I tell you that there are forces that watch over us and aid us. Although we cannot see electricity, it is there in our homes. Although we cannot see the wind, we can feel and sense its impacts. Because God is love, we have all encountered this Universal Intelligence or God. If you can experience love, you have come into contact with the most powerful force in the universe. My gift to you is the knowledge that you are not alone in your problems. There are powers available to you in the cosmos. Take a peek inside.

"In the Universe, there are no mistakes, only lessons."

—Og Mandino

CHAPTER 8

Healing is a love-language

"The whole secret of a successful life is to find out
what is one's destiny to do, and then do it."

—Henry

My Uncle Al Brenner graduated from chiropractic school in 1920. Things were tough back then; chiropractors literally got paid two dollars per visit. So not being able to make a living as a chiropractor, he went on to work for the state of New Jersey. I came to learn later, in his heart, he was always a chiropractor. I came to realize this as we would always go to his house, and we would get a chiropractic adjustment to help prevent us from getting Hay fever.

Initially, I was scared, and my father went first, then my brother, and then me. In the early years, I didn't understand it, and it scared me, but I will say this. I never got Hay Fever. I know now what I did not 100% know then, Uncle Al was on to something.

My mother always wanted me to be a doctor, a dentist. While in college, I played Varsity basketball, helped start a boxing club, was President of my class a student Senator, even an RA. Imagine today one of my star doctors in Huntington NY, Dr. Scott Banks is a client.

When I first started college I was possibly thinking about a career in politics. I enjoyed reading and loved my English classes. Science to me was pure memorization, with no imagination. I became an English major. However, I took all the prerequisites I needed for dental school to please my mother.

I remember meeting with Dr. Henry Keyishian, who was the head of the English department. I told him I was ready to declare my major, and I wanted English to be my major. He asked me, "I thought you wanted to be a doctor?"

I replied, *"Yes I still do, but I'm going to be a doctor who writes books."*
He replied, ***"You better study harder."***

Being an English major and being on the basketball team was a good mixture because we went on numerous road trips. While it was not easy to memorize with 12 to 15 other teammates on a bus playing music, playing cards, and laughing, I was always able to read. I was actually made fun of. *"Who do you think you are Bill Bradley?"* Sam Mazarra would bark. When you want something, you must do what you have to do.

The detours we have in life are incredible because I ended up not getting into dental school, so I went back to my high school and got a teaching job, coached the freshman basketball team, and took classes towards my masters at night at Jersey City State College to improve my grade point average. I taught in the day at Snyder High School, the same high school I graduated from four years earlier. The first day in the teachers' lounge I was greeted by Ms. Sheen, my ex-Spanish teacher.

"Senior Kaplan, what are you doing here, this room is for teachers only," she barked.

When I told her I was now a teacher she said,

"Oh my god, what is this world coming to."

I taught in the day, coached the freshman basketball team after school, and went to graduate school at Jersey City State College at night. I made up my mind I was going to be a doctor; I was going to do "**whatever it takes**" to get there.

Eventually, I got accepted by the Columbia Institute of Chiropractic, which later became New York Chiropractic College.

Once I decided to become a chiropractor, I remember my mother would not talk to me for a month. She would say,

"Look at Uncle Al! He's never made a living doing this."

But I had found my calling, and I thought I would never find a love so sublime as chiropractic. Chiropractic gave me the passion I lost in the gym. I was literally reborn again. To touch someone and heal them became the most excellent feeling in the world. I now had a new addiction.

Chiropractic school was where I gave my first adjustment and found that healing somebody was even more exciting than dribbling past somebody. As a chiropractor, I knew I could be great from day one, and it gave me a new meaning in life.

I knew I had great hands, hands that developed from constantly dribbling a basketball. I knew it was the sport of basketball where I developed agility and quickness. My skill set was already innately ahead of many of my peers. I knew after I treated my first patient, **"YOU CAN'T STOP ME,"** I have lived with that desire and discipline since the age of nine. Like the tortoise and the hare, it does not matter where you begin, only how and when you finish.

As someone who was initially far below average physically, athletically, academically, the fact is I had to scratch and claw just to reach mediocrity. But by that point, I had put so much effort in that I figured, "Why not just go all the way?" So, I improved my skills as a basketball player and as a student, and eventually as a doctor; average my friends is *"The best of the worst and the worst of the best."*

I did not want to be average. Now I am blessed I have succeeded in making an excellent living doing what I loved most, but I was far from an overnight sensation.

I graduated from New York Chiropractic College in 1978. As I mentioned earlier and in memory, I will mention him again, my mentor and the most outstanding teacher I ever knew, Dr. Donald Gutstein. He taught me about the importance of combining Eastern and Western medicine. A convergence of trends where egos were put aside, and the patient's health is of primary concern. He was a great teacher, and his influence is written in words throughout this book.

One night, four students stayed up late partying, even though they knew they had a test the next day. The next morning, they came up with a plan to get out of having to take their test.

Each student rolled around in dirt and then went to the teacher's office.

They told the teacher that they had gotten a flat tire the night before, and they spent the entire night pushing their car back to campus.

The teacher listened, and to the students' delight, he offered a retest three days later.

On the day of the test, the students went to their teacher's office. The teacher put all four of the students in separate rooms to take the test. The students were okay with that because they had been given a chance to study.

The test had 2 questions:

1) *Your Name* _____ *(1 Points)*
2) *Which tire was flat?* _____ *(99 Points)*
    1. *Front Right*
    2. *Front Left*
    3. *Back Right*
    4. *Back Left*

Dr Gutstein was this type of teacher, there was no fooling him. Aside from making wise decisions, **you always need to take responsibility for your actions.** This means not blaming other people for your mistakes, not complaining about the reality of the present moment, and not giving in to other people's pressure.

Chiropractic is now taking its rightful place in the mainstream of the healing arts. Today, this profession is accepted by the public, insurance companies, and almost all medical doctors. Not the case 40 years ago when I started. Who would have thought, my younger son Dr. Jason Kaplan and his wife Dr. Stephanie Kaplan would now also practice chiropractic in Wellington, Florida, where my son is taking care of a host of professional athletes and Hall of Famers? I want to say he followed in my footsteps, but I think in many ways, he surpassed me. My son now teaches with me at numerous Universities. We have offered the only National Certification Program on Spinal Decompression. Having my son who now teaches with me at this level is a wonderful thing.

With my partner, Dr. Perry Bard, we started Concierge Coaches and Disc Centers of America; we have more real estate on the Internet than any other company on disc injuries. Mentored by leading medical professions, we are lowering the number of back surgeries. Failed back surgery is now of epidemic proportions, and even has the name Failed Back Surgery Syndrome. Today with the help of modern technology, we work daily to offset the need for spinal surgery.

And because of my difficulties as a child, I felt compelled to ensure that every patient, friend, client, or colleague has the opportunity to fulfill their God-given potential and to contribute to the greater good. I was dedicated to my patients as I believe in healing them and taking them out of their misery; I did not want anyone to have the same fate as I had.

A chiropractor has always been the people's doctor. Most of the chiropractors I know are willing to work with any patient regardless of ability to pay. It is good to know that third-party payers are also beginning to recognize the value of this treatment. Without the chiropractic principles, this book would not exist, for I believe that chiropractic is as essential to good health as proper diet and exercise, and rest.

My objective in life became to make a difference in the Healthcare Crisis. The admiration of drugs and surgery that dominates our country's consciousness needs to be changed. We need to stop treating the symptoms; we need to treat and remove the cause.

As stated, there is no one cure for COVID-19. Even with a vaccine, we do not know how this virus mutates, as we are now seeing variants, so we must take care of ourselves and understand that chiropractic care will improve immunity.

There is a growing body of evidence that wellness care provided by doctors of chiropractic may reduce health care costs, improve health behaviors, and enhance the patient-perceived quality of life. My studies as a chiropractor often showed that modern medicine finds itself mired in its complexity, confronted with thousands of diseases, diagnoses, and treatments.

To succeed, we have to find an easier way, a way that anyone and everyone could control their health destiny. I want to be able to help everyone and not make anyone feel helpless.

Allopathic medicine will not find the cure to cellular-related ills because the doctors are not looking for them. They are looking for new ways to manage diseases perpetually. They spend no time considering why the body creates cholesterol, the role of renin, or what causes thick, hypercoagulation blood. The system is designed to ensure that heart disease is not curable.

Please understand, I love and respect medical doctors; I would not be here without people like Dr. Dennis Egitto MD; I have learned so much in radiology from Dr. Rob Burke, I have learned so much from Dr. Norman Shealy MD, PhD, who developed the TENS unit. Dr. Shealy with over 500 published papers is recognized as the godfather of Non-surgical Spinal Decompression. I am also blessed to have picked the brain and worked with recently deceased Dr. Alan Dyer MD. Dr. Dyer developed the first Non-Surgical Decompression table. Dr. Dyer M.D. was the minister of healthcare in Canada, also invented the defibrillator. Helping people in my life, I am blessed to have been mentored by the best. Every day I continue to work, to lead doctors and help patients all over the world avoid unnecessary drugs and surgery,

We all have the ability to heal. On day one of chiropractic school, I learned,

"The power that created the body has the power to heal the body."
And I wish that as a sick child, I knew this.

COVID has been a wake-up call to the world. Presently and unfortunately, we are a world involved in a significant war. A war that is so far-reaching that the casualties will exceed any other war known in history. War is so bold, so disastrous, that few dare to discuss it. This war on health care is sweeping America. We are now fighting a virus that has paralyzed the world. What we have learned is that people with pre-existing conditions are more susceptible. So, it is better we stay healthier.

Just consider these facts: Even before COVID, health care spending in our country exceeded 1.8 trillion dollars, which is four times the amount spent on national defense and 40 times the amount spent on homeland security. According to a recent Harvard study, 50% of all country bankruptcies are the direct result of excessive medical spending.

This is compounded by an article in the Washington Post where it was reported that every 30 seconds, someone files for bankruptcy due to serious medical problems. Some experts believe that a retiring couple will need between $ 200,000 and $300,000 to pay for the most basic medical coverage. According to Dr. David Himmelstein, associate professor at Harvard Medical School, *"We are all one serious illness away from bankruptcy."*

Another Harvard professor, Dr. Steffie Woolhander, said in an interview, *"Even the best policies in this country have so many loopholes that it's easy to build up thousands of dollars in expenses."*

If that is not enough to make you sick, in a recent article published in JAMA: The Journal of the American Medical Association, Dr. Barbara Starfield of Johns Hopkins School of Hygiene and Public Health listed the adverse health effects in the U.S. system itself, including:

- 7,000 deaths per year from medication errors in hospitals
- 12,000 deaths per year from unnecessary surgery
- 8 million unnecessary hospitalizations
- 3 million unnecessary long-term hospital admissions

- 199,000 unnecessary deaths per year
- 20,000 deaths per year from other errors in hospitals
- 77 million unnecessary prescriptions
- 77 billion in unnecessary costs,
- AIDS takes less than 20,000 lives per year, and the publicity is enormous. Yet, there are almost 200,000 unnecessary medical care deaths every year, and this statistic, this epidemic, seems to be ignored. These numbers will, unfortunately, escalate with COVID. The numbers are so skewed Governor Cuomo is now under investigation in the great state of New York about unnecessary deaths

So what do we do? It begins with prevention. Prevention begins with cellular health. Cellular health is the key. The simple truth is, in reality, there is only one disease, two causes, and one cure. Let's discuss this in detail. If you have diseased cells (and, thus, organs), the longer you take to heal them, the more expensive the treatment becomes, and the less possibility there is of correcting the problem. As the problem becomes more serious, the treatment becomes more serious.

Hippocrates, the father of modern medicine, stated in his writings, "*Drastic illness requires drastic treatment.*" Remember, time is the friend of disease. Half of the billions of dollars spent on health care in this country are spent on the last 14 days of a person's life. Many of these people waited too long, and heroic and expensive measures were used to try to save their lives. Many of these people could have been helped if they had sought care earlier. Physicians often have no protocols or established procedures for measuring the early decline in health. This is clearly present with COVID, and even Dr. Fauci has changed his position numerous times. We are learning as we go. Instead, they blame the "golden age" for so many feelings of ill health, even at ages when human beings have the potential to be in their prime.

Many physicians consistently assume that the patient is "well" until their condition deteriorates into symptoms that the doctor recognizes as a diagnosable disease. One of the most profound conclusions I have reached is that health is a choice, and we control our health destiny. The personal potential for human health and longevity is far greater than we have ever imagined or are now achieving. Scientific studies describe populations who lived longer and healthier lives than we do simply because their societies made dietary and lifestyle choices that supported human health.

With just a little knowledge and effort, we can do the same. We can choose health, but first, we must educate ourselves.

A few years back, I had the pleasure to appear on the Dr. Oz Show. What a delightful man, what a unique experience. Before the taping, we sat and talked about the changing landscape of healthcare in our world today. Dr. Oz, a Harvard-trained surgeon, believes in prevention. He believes in alternative healthcare. We agreed that the best way to treat disease and reduce healthcare costs was to change the treatment paradigm.

We must stop just treating symptoms and start attacking the cause. Often the reason is our environment, the goods we eat. We live in a toxic world. The first key is to remove your body from these toxins. Dr. Oz believes an educated patient is the key to our success in this country.

Imagine companies and maybe countries whose business and success are based on keeping people looking young naturally.

Good health starts with attitude and nutrition, not with drugs or potions. We live in fear of disease, looking for a magic pill or potion. Good health is an inside job. Even if God could not prevent you from getting the coronavirus, being healthy and strong will help you overcome that virus. You need to look that virus in the eyes and say, **"YOU CAN'T STOP ME."**

Some people may tease you for being into self-improvement. I have been laughed at throughout my life, and I vividly remember when I told people I was going to chiropractic school, and some said I was "**a quack**," but I never believed them. This was what I wanted. It was my purpose in life, and healing people was my love language. I did what I wanted to do.

Some people may think you are preachy, fake, pretentious, whatever. You can do nothing with these people, so do not even try. Better yet just ignore them, and you will infuriate them. When you keep winning, do not engage, and keep them on the outside looking in, it is more effective than any response you can ever give.

Something interesting will happen with the rest of the people around you, though. Your light will start to shine brighter, and they cannot help but notice. I remember when I got serious about self-improvement while I was in chiropractic school. I was broke on food stamps, but I was ambitious, hungry, and happy with the growth and progress I was making. I decided I was going to be a doctor, and nobody could stop me.

Soon family members, friends even acquaintances kept telling me the same thing: *"You're going places. I can tell."*

One of the most important things you need to know to fight disease and encourage your own health is the knowledge of what caused your disease in the first place and how to heal yourself. Hopefully, this book will teach you how to prepare and what to pack for a healthy journey through the rest of your life. Knowledge is power, and you are about to plug into a tremendous energy source.

We live in times of the pandemic, mostly with a cabinet stocked with medicines, a list of doctors to call, and a head filled with CNN, fear, commercial drug endorsements on television for every symptom we may have. Without understanding the vastness of any illness any virus, we can be caught up in a whirlwind of medical procedures and pharmaceuticals that suppress your cells, treat your symptoms. Still, unfortunately, it will not treat the cause of your symptoms or disease. Prevention is the key to health. Healthy people do not get sick.

We have a body so perfect that it has the ability to repair itself continually at a rate of 2 billion cells per day. If you cut yourself, the body knows exactly where the cut is and how to form a clot to stop the bleeding. The body also knows how to send more cells to heal the skin.

The continuous renewal of the body is not limited to just the tissues of our skin.

Over 98% of our body is replaced in less than one year. More specifically, we change

- *Our skin about every 20 days*
- *Our stomach about once a month*
- *Our liver about every 6 weeks*
- *Our skeleton about every 3 months*

This means that if you did not like yourself yesterday, don't worry, because today is a new day, and you are a new you. Basically, every year, we recreate ourselves. We are changing all the time; you just need to decide to change for the good.

The cells in our body contain telomeres that become shorter every time our cells divide. Eventually, the telomeres become too short, and we die. But what if that didn't have to be true? What if we could not only keep our telomeres from becoming shorter, but we could actually help them become longer? This process is possible, and I call it ageless aging.

We must also learn to have respect for our body, a body that performs miracles every day. The body is perfect when at ease. When the body is not at ease, it is at dis-ease, which leads to disease. The key is to keep the body and all of its parts working in harmony. Just look at the perfection of the body:

- *Our brain has about 8 billion cells and virtually limitless capacity to store and process information.*
- *Our brain contains 100 billion neurons, with each neuron capable of transmitting an impulse of 80 times per second.*
- *Our circulatory system consists of 60,000 miles of blood vessels.*
- *Our heart not only beats 100,000 times per day but pumps at least 46 million gallons of blood by the time we are 70 years old.*
- *Our nervous system consists of about 7 miles of nerve fibers with the capability to send messages at a rate of 100 yards per second.*
- *Our kidneys contain about 1 million filters (nephrons) that will have removed 1 million gallons of waste products from your blood by the time you are 70 years old.*
- *About 600 muscles*
- *About 200 bones*
- *About 20 square feet of skin*
- *Eyes containing about 100 million receptors*
- *Ears containing 26,000 fibers*

Let's say you're cutting up celery for a salad when the knife slips and you cut your finger. Do you immediately think you're going to bleed to death?

As stated earlier, even people who have contracted COVID are told to go home, rest, and take vitamins. You see, the power that creates the body has the power to heal the body; doctors can only help in the healing process; the body alone does the heavy lifting.

There are no shortcuts to good health, and if we do not accept this truism, we will find ourselves in the young contractor's position in a story told by Tremendous Jones.

It seems this young contractor was married to a contractor's daughter. The father-in-law wanted to give the young man a boost in his career.

"*Son,*" he said,

"I don't want you to start at the bottom where I did. So I want you to go out and build the most tremendous house this town has ever seen, put the best of everything in it, make it a palace, and turn it over to me."

Well, this was an opportunity to make a killing. He hurried out to slap together a building that would survive two fairly stiff gales.

In short order, he was back to dear old dad.

"Well, Dad, it's finished."

"Is the palace-like I asked?"

"Yes-siree, Dad,"

"Is it really the finest house ever built, Son?"

"Yes-siree, Dad."

"All right, where is the bill? Is there a good profit in it for you?"

"Yes-siree, Dad."

"Very good. Here is your check, and where is the deed?"

As he looked at the deed, the father said,

"I didn't tell you why I wanted that house to be the best house ever built. I wanted to do something special for you and my daughter to show you how much I love you. Here, take the deed, go live in the house – you built for yourself."

The young gold-bricker crept out a shattered, frustrated man. He thought he was making a fortune at his father-in-law's expense by saving money on inferior material and short-cuts; he cheated only himself.

Your body, your life is your house, you are the architect and the builder. What kind of job are you going to do? This book aims to empower, inspire, and enable people to take a more natural approach to their health and happiness. We can each enhance our health, happiness, and well-being one cell at a time.

The past is history; the future is a mystery, but this moment of life is a gift, and that is why we call it 'The Present.'

I dedicate every moment of my gift, of My Present, to coordinate conventional and alternative medicine into our system so that a sickness-based model will part of the future. The emergence of alternative medicine is the beginning of a revolution – a health revolution demanded by a public that is "sick and tired" of being sick and tired. We cannot rest on our laurels of being a super-nation if we are not leaders physically, mentally, emotionally, and morally.

Every day, researchers are becoming more aware of how specific pathways between the mind and body enable your feelings, attitudes, and expectations to play a major role in determining the cause and cure of this virus. We will survive this and learn from this, which we will pass on to future generations. In order to get the best results possible and get maximum benefits from what is currently known as cellular health, we need to integrate natural law and modern science into a single power for ageless aging. When used together, you will not only look and feel better; you will also go a long way toward preventing degenerative cellular diseases like cancer, heart disease, and stroke. These diseases, annually the top three causes of death in our country, are wreaking havoc on our health, well-being, and medical system. Please note, influenza has always been one of the leading causes of death in our country. Viruses are not new, just the Corona virus is.

Once we change the paradigm and begin treating the cause of disease, we will have moved much closer to healing all diseases. So, you can sit back and be a victim of the health system or be proactive and take health back into your own hands. To awaken the wellness within, you must understand health is an inside job. To read more about cellular health and anti-aging, read my # 1 Bestseller **AWAKEN THE WELLNESS WITHIN.**

As I look back at my life, it is almost hard to imagine that I have been a doctor for forty-two years. This was not always a blessed journey. My wife had colon cancer and was given six months to live, yet she survived and shares my spirit for health. We both overcame botulism, and it was feared we would live our lives in a wheelchair, on ventilators, if we lived at all. Not once but twice in our lives, we were given a terminal sentence, and we were told there was no cure. Yet, I sit here today, writing this book, more impressed with the human body's power and the human spirit than ever before. Our bodies were built for survival; the power that created our bodies has the power to heal our bodies. We will survive this pandemic.

God has been good to me. I worked hard and have been blessed to be a doctor helping people all over the world. Who would have thought a kid from Jersey City would reach those heights in life? Only a little boy with passion and a dream looked in the mirror and said, "**You Can't Stop Me**."

COACH KAPLAN'S LIFE LESSONS

Give yourself something of real value today. Give yourself the gift of enjoyment.

✞ *Decide today to find enjoyment and fulfillment in whatever you happen to be doing. Enjoy the little things. The little things can make a big difference. Decide to enjoy simply and honestly the real person you are. Liking who you are today is the first step to loving yourself tomorrow.*

✞ *Look beyond fleeting pleasures and set your sights on real, substantive enjoyment. Enjoy yourself in a way that says yes to life and to those things that are deeply important to you—healing, hoping and loving.*

✞ *Don't fall into the trap of thinking that you must feel guilty about enjoying each moment. We are here to enjoy life, not feel guilty about it. Guilt is fear in a different uniform.*

✞ *The most consistently enjoyable and fulfilling activities are those that make a positive difference to yourself and others. The more earnestly you seek real enjoyment, the more you'll find that you're giving of yourself and finding enjoyment. Seek and you shall find.*

✞ *Though the world has many problems, life offers boundless possibilities for true enjoyment. Enjoy being a part of it all, and in so doing you'll make it all that much better place to live.*

✞ *To achieve something, stop talking about it and start getting it done.*

✞ *To achieve, stop seeing every obstacle or fear as an excuse. Start seeing those obstacles forming a pathway to your goal.*

✞ *To achieve, stop looking for an easy and quick shortcut.*

✞ *To achieve, start putting forth a diligent, sustained effort that will create real value.*

✞ *To achieve, stop complaining about how things have been.*

✟ *To achieve, start making the most of what you have right now, today.*

✟ *To achieve, stop using your own words and thoughts to put yourself down.*

✟ *To achieve, start giving and expecting the best of yourself. Know that you're indeed fully capable of anything.*

✟ *To achieve, stop pretending that you are someone else.*

✟ *To achieve, be connected to the authentic, unique person you are.*

For many of us, material objects give us the most pleasure in life. The problem is we have to keep seeking out new objects in order to experience more pleasure. The world continues to grow and make technological progress. World disasters have given rise to all kinds of philosophical theories, but it has not brought spiritual satisfaction. Religion and dogma cannot substitute for the bliss of knowing oneness with our Creator. By chasing all these things, we may never realize that the true essence of our spirit is what brings true satisfaction. Satisfaction comes from knowing you are not alone in the universe and you can overcome anything.

"The Only Way To Do Great Work Is To Love What You Do. If You Haven't Found It Yet, Keep Looking. Don't Settle."

—Steve Jobs.

CHAPTER 9

You Can Call It Love at First Sight

*"Things Work Out Best For Those Who Make
The Best Of How Things Work Out."*

—John Wooden

Now I want to talk about one of the most important people in my life, my wife. She is everything to me, and my wife herself makes for an exciting story. I think how we met also makes for a great story, and it shows you precisely the kind of people the two of us are. It was in Florida in 1978. And at that time, in Florida, almost everyone our age (we were both in our late 20s) was from somewhere else, from either up north or another state.

My wife Bonnie happened to be working in Florida at the time; she had previously taught in New Jersey for eight years. But when she moved down to Florida, she did not go into teaching but instead went into retail. She worked in a store called the Basket Place; I on the other hand was just starting my practice, and I needed baskets for the plants in my office. When I walked into the store, it was just the two of us there, I was smitten, but I tried to act cool. The fact remains, when I first saw my wife, it was love at first sight, it may sound cheesy, but I genuinely believe it was.

I looked around a bit, and we talked, and it turned out we went to the same university, Fairleigh Dickinson University. Bonnie was a year ahead of me, and although it is a small school, I never remember meeting her. We knew many of the same people, this was our common denominator. Being the very charming person that I think I am, I asked her for a discount, and thankfully Bonnie thought it was adorable. Of course, she gave me a discount, and this was just the beginning of great things to come.

I should also mention that I was nervous not just because I had run into this wonderful woman but also because I was just opening my chiropractic clinic. I was flat broke at that juncture, and I was more interested in getting new patients to come to my clinic than I was in looking for a wife. When she heard what I did, she told me that she broke her tailbone and occasionally experiences pain. Here was my opening, so I asked, *"Would you like to come in, you know, for a visit, and I could, you know, maybe help you out."*

I was a little nervous, maybe a tad intimidated by her beauty. I could almost not stop stuttering, but a spark started there. So, she made an appointment to come to my clinic. We were not dating then, so she came to our office in a very sexy tennis outfit on her visit. *"Did she like me?"* I asked myself. Though it was difficult to maintain my composure, I tried my best to be very thorough and professional.

I took her x-rays and did a full examination as I was taught. She had some minor structural problems, and I knew I could help her. And I told her, I said, *"Let me review the x-rays and see how your coccyx bone has healed, and I will get back to you."*

Historically with new patients, we would call them up after reviewing the x-rays to let them know there was no growth, no tumors, or significant pathologies in the films to give the patient relief. So, after she went home that day, I called Bonnie the same afternoon to tell her that everything was fine.

And she said, *"Well, when are you gonna ask me out?"*

I started stuttering; completely baffled, I replied with an, *"Uh uh."*

That was the only time I think I have ever been at a loss for words. And I said,

"Well, I have to call you back."

So, I did call her back; how could I not. And I told her that we have a policy about not dating our patients.

Bonnie simply replied by saying, *"Okay, then I'm not a patient."*

"Well, in that case, how about Saturday" I replied. And we both laughed.

So that Saturday we went out, and the rest is history. We have been together ever since. She cooked me dinner, which was a good thing because I probably wouldn't have been able to pick up the check. The evening was great, and we both just knew that we were meant for each other.

We got married in May of 1980, and that is how it has been. We had been dating and quickly realized we loved each other, and we were ready to get married. It was great because I loved her more than I had ever loved any woman. She had no family, and I was glad to give her one. She had never known her mother and father, and so she became part of my family.

Now she had to meet my mother, and I wished her luck with that. Because my mother could be tough.

Plus, she was not Jewish. I never brought girlfriends home for the fear of my mom and the twenty questions she would ask. So, we flew to New Jersey, where Bonnie met my parents, brother, sister-in-law, all of my aunts and uncles. Everyone loved her, and now she finally had a family. Of course, my mother made her convert and with the help of Rabbi Joel Levine, we got married in Florida. We wanted a wedding, but she had no parents, and my parents did not have the money to pay for one. My Aunt Gloria and Uncle Herb served as her parents and gave her away. We got married at my father's condo clubhouse in Lake Worth Florida. I had most of my friends, family and classmates attend. AS she had no parents and mine couldn't afford to pay for a wedding, we paid for our own wedding with the gifts we received. The great news is we have been together ever since, and we now have been blessed with a wonderful family.

My wife has had many struggles before meeting me, and she is an inspiration to me and many more as she defeated the obstacles in her life with hard work and grace. If you ask her, she would say 'struggle' is an inappropriate word because it was the only life she knew. She was fed and clothed with donations from the church. And she was not beaten or abused, and this life was just her life; she did not know any other.

She did not have what many other children her age had, such as a family, a mother, and a father. But that was just the way it was, and it was the life she had lived. She did not grow up in a conventional orphanage; it was more of a home owned by a woman who was taking in children from the Department of Children Services. And she would take children in for whatever reason and take care of them, she was very caring, but none of those kids ever really stayed for a long time. Maybe a couple of weeks, a couple of months, so these kids were continually rotating.

It was families of children coming in for various reasons, but Bonnie remained there for a long time. She was dropped off by her parents, or one of them. She is not quite sure who dropped her off, she was never told, but she stayed in that house until she went to college.

To this day, I am in complete and utter awe of this woman. She overcame so much at such a young age, and she worked so hard even to pay her way through college; she had a '**CAN'T STOP ME**' attitude.

She always worked very hard, did not have luxuries, and honestly did not even know them. But she did go to school while she was there and cared for the other children by dressing them and feeding them. Food was never scarce because she lived on farmland, so she had plenty of food donated by local farmers. They grew their own vegetables and she spent a lot of her time working in the garden. She did the laundry and made the beds. Anything you can think of, you name it, and she did it. She slept with six kids in her bed; that is what she had to do. But she was always grateful for all she had, and it never deterred her from going forward.

And to someone who might have had great things and parents growing up, hers may seem like a terrible life, but to her, it seemed like nothing out of the ordinary. She knew she was poor, different, as the kids at school made fun of her worn clothes. It was not until she got much older that she realized through books that there was more in life and that with an education, she had a chance at a better life.

She was a voracious reader, and her foster mother, the woman who had cared for her, had a vast library. This woman was an immigrant from Kiev, Ukraine, who had brought all of her books from there; she had all of the classics.

So Bonnie read voraciously. It was books that kept her going. She knew there was something better out there, she just had to achieve it.

Bonnie had a tough life and childhood, and it was difficult just to go to school because her foster mother needed her to be there. Her foster mother was in her 60's when my wife was growing up, so she alone was not capable of raising all the children. There could have been anywhere from 20 to 50 children in the house at any given time. She needed someone young like Bonnie to help take care of the children, feed them, clothe them, do the laundry and do the cooking. And so, this was her life. It was just what she did, and it was what she had to do.

There was no going anywhere; she did not mind, she was just grateful to have a place to stay, but it was by no means an easy childhood.

Despite all this hardship, she went to college, FDU. She did this through scholarship, aid and student loans. It was here that she majored in education and realized she had a gift for teaching. So, she became a teacher and taught in New Jersey for eight years before moving to Florida. Yet when she came to Florida, it was not easy to get a teaching job, and she wanted a change. And so she decided to get into retail where she met me, and I thank God daily that I met her.

After our second son, Jason, was born, she gradually went back into teaching and eventually became a private school Principal. She loved the children and the children loved her.

As a couple, we have done everything together; we have evolved together. We share everything together; the only thing we do not have in common is that Bonnie does not play golf, while I play a lot of golf. But that is about the only thing. We are both very involved in our children's lives and their families.

We have been blessed to take trips every year, and we went on a cruise for our honeymoon and every year since. In the early years, Bonnie traveled with me when I would do my seminars and lectures. Eventually, it got a little bit much, taking the two kids to do all that. So we eventually stopped doing that, and that is when she went back to work full time. I admit I was not entirely sure about this initially; I would rather just have her spend all her time with me, but I knew this is what she needed for herself.

I was very supportive. She was independent, and a strong woman; nothing could stop her, not even me.

Soon after me taking charge of Nutrisystem she would come to Washington, DC., with the children to visit she got sick. At first we thought it was stomach poisoning, we later found out she had colon cancer. She had to have a colon surgery and ended up with a colostomy. We went to Slaon Kettering in NYC, they told her to get her affairs in order, and gave her 6 months to a year to live. With the help of her Oncologist I spanned the world for cancer treatments and we implemented a solid program combining the best of Eastern and Western medicine. To this day Dr. Henry Shapiro calls her his miracle case.

My wife never gave up, she had her colostomy reversed, in spite of the doctors' warnings against doing so, she is a strong woman.

She was loved by her students, but after recovering from colon cancer, she decided to retire. She went from being an orphan to becoming a principal. So you see, my friends, the sky is not the limit; the sky is only as far as you can see, and she saw no limitations of herself even when she was sick. She saw herself getting healthy, this is an amazing woman.

Family is vital for me, and my family completes me; it is my number one priority. And especially for Bonnie because she never grew up with a family and the concept of a family is more special. It is special for her to have the family that we have today; this is something she never had.

We now have two wonderful sons, and they are both married. We have two granddaughters, and we are all very close. We live near our kids and grandkids, and we are lucky that we see them so often. And they like to be a part of our lives just as we like to be a part of their lives. We spend all the holidays together and take several family trips. I am proud of who we are as a family, and we are very, very close and loving.

Sometimes we are a very in-your-face family, but that is the way it should be. We love each other, and we show it, it is all I ever wanted, and I am glad Bonnie has a family, that I am her family.

Let me share this story. One evening, after spending several days with his new wife, a man leaned over and whispered into her ear, "*I love you.*"

She smiled – and the man smiled back – and she said, "**When I'm eighty years old and I'm thinking back on my entire life, I know I will remember this moment.**" *A few minutes later, she drifted off to sleep.*

The man was left with the silence of the room and the soft sound of his wife's breathing. He stayed awake, thinking about everything they had done together, from their first date to their first vacation together and ultimately to their big wedding. These were just some of the life choices that the couple had made together that had led to this very moment of silence in the presence of each other. At one point, the man then realized that it didn't matter what they had done or where they had gone. Nor did it matter where they were going. The only thing that mattered was the serenity of that very moment. Just being together. Breathing together. And resting together. He knew he was blessed.

I love this story because this is how I feel every day and every night for 41 years as I look at my wife next to me. I know I am also blessed.

Friends, we can't let the clock, calendar, or pressure from external sources take over our lives and allow us to forget the fact that **every moment of our lives is a gift and a miracle – no matter how small or seemingly insignificant it is.** My wife has taught me this and reminds me often.

Being mindful in the special moments that you spend in the presence of the ones that you love are the moments that truly give your life meaning.

In life, we ALL need someone who understands us. When you appreciate where you are and hope to get more, you allow all the good things to become part of your reality. When you are negative about your ability to change your circumstances and refuse to get out of your unsatisfying present reality, you close the doors to happiness in your future. We both try to never look back at the hard times, the difficult times; we always try to look ahead.

Remember, there is no better time than now and no better day than today. The Kabbalah teaches us to live each day as if it is our last, for it says, *"one day it will be"*. Enjoy the moment. We have learned surviving cancer and botulism that doubtfulness and other negative feelings and thoughts simply block you from improving your life. We have learned that hopefulness, faith, and happiness open the doors for all your desires to come into your reality. Relax and let the flow of life take care of you. You will notice that the more relaxed you get, the less negativity you take on, and the better things that will come your way. The more days you are happy and relaxed, the more in the flow of life you get, the more your intentions manifest straight away, and you finally understand how to be happy.

Think and focus more on the great things you want to experience. Taking action in your present will guide you into your future. Never ever feel guilty about who you are or what you have done. What is done is done. You cannot relive the past, but you can change the future. Guilt will block you from reaching your goals and desires. Just trust that the universe will sort everything out for you. There are natural laws that exist internally as well as externally. I commit every day to bring myself into balance with natural laws, creating a synergy between the internal and the external. By controlling these natural laws, we can increase our life quality, the importance of our position, and the harmony of our workplace. We will be able to increase our productivity and develop inner peace. I am not talking of external law, such as the law of gravity; we do not need to jump off a building to know that a law exists. We only need to abide by it, not defy it.

Listen, not everyone's life is easy, and most of us will face difficulties and adversities in our lives. However, the less you pay attention to your reality's negative aspects, the less they resonate with you, and with time, you will be unable to recognize them at all. Your life will only resonate with good vibes as the bad vibes will drift away. Once you learn to do this, you'll learn to appreciate where you are in life. It's this appreciation of your current reality that will open the doors to a better reality. It's impossible to hate your present reality and be able to get out of it into a better one. You must embrace your present and remember it's not your future; that is why we set goals and daily state our affirmations.

A store owner was tacking a sign above his door that read *"Puppies For Sale."*

Signs like that have a way of attracting small children, and sure enough, a little boy appeared under the store owner's sign.

"How much are you going to sell the puppies for?" he asked.

The store owner replied, *"Anywhere from $30 to $50."*

The little boy reached in his pocket and pulled out some change.

"I have $2.37," he said.

"Can I please look at them?"

The store owner smiled and whistled, and out of the kennel came Lady, who ran down the aisle of his store, followed by five teeny, tiny balls of fur. One puppy was lagging considerably behind. Immediately the little boy singled out the lagging, limping puppy and said,

"What's wrong with that little dog?"

The store owner explained that the veterinarian had examined the little puppy and had discovered it did not have a hip socket. It would always limp. It would always be lame.

The little boy became excited. *"That's the puppy I want to buy."*

The store owner said, *"No, you don't want to buy that little dog. If you really want him, I'll just give him to you."*

The little boy got quite upset. He looked straight into the store owner's eyes, pointing his finger, and said,

"I don't want you to give him to me. That little dog is worth every bit as much as all the other dogs, and I'll pay full price. In fact, I'll give you $ 2.37 now and 50 cents a month until I have him paid for."

The store owner countered,

"You really don't want to buy this little dog. He is never going to be able to run and jump and play with you like the other puppies."

To his surprise, the little boy reached down and rolled up his pant leg to reveal a badly twisted, crippled left leg supported by a big metal brace. He looked up at the store owner and softly replied,

"Well, I don't run so well myself, and the little puppy will need someone who understands."

We have been through some things together. Both of us never gave up, and we just refused ever to give up; we continue to know that it is part of who we are, that life is not always easy or quick or perfect. But it is about never stopping, always trying to make it the best, not just for ourselves, but for our children and our grandchildren. I do not even have the words to express all that the two of us have been through together, what I have learned from my wife, and how resilient she is; I can only look at how we have been married for almost 42 years, and I cannot imagine not being married for another 42 years.

Coach Bonnie's Keys to a Successful Marriage

- *Communicate clearly and often. ...*
- *Tell your spouse that you're thankful for having him or her in your life. ...*
- *Make time for you two as a couple. ...*
- *Plan for some personal time. ...*
- *Understand that it's OK to disagree. ...*
- *Build trust. ...*
- *Learn to forgive.*
- *Be grateful*
- *Be there always for each other*

"Family is not an important
thing. It's everything."

—Michael J. Fox

CHAPTER 10

Being Extraordinary

"True Success Is the Ability to Get Extraordinary
Achievement from Ordinary People"

—Dr. Eric Kaplan

Heroes are ordinary people who do extraordinary things. My father was a hero. Not just because he fought in WWII, but because of the sacrifices he made daily for his family. My wife is a hero because she overcame being an orphan to become a teacher and a principal.

What about our policemen, firefighters, first responders, health care workers? They sacrifice their lives daily; they too are extraordinary; they are heroes. Where would we have been during this pandemic without them? And what about the grocery store workers that put out food and paper towels for us daily? We live in a world that allows every person to be remarkable. Choices are the difference between being a HERO or a ZERO.

I still remember September 11th; there is so much emotion when I think back to that day in 2001. I can remember exactly where I was sitting, and the news station showed the tower that the first airplane had flown into. I remember watching as that second airplane came right into the second tower – at first, I thought I must be watching a trailer for a movie rather than the actual news report. Then came the shocking realization that this was happening, followed by the horror of wondering how anyone could do something so horrible.

It was as if that day and time went in slow motion as we all sat frozen with our eyes glued to the television screen. It was one of the days that is seared into all of our memories for the rest of time.

My thoughts from that day do not go to those who carried out the horrific act of terrorism; instead, I think about the amazing number of ordinary men and women who became heroes. I think of those firemen and police officers who so bravely put themselves into harm's way that day as they rushed in to save any survivors they could find. They performed the most selfless act of service anyone could perform by willingly risking their own lives to save the lives of others.

They were ordinary men and women who CHOSE to do an extraordinary thing. That is what made them heroes – they chose to do it. They could have sat back in fear, but they chose not to. They knew the risks. They, too, had loved ones waiting at home for them, but they put thoughts of their safety aside as they helped so many people who desperately needed them.

And because of their heroism, many people survived who otherwise would not have. Because of their heroism, many of them did not make it – having given their own lives for the sake of another. Heroes. True Heroes. Those heroes set an example for all of us to follow, and I am forever grateful for that example.

On September 11th, these heroes touched the lives of countless people. They exemplified the American spirit, the American way. Not just those people they saved; it went well beyond that. It spread to all of us across the world who watched and prayed and marveled at what they did in service of others.

All of us were affected by that. All of us were touched by that. And hopefully, many of us were inspired to be better people because of their great example. May we all choose to do extraordinary things when called upon. May we live up to the legacy they left behind in loving memory of the Heroes.

Everyone starts as ordinary, and I am no different from anyone else. We all start as ordinary, yes some walk and talk at an early age, but we all begin ordinary. What separates the ordinary from the extraordinary is they do the things everyone else seems to want to do but are afraid to do. Malcolm Gladwell, in his bestselling book, **OUTLIERS**, says you need to put in 10,000 hours. He discusses how the Beatles started ordinary but put in their 10,000 hours before they were seen on the Ed Sullivan show. Find what you like to do, then do it. Put in the time the 10,000 hours.

There was once a company whose CEO was very strict and often disciplined the workers for their mistakes or perceived lack of progress. One day, as the employees came into work, they saw a sign on the door that read, *"Yesterday, the person who has been holding you back from succeeding in this company passed away. Please gather for a funeral service in the assembly room."*

While the employees were saddened for the family of their CEO, they were also intrigued at the prospect of being able to now move up within the company and become more successful."

Upon entering the assembly room, many employees were surprised to see the CEO was, in fact, present. They wondered among themselves, *"If it wasn't him who was holding us back from being successful, who was it*? Who has died?"

One by one, the employees approached the coffin, and upon looking inside, each was quite surprised. They didn't understand what they saw.

In the coffin, there was simply a mirror. So, when each employee looked in to find out who had been *"holding them back from being successful"* everyone saw themselves. Next to the mirror, there was a sign that read: *The only person who is able to limit your growth is you. You are the only person who can influence your success. Your life changes when you break through your limiting beliefs and realize that you're in control of your life. The most influential relationship you can have is the relationship you have with yourself. Now you know who has been holding you back from living up to your true potential. Are you going to keep allowing that person to hold you back?*

You can't blame anyone else if you're not living up to your potential. You can't let other people get you down about mistakes you make or their negative perception of your efforts. You have to take personal responsibility for your work–both the good and the bad–and be proactive about making any necessary adjustments.

Many people start and set goals to rise above mediocrity, but then for whatever reason, they decide it is too hard, or it is not going to happen. Extraordinary people will do "**whatever it takes**." They have a **"Can't Stop Me"** mindset. Heroes decide they will take a stand and do the things they have to do, regardless of the price.

Elon Musk has been quoted as saying, *"I think it's possible for ordinary people to choose to be extraordinary."* Now, whether you view him as a real-life hero or not, he is an exception among the humble stock of this planet. Elon Musk believes that any ordinary person – you included – can become extraordinary.

People who set themselves to changing the world and making the most of their talents are not different than you; they just cancel ordinary thoughts. Extraordinary living starts with a simple shift in mindset.

Every person on Earth has thoughts like these, *I'm not good enough,* **or** *I'll never make it,* **or** *I can't do it.* But people who behave in extraordinary ways separate themselves by the wholesale rejection of negative thinking. When a negative thought comes in, they call it out as disempowering and revert to extraordinary thinking. Thoughts like "*I am extraordinary and capable of accomplishing whatever I set my mind to*", become normal if you initiate phase one of becoming extraordinary.

To build my practice early on I conducted lectures on health and wellness. I personally thought I was pretty good, so I invited my parents to a dinner talk to show off. I thought it was off to a good start when one person in the front row raised his hand, and stupidly I said, "*Yes, how can I help you?*"

He yelled out, "*When do we eat?*"

The whole room started laughing, and then another said, "*Yes, I'm hungry as well. Let's eat.*"

The whole room applauded at this. I was thoroughly embarrassed and humiliated, but I did not give up. I ended my speech and had dinner served. But that is what I did then, rather than going to hide, I walked around to every person while they were eating, introduced myself, spoke to them. I ended up getting ten new patients from that evening, and even though that could have been a total disaster, but it became an extreme success because I put my ego aside.

I like to call this process 'extra-ordinification.' If you stick with me throughout this book, I will teach it to you. Spoiler alert: You may not turn into Paul McCartney or Elon Musk, but that is not the point. The point is to maximize your God-given talents to create an extraordinary impact in the ways that only you can. This might involve millions of dollars; it might not. But it will lead to the happiest and most significant version of you possible.

Everything in life starts with a dream. Those who move on to attaining their goals understand how important doing that little bit extra is with dreaming. You have to dream big. Your dreams should be so big that they scare you. Do not allow thoughts of limitations and excuses as to why those dreams cannot come true. Do not let these thoughts enter your head. Just dream your wildest dream. Tell that genie precisely what it is you desire.

There are two essential steps you must undertake when dreaming, "The only difference between ordinary and extraordinary are the actions you decide to take."

Say yes to the dream; understand that you deserve it. In saying yes to the dream, you are saying that you deserve this to be a reality in your life. If you don't stand up for your dreams, then no one else will. Whatever you are dreaming, you are dreaming it because it is the life that was purely destined for you. Of course, you deserve it. Why wouldn't you?

Saying yes to the dream means that you commit yourself 110% to the attainment of it. You understand that the "yes" starts the wheels in motion to move the dream from absent-minded wishing on the couch to full-fledged participation in making it become a reality.

Start learning to learn again. You cannot move into the realm of success without first learning how to get there. All successful people spend years learning how to perfect their craft and develop a mindset destined for success.

"The road to success, it's always under construction."

Do not waste time filling your heads with gossip, reality TV shows, negative news, dis-empowering emotions, or anything else that will interfere with you moving forward.

The key is to find out who are the successful people in your niche and then learn how you can follow in their footsteps. Follow their process, put in the time, the energy, the effort, the 10,000 hours.

There is rarely a spare moment that goes by where I do not have a book in my hand, a positive message in my ear, or in which I am not having a conversation with someone who can help me move forward to achieving my goals.

Invest your time and money into learning and growing yourself. Sitting on the couch dreaming will never be enough to make your dreams your reality. You have to take action. Achieving success means playing full out and giving 100%, a 100% of the time. Doing even 10% more than everyone else will propel you in front.

For every action, you undertake, push yourself just that little bit more. Take on that extra hour of work each day, write that one extra chapter or blog post, and talk to that one extra person who can help you be where you want to be.

Taking action requires you to stretch your comfort zone, which means there are times when you will have to get uncomfortable. We only grow by stretching. By all means, take baby steps if you need to. From being a high school basketball player to be a college basketball player to a high school teacher to a doctor, becoming a renowned lecturer, running a public company, every step had me overcoming the fear of failure. Eleanor Roosevelt said, *"To conquer your fears, you must confront them."*

From this day forward, every day, do at least one thing that makes you feel uncomfortable. You are entering a new world; it will scare you, but do not let that fear prevent you from attaining the dream you deserve. If you don't know where to begin, get my book "The 5 Minute Motivator." 300 seconds a day can change your life.

Make sacrifices because you cannot get without giving something in return. Understand that you will have to make sacrifices for you to go from ordinary to extraordinary. This could be a sacrifice of time, money, relationships, comfort levels, character traits, or material possessions.

What does living an extraordinary life look like? Well, to see the *"extra,"* let's look at an ordinary life first. When I say ordinary, I mean you are in a job you do not particularly love, you are plodding along day to day, and you are just kind of existing.

An extraordinary life, on the other hand, is one you design. You live a life that you want to live, a life that's exciting and stimulating. You do not have to live a life of extraordinary wealth, though there is nothing wrong with that. But you are in charge of your life. You are doing what you want to do, you are being paid for doing something you would be doing anyway, and you are genuinely happy. To me, the best definition of an extraordinary life is a happy life.

There are seven specific ways to transform your life from ordinary to extraordinary:

COACH KAPLAN'S RULES FOR SUCCESS

1. Understand yourself.

You need to figure out what motivates you. What excites you? What are you passionate about? What is it that you love to do?

If you are not sure, spend some time understanding yourself. Observe what makes you happy, what makes you excited to get out of bed in the morning, and what makes you feel fulfilled. Focus on doing the things in life that you are dramatically excited about and nothing else. Everything else is nothing but a waste of time.

2. Get paid for what you love to do.

Once you figure out what motivates you, try to design your life to maximize your time doing that activity. Maybe that means setting aside time in the morning or on the weekends at first. Then try to design a life where you are being paid to do what you love. The goal is to earn your living doing something you are passionate about and do not do it for free.

3. Invest in lifelong learning.

If you want to live an extraordinary life, you have to focus on improving yourself every day. At the end of the year, you should understand and know something that you did not know at the beginning of the year. The only way you can coast in life is downhill. Ray Kroc, in his book, "GRINDING IT OUT," said when asked his key to success, "I am for Evergreen, perform green, and I am still growing."

Stay green and growing. challenge your body and brain by mastering something you did not know before.

4. Have high expectations.

This is critical to leading an extraordinary life. Do not become cynical and think, good things do not happen to me. Things always go wrong for me. Have high expectations for yourself and your life. Dream big and let yourself get excited about a big goal or a big idea. Stay inspired to move forward and continue growing. A big dream can help you do that.

5. Be financially independent.

There is a difference between financially independent and rich. Financially independent is where you live within your means. You do not have massive amounts of debt. Out in the world, you might look at some people and think, wow, they must be rich: Look at that car, look at that house. But in reality, they might owe everybody known to man. To me, that is not extraordinary. Extraordinary is where nobody—no institution, no bank— has their thumb on you. Dream big, but prepare for adversity. Expect and plan to succeed, but realize life does not always go great.

Being financially independent means you are never in a position where you would be ruined if the world around you went downhill. Live below your means. And do not worry about keeping up with the Joneses; who are the Joneses anyway?

Whatever level I have been at in life, I have always believed in the idea that a paid-for car is a good car. A car you owe a gazillion dollars just to impress other people is not a good car. Become financially responsible, and that will help you become independent.

6. Deal equally well with success and failure.

If you try many things, if you live a life of adventure, you will have a lot of success and a lot of failures.

"You may see me struggle,
But you won't see me fall.
Regardless if I'm weak or not,
I'm going to stand tall.
Everyone says life is easy,
But truly living it is not.
Times get hard,
People struggle
And constantly get put on the spot.
I'm going to wear the biggest smile,
Even though I want to cry.
I'm going to fight to live,
Even though I'm destined to die.
And even though it's hard
And I may struggle through it all,
You may see me struggle.
But you will NEVER see me fall."

Things are never as good as you think they are when everything's going good, and on the other side, things are never as bad as you think they are when things are going crappy. What sets you apart is the ability to go through life, grow through life, and weather the storm. There are going to be sunny days and stormy days. That is just fact. Put yourself in a position where you can financially, physically, emotionally, and mentally make it through.

7. Work harder.

The founder of Primerica, Art Williams, used to give a speech on "*A Little Bit More.*" He talked about the difference between the super successful person and the average person. He said the winner does what it takes and a little bit more. You cannot go through life just doing what is necessary. You have to do what is beyond necessary. If one level of effort will get you ahead, then the next level of effort will get you to an extraordinary life.

Succeeding in life is not easy. It takes hard work. The only place where success comes before work is in the dictionary. Work hard. Pay the price. But make sure that you are working hard and paying the price toward a goal that you want to achieve. Do that, and an extraordinary life is within your reach.

My journey from ordinary to extraordinary was simply about me always giving the extra. My life's philosophy has followed the great Winston Churchill 's famous speech when he looked upon the audience and said the great words **"Never Give Up."**

How did I go from last to first, from ordinary to extraordinary? I never gave up. I never stopped believing in myself. I developed the mantra, **"You Can't Stop Me."**

For me, it is not okay to be average. I am not saying there is anything inherently wrong or bad about anyone being average, but from a pragmatic standpoint, being average is a bad idea because the average person does not like their job. The average person has no real money saved up and is in a ton of debt.

I often believe if you looked into the eyes of an average person, you would not see signs of real life. You can visualize them going through the motions like a mouse on a treadmill. People realize that as many are trapped in a cage or treadmill, they allow themselves to be trapped. Some of my most rigid teachers were some of my best teachers. They were not abusive; they were demanding; they wanted you to meet your potential.

That was why I so enjoyed my time playing basketball under Bobby Knight's eyes; that is why I enjoyed my time in the clinic under the direction of Dr. Donald Gutstein. Many people hated him; he was a strong personality, some might even say he was abusive, but I would not be here without him today.

I remember one day on my drive to the clinic; my clinic hours started at 3 o'clock, and those days which is 1978, I drove a 1966 Cutlass, with no heat, no air conditioning, no radio, and it leaked. I had to drill a hole in the floor, I never wanted the car to get rained on because when it rained and I stepped on the gas I would feel the water easing through my shoes. Not fun, which is why I drilled a hole to drain the water. My tires were always retreads, and I always took other people's throwaway tires. One such day my car broke down, and I called the clinic and told Dr. Gutstein I would be a little late because my car broke down.

He said, *"If you're not there by 3 o'clock, you will fail the semester."*

I was shocked by his words, and I had already met my year's annual numbers that were needed to graduate. I had set a record at New York Chiropractic College for reaching their annual numbers within the first 30 days. But the moment I heard that, I left my car on the side of the road and hitchhiked to the clinic. When I walked in, Dr. Gutstein was there to meet me.

"It's 3:05," he said, *"you're late. I'm failing you."*

"Why?" I asked, *"I have exceeded all my quotas in record time; it's not fair!"*

He responded, *"Life's not fair."*

Then came his lesson,

"Kaplan, you have great potential, you might even one day be a great doctor, but being cocky, too confident, are not the qualities of being a good doctor. Being above average, being great, it's not just a thought process. It's a mindset. If your first patient is scheduled for 3 o'clock, you need to be here at 2 o'clock, review their x-rays, review the treatment plan, and ensure that you give the best care. Do you want to be an ordinary doctor or an extraordinary doctor? That is a choice that you have to make. The only way I'll pass you is if you are here an hour early for the rest of the semester, not 55 minutes, one hour."

To make a long story short, I was there an hour earlier each day from that day forward, and the lesson I learned was preparation is as essential as perseverance. He taught me how to be prepared. He taught me the value of a patient, the gift of being a doctor.

Sometimes in life, you have to be shocked out of complacency. The feel-good stuff does not tend to do that. I write this way to compete against the narrative that is ruling your life: People always tell you just to be yourself. If you do nothing to improve yourself and expect to be treated well and become successful for no reason, it will not happen.

If you do not calibrate yourself to situations, you cannot achieve success; change is necessary. It is normal.

To sometimes admit that the way things turn out is on us. We often like to believe that nothing is our fault. You may think you had the wrong parents, and they looked the other way; they were not hard enough on you. WRONG! You make choices; they just oversaw them; right or wrong, you make the choices. My wife was raised in an orphanage, and my father worked in a factory; many of you, many of us, did not have the right resources, but do not let the past dictate your future. My father used to always say, *"**Don't give me reasons. Give me results.**"*

The key is to make the right choices regardless of your situation.

Ever notice how the idea of improving yourself and becoming extraordinary can elicit such negative reactions from other people? I have heard this my whole life, as I read books, attended seminars, and had many mentors and a bunch of failures on my road to success. Even today, I always try to mirror what was successful and never listen to the people telling me what I could not do. That was the "**Can't stop me** attitude."

I cannot tell you how often I would hear some of the following phrases or look in other people's eyes. I can hear them now.

"How dare you try to make more of yourself?

Are you ever happy?"

Your obligation is to get in excellent shape, find your purpose, make an impact, or build a legacy.

You only get one life. It is your job to live it to its maximum, and I start every lecture with *"**Life is for living, laughing, loving, and learning. Not just whining, worrying, and working**".*

No one can stop you but you. Does it rationally make sense to spend a third of your life doing something you tolerate or hate? Does it rationally make sense to have many goals, dreams, and accomplishments on your mind but never do anything about them in a short lifespan?

Being as successful as possible is not selfish; it is one of the most pragmatic and sane things you can do. Focus on yourself. Focus on your true nature. If you escape the machine, they will not notice you are missing. Understand your true nature. If I am hard on you because I care enough to tell you the truth. Everything I have ever accomplished is because I was always harder on myself then on anyone else.

See, as much as I harp on the idea of you possibly being average, I do not think you are average at all. At least not innately. You are not supposed to be the way you are right now. You think you are *the real you* right now, but you are not.

You may not be the shy, passive, obnoxious, timid, sensitive, overly modest, trepidatious version of the real you. You do not have to have a 'governor' on your soul and spirit — a governor keeps vehicles from going too fast. Only you know if you are operating way below your potential, like way below. And this is not good. I am harsh because I know that following this route may not end well for you.

To this day, I try to push my doctors to be the best doctors, like Dr. Gutstein pushed me. I could easily blow smoke up their rear ends and tell them everything will be okay, but that would not sit well with my soul, and it would not help them.

Honesty is the best policy, to be honest with your friends, your family, your peers, and most importantly, yourself. Every night when you brush your teeth, look in the mirror and ask yourself were you the best you could be today.

COACH KAPLAN'S CORNER

First, understand your true nature.

Second, understand that you may have been systematically robbed of it. It is easy to blame others, a mother, a father, a teacher, a preacher, they might have guided us, but they did not shape us. We make choices.

Third, and most importantly, reclaim it.

Remember, from this day forward, that you are not average. You have just been tricked into feeling like you are average and feeling like it's not only okay to be average but that it is a source of pride. I call this "*Head trip syndrome.*" Some people get a perverse high from seeing others as being unsuccessful.

They think it makes them *"authentic," "real,"* or *"down to earth."* Deep down, they know the truth, though. They want more. You want more. But until you admit it to yourself, you will not have more. Until you admit **YOU CAN'T STOP ME"** you will be stopped.

Once you take that **can't stop me** attitude, you remove the limits and become limitless. If you want to become extraordinary and see exceptional results, you must put in the hard work and maintain that "**CAN'T STOP ME"** attitude.

One day a traveler was walking along a road on his journey from one village to another. As he walked, he noticed a monk tending the ground in the fields beside the road.

The monk said "Good day" to the traveler, and the traveler nodded to the monk.

The traveler then turned to the monk and said, "Excuse me, do you mind if I ask you a question?"

"Not at all," replied the monk.

"I am traveling from the village in the mountains to the village in the valley, and I was wondering if you knew what it is like in the village in the valley?"

"Tell me," said the monk, "What was your experience of the village in the mountains?"

"Dreadful," replied the traveler, "to be honest, I am glad to be away from there. I found the people most unwelcoming. When I first arrived, I was greeted coldly. I was never made to feel part of the village, no matter how hard I tried. The villagers keep very much to themselves; they don't take kindly to strangers. So tell me, what can I expect in the village in the valley?"

"I am sorry to tell you," said the monk, "but I think your experience will be much the same there."

The traveler hung his head despondently and walked on.

Later that same day, another traveler was journeying down the same road, and he also came upon the monk.

"I'm going to the village in the valley," said the second traveler, "Do you know what it is like?"

"I do," replied the monk. "But first tell me, where have you come from?" "I've come from the village in the mountains." said the traveler.

"And how was that?" said the Monk.

"It was a wonderful experience. I would have stayed if I could, but I'm committed to traveling on. I felt as though I was a member of the family in the

village. The elders gave me much advice, the children laughed and joked with me, and people were generally kind and generous. I am sad to have left there. It will always hold special memories for me."

"And what of the village in the valley?" he asked again.

"I think you will find it much the same," replied the monk,

"Good day to you."

"Good day, and thank you," the traveler replied, smiled, and journeyed on.

In life, as the monk revealed in the story above, your attitude will carry you from town to town, person to person, and situation to situation. Your attitude can be altered by merely altering your way of thinking. We're all masters of our own thoughts, our own destiny. Our thoughts are the seeds of our actions, and our actions are the seeds of our future. Plant your seeds of positive thinking daily and watch your dreams grow."

"Don't wait for extraordinary opportunities. Seize common occasions and make them great. Weak men wait for opportunities; strong men make them."

—Orison Swett Marden

CHAPTER 11

The Vitamin of Friendship B-1

*"Friendship is the only cement that will
ever hold the world together."*

—Woodrow Wilson

Another essential aspect of building ourselves is having friends and people we trust. The importance of having people in our lives who push us to our limits and help us reach our goals is immeasurable.

I've come to learn on my journey, the power of friends. Friendships are one of the most underrated yet important facets of life. Friends can enhance and help us celebrate the best times—from weddings to graduations and new careers—as well as help us get through the worst of times (i.e., divorces, deaths, and layoffs). At the end of your life you will basically have three things.

1. ***Your Friends***
2. ***Your family***
3. ***Your memories***

That's why friendships are so crucial to helping maintain our mental and physical health. Simply put, it's incredibly important that people have a dependable social network in place to help them weather the storm of life. So, in a specific way, let's examine how friendship affects our health and wellness?

The power of friendship is an absolute game-changer. Who would have thought some 34 years ago a man would walk into my office who would change my life. His name was Dr. Perry Bard. Our office was in North Palm Beach, and I was looking to add an associate doctor and in walked Dr. Perry Bard.

There was something charismatic about him from the beginning. He was in great shape, handsome, with a pleasant smile, and he made excellent eye contact. He was perfect except for one thing. He was not yet licensed.

There is always a risk of hiring a non-licensed doctor, yet we all start out that way. The risk is they learn whatever they can and leave you as soon as they get their license. My interview with Dr. Bard was funny. I offered him less money per week than I knew he was worth, not to be cheap, but more as a challenge. I wanted to see how much he wanted the job. Perry stayed with me for three years. He was not as bright or talented as I initially thought he was. He was actually brighter and more talented than any man I ever worked with.

The Vitamin for friendship is B1; if you want a good friend, ***BE ONE***. Your best friends are the ones that bring out the best out in you. Dr. Bard has done this for me. When Dr. Bard first came to my office, he was looking for an associate contract, but he was more than a charismatic man, he was a man with great chiropractic tools, a man with excellent business acumen, a man who understood the value of patients, the value of ethics, the value of dedication and the value of discipline. With all my success today, I am grateful to this man, along with his wife Laura (who one time ran my main clinic) for accepting me in spite of my flaws, through thick and thin. Dr. Bard teaches *"Success leave clues"*. As a Bestselling author himself he goes into detail in his book Success Spotlight Book, geared toward doctors. As a gift to my readers, he is offering this book for free to doctors go to, https://www.freebooksuccess.com/drspotlight-order1

It's funny how life works out. One day, one person, one thing can change your life. I knew from the first 5 minutes I was going to give Dr. Bard the job. Who knew it would be a decision that would change my life?

Yes, he got the job, but in reality, he was looking to suck my brain dry, get as much knowledge as he could and then move on. But the fact is I thought at the time he would probably leave me in three months. Yet, he stayed as an associate doctor with me for three years, helped me develop five offices. If you met him, he would always tell the story of how much he learned from me, but there was much I learned from this man.

Initially he innately wanted more than a job. He wanted the secrets to success. In those days I was seeing over 200 patients a day. I had one of the largest practices in the country. But I needed help to maintain and sustain my practice. Dr. Bard had a unique confidence for a recent graduate. Dr. Bard understood visualization. He had that "**CAN'T STOP ME ATTITUDE**" and I saw it in him immediately. Like oxygen we need to breath, like the wind or electricity, you can't see it, but you can feel it.

Dr. Bard was a young man from Brooklyn, he came from humble means, his father was a TV repairman. His mother a saint. He had an advantage of great parents. And now he is a great dad. When I first met him, I likened him to Mickey Rourke in the movie Diner. Handsome, confident, charismatic, a true leader. His road to becoming a doctor was not an easy path. After numerous junior colleges and many major changes, he heard his calling and decided to become a doctor.

Once he made up his mind there was no stopping him. Weekly he would go to the local Jaguar dealer and just sit in new cars. Visualizing his future, motivating his subconscious and yes Superconscious, to give him the powers to realize his dream.

Even as the years pass by, one of the most memorable things was when I was in the Shepherd Center in Atlanta, Georgia. This was a game-changer. This day changed my life.

Dr. Bard came to Georgia to visit me when my wife and I recovered from Botulism after receiving raw botulinum Toxin injections versus the real Botox we thought we were getting. Remember the CDC said we had enough toxin in us to kill 2400 people each. Our prognosis was initially grim and to honest I don't know if Perry was expecting to see what he saw.

Prior to his visit he knew they expected us to live our lives in a wheelchair and possibly on oxygen for the rest of our lives. However, when the going gets tough, the tough get going, and that is when you dig deep, that is when you know what you are made of. During those times, friends, family, and memories can take you to another level. I was blessed to have friends like Dr. Perry Bard.

Before that day, we had not spoken for a while; he was the last person I expected to fly to GA to see me. But that is the type of man he is. This was a good day for me because I saw someone I loved and admired. It was one of my first few days off of a ventilator after ten weeks. Georgia is known for its weather changes, and this was a cold, windy day. I was excited to talk to Perry and walk with him. I was happy I was getting stronger every day. I was glad he didn't see me at my worst. Today he saw and knew I was getting better. Bonnie was still in bad shape, still on a ventilator and struggling, but my progress gave him hope for her.

Dr. Bard was a marathon runner, and each day for me being on a ventilator felt like a marathon; walking was work. But on this day, I was excited to see Perry; his smile is infectious. I wanted to show him not to believe what he was reading in the papers, that I would get well, and I would conquer this. I was now able to walk, and we went for a walk outside, feeling the air upon my face; breathing fresh air was a gift from God.

This was only my second day outside as we walked on the grounds of the Shepherd Center. Often patients were wheeled around in wheelchairs, but I was walking again, I was talking again, I was showing that **"You can't stop me."**

At the Shepherd Center, most of the patients were quadriplegic and paraplegic; not many people, patients, walk these grounds. Yet on this day, I could feel the love from Dr. Bard. His love and appreciation were with me and providing me with tremendous inspiration. Who would have thought Monday would change a man's life forever, remember one day, I was on top of the world, and the next day the world was on top of me?

On that day in the garden, Dr. Bard said to me,

"I see you're getting better; what next? I know you're not done yet."

I said, *"I have an idea."*

He smiled that Perry smile and said, *"Let's discuss it."*

And discuss it we did.

During my many hours in bed, I thought of my time working with Nutrisystem, I thought about the power of the *"**BRAND**"*, and on this day, I told Perry what I thought would be the future of Chiropractic, and I was hoping we could do something together. Imagine one day, one thought, one memory, one idea, one person, can change your life.

It was on this day, we talked of the future; till that day, my battles were continually fighting the present. Now on this day, we talked about the future, and Concierge Coaches was eventually born. Today Concierge Coaches and Disc Centers of America has over 160 clinics nationwide. We are considered by many to be the largest group of doctors specializing in non-surgical Spinal decompression. Dr. Bard leads by example; his two sons Devin and Justin, are now in Chiropractic and Dental school respectively.

It was so exciting to talk business again, to look into the eyes of someone who believed in me. Dr. Bard believes in me as much as I believe in myself, and I knew my future would not be remembered as the *"**Botox Boy.**"* I wanted to make a difference. Together we have made a massive difference by saving thousands of people from having back surgery.

Disc Centers of America doctors offer Non-Surgical Spinal Decompression, which is a conservative approach to disc restoration, maintenance, and support through TDC Therapy, exclusive to Disc Centers of America.

Millions of Americans who have suffered or know someone suffering from back pain now there is a non-surgical, non-invasive solution. Back Pain has reached epidemic proportions. Now to understand how severe this epidemic is, consider that Low back pain is the second most common symptom related reason for seeing a physician in the United States, or approximately 19 million physician visits annually. It is estimated that 85% of the US population will experience an episode of **Low Back Pain**, in their lifetime.

The cost for the treatment of low back pain is staggering. Back pain is a billion-dollar industry. According to Newsweek magazine in an article "THE PRICE OF PAIN", by Karen Springer, that in the year 2005 Americans spent $85.9 billion looking for relief from back and neck pain through surgery doctor's visits, X-rays, MRI scans and medication, up from $52.1 billion in 1997, according to a study in the Feb 13 issue of the Journal of the American Medical Association (JAMA).

She went on to report *"Not only are more people seeking treatment for back pain, but the price of treatment per person is also up."* In the JAMA study, researchers at the University of Washington and Oregon Health & Science University compared national data from 3,179 adult patients who reported spine problems in 1997 to 3,187 who reported them in 2005—and found that inflation-adjusted annual medical costs increased from $4,695 per person to $6,096.

Spinal Decompression has been proven effective in relieving the pain associated with bulging and herniated discs, degenerative disc disease, sciatica, and even relapse or failed back surgery. Since its release, clinical studies have revealed an amazing success rate in treating lumbar disc related problems with Spinal Decompression.

Spinal Decompression uses state of the art technology to apply a distraction force to relieve nerve compression often associated with low back pain and sciatica. Today, you don't have to live with that pain anymore. Thanks to the concerted efforts of a team of top physicians and medical engineers, Spinal Decompression was developed to effectively treat lower back pain and sciatica resulting from herniated or deteriorated discs. Spinal Decompression not only significantly reduces back pain in many patients, but also enables the majority of patients to return to more active lifestyles.

I am proud of the work Dr. Bard, and I do with DCOA, imagine from my sickness, from his visit came a business idea that is saving thousands of patients from having unnecessary back surgery.

Life can be hard and for some it is battle after battle to stay afloat. If your life is war, then your friends are your best allies. They are the ones we call up when there is a battle ahead, and we will need some help. They are the ones who come in when we are weak and close to defeat. They are the ones who have been there, supporting you throughout life's numerous losses and gains. Like allying nations, we are friends because we trust each other. We need each other for resources and support. We depend on each other; our strength and health are vital to each other's wellbeing.

It is a support system necessary to our sovereignty because every great power would be nothing without its allies if you think about it. Our strength is dependent on the strength of our friendships.

This was a time in my life when I learned who my true friends were, people like Peter Brock who came to visit me every day. His brother Andy Brock and people like Harold Rosen, a plastic surgeon who told the doctor they put my tracheotomy on wrong, made them redo it. I was blessed with people like Dr. Dennis Egitto, who literally saved my life, and his wife, Barbara who we still dine with every Thursday night. Bill Meyer and his wife Denise (who has since passed) worked with Peter to preserve my life and my estate in the early days. Joe Littenberg came to visit me when I was paralyzed and made me laugh. The list goes on and on. To all my friends too many to mention, you know who you are, thank you.

So many people came to GA to sit with my wife and me. I can never express just how much their visits meant. I was blessed with family and friends who cared so much for us.

Michael, my older son, literally gave up his life and moved to Georgia and tended to us every day. These are things in life that you do not forget. He had to drop out of college for a year to do this. My father used to say, ***"Be good to everybody because you will see the same people on the way up that you see on the way down."***

You never know when you will need friends, but you need to cultivate them, and like seeds, you need to water them constantly. We take care of our friendships the same way we take care of our allies. We support them, advise them, go to them in times of need, and rely on them during our own moments of weakness. They will be the first ones there when we've been attacked and the last ones to leave in recovery.

We choose people based on the notion that they will provide aid and care when we need these things most. They are a support system we need to create for those tough battles against all the A-holes of the world. We all have a few enemies in life, and we are all bound to fight a few battles. And we feel stronger going into life knowing someone has our back. Neal Chapnick was that type of friend. He always had my back. I mentioned earlier how tough he was, he literally was the toughest Jewish kid I ever knew. He'd fight anyone, anywhere, just for the fun of it. So often we go to a dance on a Saturday night and Neal sat in the back of the car drinking Southern comfort or whatever.

Neal, we say, *"don't get into a fight tonight"*

And he said, *"I promise I won't"*

And he always did.

We can take the blows and the setbacks, knowing someone is there to keep pushing us forward. They are our lifelines to the outside world and provide aid in times of need. They are the people we trust most in life and the only ones who would take a metaphorical bullet for us.

Friendships are born and forged without any necessary expectation that they will receive anything in return anytime soon, but knowing that support is there when they need it makes all the difference. **"Good friends care for each other, close friends understand each other, but TRUE FRIENDS stay forever. Beyond words, beyond distance, beyond time!"**

Many of us have friends in our lives over the years. Some friends we make as children and then lose contact with as we grow older. Often the friends we make as adults and stay in touch with, are friends as long as we are nearby them. It is convenient to keep in touch, but then over time, one moves away, or busy schedules slowly pull us apart, and we start to lose touch.

Those friendships fall into the *"good friends"* or *"close friends"* category. But then there is that last group of friends – those we call true friends – they are those we have a mutual caring about. We understand each other's hearts, and where bonds are formed between us that span any distance in proximity and where the bonds run so deep that no amount of time apart or lack of words will change the way we feel about that friend. These are our true friends, and when one comes into your life, cherish it! Dr. Bard is more than a partner. He is a true friend.

I have been blessed to have many friends over the years, and friends always forgave me for the times when I may have been grumpy or obstinate. They loved me without judgment and expectations. During my bout with Botulism, I needed friends; I appreciated friends and hopefully became a better friend.

As my wife and I healed, it was our friends and family that gave us hugs, even at times that I may not have deserved one. These faithful friends were there for me, maybe not always in person but always in heart; knowing this helped me through incredible challenges throughout our lives. True friends help us grow and change for the better. They support us in good and bad times and make us laugh when all we want to do is cry. So today if you know someone fighting this dreaded virus, call them up, offer some words of encouragement, it may mean more than you might ever know.

True friends stay forever, no matter how far apart time and distance may cause us to grow from one another, we always have the comfort of knowing that these true friends are still there for us, even if only in spirit—cheering us on and wishing us the best because that is what true friends do for each other. *"A strong friendship doesn't need daily conversation, doesn't always need togetherness as long as the relationship lives in the heart, true friends will never part."*

When someone is your true friend, they leave an impression on your heart that will never go away, not with time and not with distance. I dedicate this chapter to my friends, and you know who you are. I am forever grateful for the true friends in my life, both those who are alive and those who have passed away; thank you so much for being my faithful friends!

How do I define friends? What do friends mean to me? How can you master friendship?

Always remember, no harm can ever come from loving people.

Let's agree that true friends are pretty amazing, right? No wonder I love them so much. Lastly, as I thought about what I have learned about friendship over the last 69 years, I wanted to share a few of those things with you.

COACH KAPLAN'S CORNER

1) **Friendship** *to me is someone believing the best about you at all times; my wife Bonnie is my best friend. A true friend defends you when you cannot defend yourself, someone standing in your corner ready to sacrifice on your behalf at any given time. It is someone who pushes you to be the best version of yourself and is the first to stand and clap for you when you succeed. True friendship is God's Way of reaching down and hugging you at your best, and more importantly, at your worst.*

2) **A true friendship is never easy.** *There are so many things in this world that demand stress and force heartache, so someone you genuinely care about and want to spend time on should not be one of those things. Friends are healers, helpers, and they are integral to a happy life. I want to be the friend that is always there no matter what, supportive, trustworthy, loyal, and down for a good meal, a good glass of wine!*

3) **True friends are forever.** *Somewhere along the way, there is a shift – from the ties of childhood and the memories of college to the actual connection that goes beyond social commitment. Our extra time dwindles as our ability to smell the BS heightens, and that is when we identify with those that will be with us for the long haul. We may not speak every day or every week, but it matters when the conversation happens, and it lasts over several cocktails. Those that will drop everything when you call are now able to be listed on the one hand, and it is no longer called friendship – it's called family.*

4) **Friendships grow over time.** *Friendship to me has a whole new meaning in this time of my life. Friends to me form my A-Team. Your gift is to pick and choose and build your team member by member knowing the value of the power and bond you share. A true friend loves the imperfect you, the confused you, the wrong you – because that is the real you. All at the same time, they celebrate you, cheer for you and show up for you, no questions asked. This may not be a big group, but a solid and genuine group that expects nothing more than your company in return.*

You can see how important friendship is to me because, without these people who support me, I never would have been able to grow and reach my goals. They pushed me to my limits, and they are the people I would sacrifice anything for FRIENDS.

COACH KAPLAN'S RULES ON FRIENDSHIP:

• Make the Time

We live in a world where information and life updates are at our fingertips but do not let social media be an excuse not to reach out. I have learned that a simple phone call or impromptu lunch date is so much more effective. For example, one of my best friends calls A LOT, and when we first became friends, it really annoyed me. However, I quickly learned that is her way of showing love. She is so genuinely invested in what is happening throughout my day.

And it is a lot easier to pick up the phone and have a 30-second conversation than it is to have a 45-minute conversation and catch a friend up on the last month of your life. The bottom line is making an effort to connect shows how much you care.

• Love Who They Love

When it comes to having a genuine relationship, it is important to love who your friend loves. With each of my best friends, I love their spouse just as much as I love them. And if they have kids, I love them like they are my own. It is a package deal. When it comes to the friends I am so invested in, I want every part of them – from the good and the easy to the messy and the imperfect. With that comes a fierce loyalty to love who they love.

When it is authentic, it is easy. It strengthens your relationship in a completely new way and creates this beautiful, vulnerable extended family.

• Never Let Insecurity Get in the way

Friends, male or female, can be brutal at times, and even that is an understatement. I have never been one that deals well with making things more complicated than they need to be, but I have learned that judgment, competition, jealously, and little mistruths have no place in friendship. However, what all of those things typically come down to is insecurity.

When you genuinely want what's best for someone, all of those toxic emotions are replaced with selfless love. You want them to have more. Judgment turns into understanding, competition completely dissolves, jealousy turns into things you are allowed to say out loud, and mistruths are not given a second thought. Never let insecurity get in the way of friendships, as actions always speak louder than words.

• Do Not Force it

I read a quote a while ago that said, "I no longer force things. What flows, flows and what crashes, crashes. I only have the energy for things that were meant for me." I love that for so many reasons, but when it comes to your friends and who you choose to spend your life with, you know without a doubt who your soul connects with. I have learned that just because you have a history does not mean you have a future. There are too many hardships in life as it is, do not let your friendships be one of them.

Know when to take a deep breath and let it go – sometimes the lesson to be learned is in the inevitable truth. Or, know when to fight like hell for someone who you cannot imagine doing life without.

• Be Present for the In-Betweens

Most days, life is full of lunch dates and uncorking a good bottle of Italian red wine. Endless laughter and sweet conversation are common amongst my friends. Other days, when we are tired or run down, I do not even know if I can function. Yet I pick up the phone and call a friend, a true lifeline. Friends are not only there for the big things, and they were there for me when I literally could not get out of bed.

When I needed endless prayers, they prayed for me. We all have bad days, challenging times. I lost my brother at the young age of 65. My friends were there for me. Many flew to Jersey for his funeral to support me. Friends love you at your best and worst. From the life-changing days to the small fleeting moments. That type of connection creates a bond that is not quickly broken.

Friendship is so important that I do not think I can ever completely express how meaningful these people are even now. We all need true friends who help build us up.

"The most beautiful discovery true friends make is that they can grow separately without growing apart."

—Elisabeth Foley

CHAPTER 12

Build Your Dreams

"A dream doesn't become reality through magic; it takes sweat, determination and hard work."

—Colin Powell.

We can build our habits and turn our failures into successes by just being more present in the moment. I am sure that we have all felt the fear of failure at one time in our life. What begins with a conservative attitude of playing it safely soon enlarges itself to become a total obsession with fear and failure. By focusing on our successes and not on our fears with the aid of imagination, one can overcome these hurdles in one swoop.

Think of what you are most afraid of. Picture it until you can feel the emotions. Are you experiencing anxiety? Good. Now push that picture aside and imagine yourself in the same situation but triumphing over your fears. It feels different, doesn't it? You can create your own emotional responses, so why not create the most pleasant ones?

Having heart means doing "Whatever It Takes." Combine this with a **"Can't Stop Me Attitude,"** and you become unstoppable, invincible. If you do not believe me, read on.

The key that will unlock the vast treasure chest of greatness lies deep within each person. Deep in your heart. We may need to stop looking outside of ourselves for the answers since the entire Universe's answers lie somewhere within. One unsettled man chose to embark on a journey, a quest. After looking around at what he had, he became more concerned with what he did not have. So, he sold all his worldly possessions in search of the secret of life and flew to India.

Upon arriving in India, the natives looked at the man and said, *"How can we help you?"*

The man said, *"I am here to find the secret of life."*

The natives pointed to a local mountain and said, *"If you climb up that mountain and you ask to speak to the Maharajah Mukesh, he will tell you of the secret of life."*

So, the man picked up his gear and climbed the mountain. On top of the mountain in a shack surrounded by sheep, there was a tattered old man whose eyes were illuminated by strength, not weakness.

The Maharajah looked at the man and asked,

"How may I help you, my son?"

"I am here to learn the secret of life," said the man.

"My son," said the Maharajah, *"you have traveled all this way to learn something you already know."*

The man looked at the Master and said, *"Maharajah, if I knew the answer, I would not ask the question."*

"The answer, my son, is not complex," answered the Master, *"but it is something you must understand. The secret of life is, 'I AM.'"*

The man was surprised and repeated, *"I am?"*

The Master looked into the traveler's tired eyes and replied, *"Yes, my son. I AM."*

The man became irritated and retorted, *"Well, there has to be more to life than that! This is something that I already knew!"*

The Master looked at the man and said, *"But is it something that you believe?"*

The man then declared, *"You're a phony,"* and he left. He went back down the mountain and found the man who had recommended that he seek the Master.

The man fumed.

"He was no visionary! He didn't know the answer! Have you seen the way he lives? He lives amongst sheep in a broken-down shack with tattered clothes. This man could not know the secret of life!"

The guide looked at the man and responded,

"There is only one master of equal knowledge. To see him, you must travel a great distance. This journey will take ten days through the mountains, to the peak of the Himalayas."

So the man hired a party, and for ten days, he traveled through the Himalayas. On the tenth day, the sun rose as they began their march, and on the slope of the mountain ahead, the man saw one of the most beautiful temples he had ever seen, a temple that sparkled with gold and silver. The closer he got to the temple, the more impressed he became with the magnificent dwelling. He walked in and asked to meet the Master.

Soon, the Master came to meet the traveler. He had silver hair, his eyes shone, and an aura of peace and contentment surrounded him. When he spoke, his words were gentle:

"My son, you have traveled a long way. How can I help you?"

And the man replied, *"I have come here to learn the secret of life."*

"Ah, the secret of life," said the Master. *"So many people travel to our country to learn something that they already know."*

And then the Master asked, *"Have you not already asked this question of any of the other masters along the way?"*

"Yes," said the man. *"I asked this question of Master Mukesh, but he gave me the answer, 'I AM.' How could a man who lives on the side of a mountain, in a broken-down dwelling, surrounded by smelly sheep, possibly know the secret of life?"*

The Master looked at him and spoke in a soft voice, *"My son, I see that you do not know the secret of life. I will teach it to you, but there will be a price."*

The man smiled back and said, *"Well, how much? I am prepared to pay any amount that you may ask."*

"My son," answered the Master, *"look around you. You cannot buy the secret of life. That is an investment you must make in time. If you will spend five years living in my barn amongst my animals and be their caretaker, on the first day of the sixth year, we will meet again, and I will tell you the secret of life."*

The man agreed. So, for five years, the man lived within the dwelling. He milked the cows, brushed the horses, chased the goats, and swept the floors. On the first day of the sixth year, he re-entered the temple. The five years had taken quite a toll on the man. He did not appear happy. His face was pale, his eyes sullen. His hair was now gray, his posture weakened, and his teeth were discolored.

He stood in front of the Master and said,

"I have done everything you have asked. I lived amongst your animals and was their caretaker for five years. Now, Master, I have come on the first day of the sixth year to ask you for the secret of life."

The Master sat down, and he said, *"Give me your hand."*

The man held out his now callused hand to the Master, whose hands were soft as silk but still suggested both strength and power, yet his hands also had warmth that emanated into the hands of the weary traveler.

The Master then looked into the traveler's eyes and said, *"My son, the secret of life is hidden within. The secret of life has always been within you. The secret of life is, I AM."*

The traveler pulled his hand back, jumped up, and shouted,

"I AM? I am WHAT? I am five years older! I am five years more tired! I am five years more broken down, and you tell me something that I already know? How dare you deceive me!"

At this point, the Master stood up and said,

"Deceive you? I never deceived you. Five years ago today, you passed the Master Maharajah, who was once my master, and you looked at him, and you judged him because he lived on the side of a mountain, surrounded by sheep that he adored. You asked him the secret of life, and he told you, 'I AM.' But that was not good enough. It was too easy, too simple. So, you came to my opulent palace, and you again asked the question that had been already answered; this question whose answer existed within you. If I had given you the same answer, you would have gone on to the next, even more, opulent castle and asked the same question. But the answer remains the same: 'I AM, YOU ARE.'"

He continued,

"You see, I am responsible for where I sit; I am responsible for everything that I have, as are you. You chose to travel to my castle; you chose to live in my barn. There were no restraints. You could have left any day you wanted, but your desire to know kept you there and kept you going. Now, the price you paid might have been steep, but maybe this time, when you leave, you will realize you chose your destiny. You chose to come to this country; you chose to live amongst my animals, and because you chose to do this, this choice led to the direction of your life, and it paralleled your existence. Yes, my son, I AM. YOU ARE. The secret of life exists within each and every one of us."

Here's the premise: We are all, right now, living the life we choose. This choice, of course, is not a single, monumental choice. The choices I am talking about here are made daily, hourly, moment by moment. Do we try something new or stick to the tried-and-true? Do we take a risk or eat what's already on our plate? Do we ponder a thrilling adventure or contemplate what's on TV? Do we walk over and meet that interesting stranger, or do we play it safe? Do we indulge our hearts or cater to our fear? Do we pursue what we want, or do we do what's simply comfortable? For the most part, most people choose comfort—the familiar, the time-honored, the well-worn but well-known. After a lifetime of choosing between comfort and risk, we are left with the life we currently have. Here today, we can begin a new adventure, right here, right now. Are you ready?

The answer should be, *"I AM!"*

Life gives us chances, and now it is on us to make the most out of it. I encourage you all to take control of your lives and aim for your goals.

My mantra is: "**Whatever it takes**". "*The road to success is always under construction, and in life, there's no free ride*". This road to success often has many detours. Choose your dream job, car, relationship, house, or family. Each day, like an architect, design your dream life. Think about the materials you will need, the time it will take to build this life, the site of your new life. You are the architect of your dreams, your destiny. Just imagine if God said, *"Be the architect of your life. You can become whatever you design."*

Now, realize you are. Life supplies us with all the tools, materials, and abilities that are needed. It's now up to you to develop the blueprints and build your future. It takes as little as you willing to lead yourself to success, to plant daily all the seeds of success that will lead to a fruitful harvest of greatness that lies within your spirit. If you plant your dreams into your heart, spirit, and soul, their roots will anchor your vision and create your reality. Are you ready to grow, to lead, to live the life of your dreams?

My father once told me there are three ways to lead in life, which I've shared with my children,

1. **Is by example**
2. **Is by example**
3. **Is by example**

As a doctor, as a father, I have always tried to lead by example. My partner Dr. Perry Bard and I have always looked for the secrets of life; what separates winners from losers? The secrets to success, lies inside every one of us.

According to an ancient Greek story, a gathering of the gods took place on Mount Olympus when the world was young. Having created the earth, man, all the animals and birds, the creatures of the sea, flowers, plants, and all other living things, the gods still had one thing left to do. They had to hide the secret of life where it couldn't be found until mankind had grown and evolved in consciousness to a point where they were ready for such wisdom and understanding. The gods argued over where to hide the secret of life.

One said, *"Let's hide it on the highest peak of the highest mountain. Mankind will not find it there."*

But another god responded, *"We have created mankind with an insatiable thirst for knowledge, and an insatiable curiosity and ambition. It's because of these traits that he will eventually conquer the mountain and obtain the secret of life."*

The gods continued to talk of mankind's strengths and weaknesses, realizing that a person's strength was derived from his or her weaknesses many times. They knew that mankind was born without the ability to climb, yet that weakness could be turned into strength because it could give the incentive to learn to climb. Man was not born knowing how to swim, a weakness. The ability to learn to swim was a strength.

"We should not underestimate the power of mankind," one God said to another.

And, they continued to dialogue and make suggestions until one God suggested,

"We need to hide the secret in the deepest part of the deepest ocean."

To this, another God responded,

"That won't work. We have designed mankind with unlimited energy, a boundless imagination, and a burning desire to seek, dream and explore the world—to succeed at all costs. Mankind's inherent ability to succeed will provide him with the ability to conquer even the greatest ocean depths."

Finally, one of the gods came up with what he felt was the solution:

"Let us hide this in the one place where mankind will never look. A place they will only come to when they have exhausted all other possibilities and are finally ready."

"And where will that be?" the gods chorused.

Zeus stood up and replied,

"We will hide it in the deepest part of the human heart. For mankind will not look there until he has truly evolved."

And so they did. Man's quest for the secret of life spans 5,000 years of recorded history and has occupied some of the world's wisest men and women, as well as some of the greatest leaders of all religions.

Having a heart "means doing whatever it takes," combine this with a "Can't Stop Me Attitude," and you become unstoppable, invincible.

People who are successful in business and in life are leaders rather than followers. **Leadership is a quality made up of a number of attributes, including:**

COACH KAPLAN'S CORNER

A leader must have the following qualities.

1. *Courage*
2. *Self-control*
3. *A sense of right and wrong*
4. *Decisiveness*
5. *Giving more than necessary*
6. *A pleasing personality*
7. *Sympathy and understanding*
8. *Willingness to accept responsibility*
9. *Attention to detail*
10. *A spirit of cooperation*

Consider how prominent these attributes are in your own life. Maybe you would like to eat a candy bar. If you lack self-control, chances are you will eat that candy bar. But if you are willing to deny yourself a small, transitory pleasure, you will eventually achieve enormous, long-lasting satisfaction.

Leaders take action. My goal is to help you turn positive thinking into positive doing. Don't wait until tomorrow; take action steps now!

Do not wait until conditions are perfect. They never are. Expect difficulties, and then use your creativity to overcome them. Do not be stopped by past failures. Today is the first day of the rest of your life. *"Plan your life and live your plan."*

As I mentioned before, set goals. Determine how you will reach those goals. Perseverance is required to reach your goals, and the secret to perseverance is persistence. This may sound like circular reasoning, but the fact is that successful people refuse to succumb to setbacks. They put themselves on the line of their dreams, and they do it over and over again. They know that they must take risks and that there are no guarantees, but they also know that they have to lose. Successful people are people who dare to be successful.

In life, we have the doers and the talkers. Talkers are usually characterized by their lack of enthusiasm, lack of commitment to their work, lives, and themselves. Doers, by definition, are people who get things done. Talkers nourish every failure until it becomes powerful enough to overcome their hopes and success. Doers learn from their failures, then let them go. Talkers spend a lot of time wishing that things were different. Doers make them different. Nothing in this world is for free. Success takes work. But then, so does failure. If you want to be one of the doers instead of one of the talkers, you must develop certain characteristics.

COACH KAPLAN'S CORNER

Willpower – *By focusing on your goals instead of your distractions, you will be able to persevere in the face of obstacles and temptations. Use your imagination to see yourself as you want to be, and you will also develop your willpower.*

Self-esteem – *Understand that you are in control of your destiny and not vice versa. This belief provides you with the courage to follow through on your plans.*

Purpose – *Vague ideas bring vague results. You must know why you are here, what you want, and what you are willing to do to achieve it.*

Answer the following questions to see where you rate on the Purpose Scale:

A. Do you fail to clearly define your goals? Do you procrastinate?

B. Do you waiver when making decisions?

C. Do you settle for the second-best?

D. Do you care who you are?

E. Do you blame others for your mistakes rather than accept responsibility for them?

F. Are your desires weak, shallow, and lifeless?

G. Are you motivated to achieve your goals?

H. Do you quit at the first sign of defeat?

I. Do you have specific plans for your success?

J. Do you wish for things to happen rather than make them happen?

K. Do you lack ambition?

L. Do you look for shortcuts?

M. Are you stopped by criticism?

If your answers do not satisfy you, then you need to work on the areas in which you are weak. Do not just do the minimum; always go the extra mile! In order to succeed at anything, you must give it all you have and then give some more. This is as true for success in life as it is for a business plan. My formula will work, provided you bring the necessary commitment and perseverance.

Keep in mind that you have nothing to lose but your past history of failure. There are risks in this approach, but there are far greater risks involved in doing nothing. And there are no rewards involved when you do nothing, but ask anyone who has ever persisted in reaching a goal whether the effort was worth it.

Yes, there may be times when you feel discouraged. This is a normal emotion, not your enemy. During these times of emotional weakness, look to your allies. Through discipline, controlling your emotions, stating your affirmations, and utilizing your imagination, you will shed pounds and thus will increase your success level. Allow your awareness and desire to become a result rather than a mere image. Look to yourself for courage and look to others for additional help. We are all here to help each other in loving and sharing. What better success could there be than the offering of these to another?

I have often found how failure and lower self-image comes from comparing yourself to others. As a basketball player, as a doctor, I tried never to compare myself to others. My father used to say there are three sides to every story, his side, her side, and the truth. Do not worry about keeping up with the Joneses; just be the best you can be.

Two men were thrown into the army guardhouse. One prisoner asked his cellmate, *"How long are you in for?"*

The other prisoner replied, *"Twenty-four hours."*

The first prisoner asked what offense he had committed.

"I killed the general," he said.

Confused, the first prisoner asked, *"How come I got 30 days for going AWOL, and you only get 24 hours for murdering the general."*

He replied,

"Because they're hanging me tomorrow."

Do not think about what you do not have; look at your life for all the answers, never give up, never give in. I am asking you from this day forward to put aside any thoughts of failure and lack and replace them with positive, vital images. Use your imagination – it is more powerful than you may realize. Try this simple experiment. Close your eyes and picture a lemon. Imagine the sharp, citrus smell. Now imagine yourself biting into it; feel the tart, juicy pulp on your tongue.

Are you drooling yet? The lemon is not real, but your subconscious does not know that.

Now use that same power of imagination to picture yourself at your ideal place in life. Your imagination is the tool that carves the way. Imagine yourself buying a new car, a new house, hear yourself telling your friends that you have never looked or felt better, never been happier. Say it out loud.

Write down your favorite goals and affirmations and place them where you will see them frequently – the bathroom mirror is a good spot. Say your affirmations frequently and with conviction until you make them a part of yourself.

Imagine if God said to you, *"I want you to be the architect of your life, I want you to design the life that you've always wanted,"* but God did give you this gift, and it sits within your heart.

Now friends, create an image of what success means to you and then write down the attributes needed to make this image a reality. Do your ideas differ from those you held before you started this book?

Now take your image further, to the outer limits of what you believe possible. See yourself not where you are but where you want to be. Imagine what it would be like to have no limitations in life. Think of how far you could go if you knew that your past could not hold you back. Now realize that these images can become tangible, that the only limitations you have are those which you place on yourself.

I know from personal experience that this is true. You are reading one of my dreams right now. I had a great desire to become a writer, and I used affirmations, imagery, and the other techniques I am sharing with you to help myself realize this dream. Who would have thought that I would have written seven books and already have four #1 bestsellers?

No one thought I would have met with Presidents and sat with leaders of the free world. No one even thought I would be a varsity basketball player in both high school and college.

Who would have thought I would've been not only a doctor but a highly successful doctor?

Who would have thought when I started Disc Centers of America that I'd have 160 clinics underneath me? I did. I believed in myself.

Perhaps you are telling yourself that I started out with certain advantages that I am not sharing with you. Well, my education was also once only an idea. In today's world, an education is open to anyone who desires it. My wife was raised by the state, read books to escape, wanted an education, became not only a teacher but a principal; she survived cancer, botulism, she turned her dreams into a reality. Her youth was spent with hand-me-down clothes, she went to college on a scholarship and student loans, she wanted more out of life than what she had, and she was willing to do "**whatever it takes**".

And what is true for us is true for everyone who ever lived. Successful men and women enter the world as naked babies; they do not leave the womb wearing a three-piece suit or reading The Wall Street Journal. They learned the secrets of success and – just as important – used them in their own lives.

Whatever you desire, you can acquire. Do not let obstacles get in your way – use them as steppingstones to success. And do not promise yourself that you will *"try"* to reach your goals because that attitude will only hinder you. In the successful movie, The Empire Strikes Back, Yoda, the Jedi teacher, explains to Luke Skywalker how to use the Force, the greatest power in the universe. He says to his prize student, *"Luke, there is no try; there is either do or not do."*

If faith can move mountains, it can also enable you to scale a mountain. Do not be afraid to aim for the top or be tempted to rest on a comfortable plateau. You are an infinite source of energy, so there is no reason for you to settle for a limited existence. Give of yourself in any way imaginable. Life will become something that you experience rather than something that you have become a passenger in. You can follow a rainbow that never ends but leads to an infinite combination of colors that culminate in one bright light.

Your dreams are not illusions, but your fears are. In the phrase made famous by Franklin Delano Roosevelt, *"We have nothing to fear but fear itself."* In *"Think And Grow Rich,"* Napoleon Hill claimed, *"Confront your fears, and you can make them disappear."* It's true. Our fears of failure are incredibly destructive and unnecessary.

Napoleon Hill interviewed Thomas Alva Edison, who provided an enlightening perspective on what most of us call "failure."

Hill asked the great inventor, *"Mr. Edison, what have you got to say about the fact that you've failed thousands of times in your attempts to create the light bulb?"*

Edison replied, *"I beg your pardon. I've never failed once. I've had thousands of learning experiments that didn't work. I had to run through enough learning experiments to find a way that did work."*

All I hope you learn from this is to work on yourself, do what you want to do, and succeed. Learn from your failures, and you will eventually succeed.

"Failure Will Never Overtake Me If My Determination To Succeed Is Strong Enough."

—Og Mandino

CHAPTER 13

Goal Tending

"Success is the progressive realization of a worthy goal or ideal."

—Earl Nightingale

Once there was a boy who lived with his family on a farm. They had a beautiful dog who would go down to the pond for hours every day in the spring and summer with the boy to practice retrieving various items. The boy wanted to prepare his dog for any scenario that may come up during duck season because he wanted his dog to be the best hunting dog in the whole county. So, he made a goal to himself that he would make his dog great.

The boy and his dog had vigorous training sessions every day until the dog was so obedient, he wouldn't do anything unless he was told to do so by the boy.

As duck season rolled in with the fall and winter months, the boy and his dog were eager to be at their regular spot down at the pond near their house. Only a few minutes passed before the two heard the first group of ducks flying overhead. The boy slowly raised his gun and shot three times before killing a duck, which landed in the center of the pond.

When the boy signaled his dog to retrieve the duck, the dog charged through the duck blind and bushes toward the pond. However, instead of swimming in the water like he had practiced so many times, the dog walked on the water's surface, retrieved the duck, and returned it to the boy.

The boy was astonished. His dog had an amazing ability to walk on water–it was like magic. The boy knew no one would ever believe this amazing thing that he had just witnessed. He had to get someone else down there to see this incredible phenomenon.

The boy went to a nearby farmer's house and asked if he would hunt with him the next morning. The neighbor agreed and met up with the boy the following morning at his regular spot by the pond.

The pair patiently waited for a group of ducks to fly overhead, and soon enough, they heard them coming. The boy told the neighbor to go ahead and take a shot, which the neighbor did, killing one duck. Just as the day before, the boy signaled to his dog to fetch the duck. Miraculously, the dog walked on the water again to retrieve the duck.

The boy was bursting with pride and could hardly contain himself when he asked his neighbor, *"Did you see that? What do you think?!"*

The neighbor responded, *"I wasn't going to say anything, but your dog doesn't even know how to swim."*

The boy sat in disbelief as his neighbor pointed out a potential flaw of the dog rather than recognizing the fact that what he had just done was a miracle. People will often downplay others' abilities or achievements because they're unable to accomplish the same thing. Don't let this bring you down. Just move on and keep working on improving yourself. Maintaining a positive mindset is a key part of being successful. Friends when you set goals set them for yourself, not to impress others.

Goals are the first step in making plans for the future, and they are critical in the development of talents in various areas, from job to relationships and everything in between. They are the symbolic target for our metaphoric arrow.

Understanding the significance of goals and the tactics for achieving them pave the route for success.

Pablo Picasso said it best:

"Our goals can only be reached through a vehicle of a plan, in which we must fervently believe, and upon which we must vigorously act. There is no other route to success."

The Power of Goal Setting

Setting goals, as we've heard many times, is the first step in realizing our aspirations. If we only fantasize about it without any goals in mind, our dreams will never come true. I've always established goals in my life. Lee Hackett, a former teammate from Fairleigh Dickinson University, and I recently met with each other.

Lee was one of the most extensively recruited talents at FDU at the time. He had a high school career in which he scored over 1,000 points and grabbed over 1,000 rebounds. He was the talk of the town and larger than life. We expected to see someone between the height of 6'8" or 6'9" when he arrived on campus. Lee stood at a svelte 6'3" height.

On the first day, he declared, *"I'm going to score 1,000 points and collect 1,000 rebounds, and nothing is going to stop me."*

We reconnected through a friend Dennis Kelly here in Florida. We met at my home, here we were more than 45 years later and it seemed like yesterday. Lee was a poor man's Larry Bird, and I was proud of him. This is not meant as a slight, but rather as the ultimate compliment, as Larry Bird is a consummate overachiever, even standing at 6'9" tall.

I remember Lee as a tenacious player who, more often than not, caught the ball after it flew through the air after it hit the basket. Yes, he achieved his goal. He is a "Hall of Famer" who got his 1000 points and 1000 rebounds.

"GOAL SETTERS ARE GOAL GETTERS," remarked Mark Victor Hansen, author of the "Chicken Soup for the Soul" series.

We can imagine ourselves in the same situation in our lives after wasting years, attempting to achieve our goals in various methods, only to discover that we never actually achieved any goals that brought us closer to our ambitions. From the start, it would have been a colossal failure.

I started setting goals before I even realized what they were. My initial goal was always to make the team, and my second goal was to one day be the best player on the team. My ambition was to go into chiropractic school and become the best chiropractor in the world once I got there. Now that I've specialized in disc injuries, my goal is to become the country's number one professional in Decompression therapy. **"Disc Centers of America,"** founded with my partner, Dr. Perry Bard, and with the help and mentoring of Dr. Norman Shealy, we are achieving these goals. We are honored to be endorsed by him as the leaders in our profession.

The general definition of a goal is something that anybody desires to achieve, but only we can fully describe our ambitions.

Every accomplishment of the human race stems from the ideals and efforts of our forefathers and mothers. Many people have united since then and aspired to attain goals in their different industries. When we desire to reach a specific goal in life, we have discovered meaning in our lives in different ways in each generation. We shall, without a doubt, put up our best efforts to attain these objectives.

Then, as a result of these accomplishments, the next generation is inspired to better and do more than our forefathers did. Industry experts, business leaders, motivational speakers, and entrepreneurs have all shared their knowledge, methods, and abilities with us to help us achieve our goals or mimic their success. Despite this, many people miss the significance of clearly defining their objectives to make the best use of the information and skills they have.

So, how can we create goals that will propel our work forward?

Before we can answer this issue, we must first comprehend why so many people have failed to develop their objectives.

When walking through an elephant camp, a man noticed that the elephants were only secured with a small rope that was tied around one ankle. He wondered why the elephants didn't break free from the rope, as the elephants were certainly strong enough to do so.

He asked a trainer why the elephants didn't try to break free, and the trainer responded by saying that they use the same size rope for baby elephants all the way up to adulthood. Because they're too small when they're babies to break free from the rope, ***they grow up being conditioned that the rope is stronger than they are.*** *As adults, they think the rope can still hold them, so they don't try to fight it.*

What's holding you back from achieving your goals in life. In this story the elephants in this case are experiencing learned helplessness. This phenomenon occurs when someone has been conditioned to anticipate discomfort in some way without having a way to avoid it or make it stop. **After enough conditioning, the person will stop any attempts to avoid the pain, even if they see an opportunity to escape.**

Imagine Michael Jordan didn't initially make his High School basketball team.

If you go through life thinking that you can't do something just because you have failed at doing it in the past, you're living with a fixed mindset. You have to let go of your limiting beliefs in order to make the breakthroughs that are required for your ultimate success. Don't let other people tell you that you can't do something, and don't hold onto an assumption that you can't grow and learn from past failures.

To comprehend where we should take our next few steps or goals in order to achieve success, we must first recognize the six important reasons for us to set our goals correctly.

Number 1: Goals Force of Motivation

Goals motivate us to achieve our objectives because they operate as a driving force. Goal setting is the first step toward achieving our objectives since it allows us to connect to our inner energy or desire. It provides us with an objective to aim for, a location to visit, or even a certain figure to reach in the short and long term.

Number 2: Goals are Visual Representations of Our Dreams

If we have set our aims towards them, imagination, visualizations, fancies, and even dreams are not enough. You will still have impractical concepts based on your utilizable knowledge. As a result, goal setting is critical in guaranteeing your faith in your methodology, your analysis of your findings, and your pursuit of every resource required.

We can think of our dreams as a series of puzzles, and the goals we set as parts of puzzles we need to design, correct, or even match to complete this set of puzzles, rather than setting one goal as the sole way to achieve our aspirations. Each aim can also be viewed as a steppingstone on the way to our desired destination.

We are closer to completing the overall image of our dreams due to completing each goal, similar to finding each puzzle (the complete set of puzzles).

So, don't be frightened to fantasize!

Number 3: Goals to Track Progress

Because certain goals serve as a foundation for us to build on to achieve another, prioritizing them for completion will help us track our progress. Goals, as previously stated, act as steppingstones to our main objective, but they also serve to track our progress in our job. This might be understood as achieving each goal bringing us closer to our ultimate aim.

While accomplishing our objectives increases our chances of success, we must also keep track of our work in progress. This is done by determining how a task may be completed and the amount of time required. These objectives or goals may be interrelated since we cannot advance with a specific task if one objective or goal is not met.

The task of planning a birthday party for our family is an excellent example of this principle. The initial stage is always to send out invitations, followed by a confirmation of the number of guests expected to attend. It would be difficult to plan the venue, the amount of food and drinks, the decoration, and other components of the party without these first two phases. The success of the party is determined by the invitations and the number of attendees who arrive.

Ultimately, certain projects cannot move forward without first accomplishing specific objectives.

Number 4: Goals as Promises to the Self

The objectives we've established for ourselves are also promised to ourselves. It's also critical to document our goal-setting process to ensure these concrete targets and give ourselves a specific timetable to reach each one.

Apart from that, these 'promises' hold us accountable. This relates to all of our actions that result in the failure or success of our objectives. We can re-evaluate our actions and study the effects, whether in the short or long term since we have developed a feeling of responsibility.

When one considers the judgments made two years or even 20 years ago, one might be very proud of their accomplishments. If, on the other hand, one fails or falls short of the stated target, it is a clear indication that something is wrong. On the other hand, if one fails or accomplishes less than the set goal, it is a definite sign to change things in order to improve and achieve the goal.

Number 5: Goals as the Direction of Our Focus

Setting objectives entails aligning our intellect, heart, and soul with the target. We simply cannot shoot an arrow without a target in another metaphorical sense. We will know how, where, and when to employ our talent and abilities once we have determined our goals.

Like how when you take a magnifying glass and concentrate the sunlight towards a particular area on a leaf or paper, it will burn. The sunlight represents our abilities, whereas the magnifying glass is likened to our focus on the target which is the leaf.

Without the magnifying glass (our focus), the target would never be reached despite the amount of heat the sunlight supplies (our potential).

We can only have this sense of direction on our journey to our dreams if we clearly define our objectives from the start. We can't always ignore the reality that our focus shifts, and we must maintain or, in some cases, defend our attention to achieve our objectives. Changing our routines to avoid distractions, such as denying invites to useless parties or saying no to outings with friends, is one of many methods to retain attention. This saves us time and money by reducing the amount of time we spend on distractions and allowing us to focus on our goals.

Number 6: Goals to Develop Our Potentials

Our potential is fostered as we make progress toward the objectives we set for ourselves at the outset. Setting goals that provide immediate possibilities for us to broaden our knowledge, polish our talents, and broaden our experience will help us in the future.

We may not be able to grow ourselves outside of our comfort zones if we do not have such goals, as we are subjected to the comfortable and safe routines of our daily life. Some of our potentials never flourish or are locked within ourselves because we don't create goals or don't have the right goals.

On the contrary, the goals we have set will enable us to challenge ourselves to adapt to new environments and new situations. Besides, setting certain expectations would only convince us to do our best and expand our limits. Weight loss or gain targets, running time limit, business profits or even following a planned diet are all personal goals for us to challenge ourselves. Obviously, we reap what we sow and sometimes, it might be more than just the reward itself.

Once we can appreciate the improvements we gained through accomplishments, we will also achieve a sense of self-fulfillment. With this feeling of satisfying ourselves, we can work on other goals with better motivation and energy. We might not even feel that the obstacles in the later stages are as challenging as before too.

COACH KAPLAN'S CORNER

10 Reasons Why People Fail at Setting Goals

There are 10 simple reasons why people fail to set goals. We're going to take a closer look at them here.

Number 1: Not Realizing the Importance of Setting Goals

The most habitual mistake during the planning stage is to ignore the importance of setting goals. In fact, most do not understand that specifying goals for both the short term and the long term cannot find purpose, meaning, or even inspiration to achieve the goals set.

Such mistakes affect an individual or organization's course of actions and their attitude towards the goals. Without a sense of purpose or meaning of the goals, one cannot simply use passionate effort to achieve success.

Goals are not just tasks on a to-do list, which you can tick off once you've completed it. Goals can also be steppingstones to a bigger cause in life. Therefore, we should define our goals clear enough before we set ourselves on our journey.

Number 2: Writing Only the Long-Term Goals

Our focus on the end results s often derailed us as our progress is not constructively planned when we have only set long-term goals but not the short-term ones required to accomplish the long ones.

For instance, if you wish to start a bakery, you must be good at baking cakes confectionery treats and pastries. You must also know how to manage the business and employ the right people to help you operate the bakery.

Those are the short-term goals of getting everything prepared before realizing the long-term goal of operating a bakery. Setting short term goals in sight of the long one is to help us focus on one goal at a time and build on each success to reach further and achieve our long-term goals. Usually, this sort of achievement satisfies us even more in the end.

Number 3: Belief that it Won't Work

Those who have such belief usually have very consistent reasoning on rejecting certain ideas before reaching the final stages of setting their goals. As such, during the stages of setting goals, one should embrace the foreseeable challenges after sufficient analysis and not discouraged by them.

However, over-analyzing and constantly filling ideas and efforts with doubts will definitely end the goal-setting process earlier than expected.

During the goal setting goals, we also must acknowledge that it would not be possible to answer all the questions and create substantial plans to overcome the foreseeable challenges.

Number 4: Writing Our Goals as Negative Statements

Instead of working towards something we want, writing our goals as something we try to avoid or as obstacles we do not wish to overcome may affect our motivation to finish work. How we write our goals down can really affect how we view them. In other words, nobody wants their goals to sound discouraging.

Writing *"Don't lift less than 120 lbs. for your bench press,"* definitely does not sound as inspiring as *"Good job on lifting 100lbs on the bench press. Try lifting 120 lbs. next week."* The way the goals are written should inspire us to be dedicated to accomplishing them and not instill fear of failure in us.

Number 5: Generic Goals

Having goals that are often too similar to others around your age usually means the goals you have set are not specific enough. So how does this deter you from being successful?

Not having enough details of how your goals should specifically be means the effort you will use might not help you achieve whatever targets. For instance, if you wish to buy a house, you must find out the market price of the house, its size, its design, the loan repayment, interest rates of the loan, the location of the house and many other necessary factors for you to purchase the house successfully.

Whether it's a vacation you're planning or increasing your business's profits, the more you specify your goals, the clearer it is in your mind that you are convinced these are the goals you really wish to achieve.

Number 6: Measuring Results

Business leaders and entrepreneurs often face the problem of utilizing the right tools to measure the progress of their businesses. Those who have no idea how to measure the progress of their work during the goal-setting process are doomed to fail. Most are disillusioned by the monetary profits they gained earlier on.

Measuring results is not only a good way of ensuring you are on the right track to your long-term goals. Besides, it gives you the chance to improve results based on the goals you have specified during goal setting.

Number 7: Setting Irrelevant Goals

Wasting time on goals that are not relevant to the aim of missions in your life will not benefit you in the long term. Besides, having too many goals at one time and not being able to produce results for each goal after so much effort will only damage your progress towards the long-term goal.

Stay focused on the goals and try to achieve one goal after another.

Number 8: Setting Unrealistic Goals

If you set goals that you could not realistically achieve over a certain period of time, you will feel discouraged and eventually chase after your goals.

So, don't kill your chances of achieving your goals by being unrealistic. In setting your goals, you must set short term goals or steppingstones to reach the bigger goals. These *'steppingstones'* will also nurture you to face bigger challenges in the pursuit of your dreams. At the end of the day, it's important to be ambitious but not too unrealistically excited.

Number 9: Not Having a Reasonable Time Frame Achievement

While you can measure results with the realistic goals you have set, time is always an important factor as any delay in achieving your goals means less can be done to achieve it.

Some goals have their time limits, so progress must be measured over a certain amount of time. For instance, you worked out that, to have your dream vacation on July 3 years from now, you must save up about 10% of your salary every month. Otherwise, you will not have enough money for the vacation by then, so it's crucial that you save as much even if the amount you save each month can be different.

Number 10: Opinions of Others

The opinion of others may have considerable weightage in our goal-setting process, especially if these people are close to us like our family, colleagues and friends. It is therefore understandable that we may have set our goals based on most of their opinions. The risk of setting the 'goals of others' under the illusion that you share those goals might actually be similar to the risks of setting irrelevant goals, as you have read in mistake no. 7.

If those goals are solely based on the opinions of others, you will not be able to feel the satisfaction of achieving them, especially if they are not truly your goals.

After learning about the most common goal-setting blunders, it's simple to assume that we can reach our objectives to identify the obstacles and strategies for success. However, most people have overlooked the sheer determination to sacrifice many other things along the way in their pursuit of achievement. Instead of asking ourselves, like:

"What would you do if you were in my shoes?"
"What level of access do you want to achieve?"
We must be able to respond to questions like
"How desperately do you want to do this?"
"How much resources are you willing to expend to attain your goal?"
"How much are you willing to give up for this?"

There's no limit to what you can achieve. Everyone aspires to win a gold medal. Yet, few people are willing to train, eat, and live as if they were a world champion.

To put it another way, creating objectives with simply the future rewards in mind will not mentally prepare us adequately. To be the best, we must be willing to pay whatever price to achieve our objectives. Smart goals, *Specific, measurable, attainable, timelines.*

Specific

Goals that aren't clearly defined won't get us to where we want to go in life. Even if we are supplied with many approaches to reach our goals, if the goals are our destinations, but we cannot describe them, we will most likely lose our course during our task. We will waste many resources if we do not believe in the specificity of our aims, as indicated in this chapter and the previous one. Remember, goals point us in the right direction. Thus, we must spell out every single detail to lead us there.

Measurable

Immeasurable goals are weakly defined, and as a result, we will be unable to track our progress. We can determine our performance and success rate by quantifying our progress and our goals and then comparing them. Such data could be used to analyze how we might increase our performance even more. Absolute quantification is used in body weight management programs, budgeting, running distance and time, building development, and many other goals.

We can tell how much we've improved or developed by measuring results, and we won't miss the celebration if we know we've met particular objectives!

Attainable

Setting goals that are genuinely achievable involves stacking success on top of success. Working on goals that are impossible or too difficult to reach, on the other hand, will only break our perseverance and determination in the long run. We will quickly lose motivation if we cannot obtain the benefits we desire despite our best efforts.

Despite this, we should always resist the temptation to create goals that are too easy to achieve. This is because we will develop a comfort zone if we continue to set easy goals. We become insensitive to our desires to progress when we are preoccupied with attaining these simple tasks. Finally, we are so terrified of failing and failing to achieve that we will not risk setting a more challenging goal. The goal is divided into measurable upper and lower boundaries, which is a unique manner of creating such goals.

Instead of running the same distance in the same amount of time, you might aim to go further in 30 minutes or run the same distance in less time if you have reached the lower border of your objective, such as 5 kilometers in 30 minutes. These objectives can be altered as needed, but we can confidently attempt a greater distance knowing what we have accomplished during the run in some instances, such as running.

To put it another way, we create attainable goals to be aware of the degree of difficulty and the benefits of our efforts. To avoid falling into our comfort zone or feeling demotivated in the future, we must alter the degree of difficulty to our preferences.

Concentrating on relevant goals not only prevents us from becoming distracted by other things. It also allows us to put our greatest skills to the test, broaden our knowledge in a particular field, and obtain significant experience for future advancement. It might be tough to distinguish between goals that we are eager to achieve, and those that we believe are relevant and beneficial to our future. As a result, it is a primary but crucial step in ensuring that our objectives are always appropriate.

We can set deadlines, time restrictions, or even day-by-day progress goals for ourselves to assure growth. Furthermore, creating goals with a specific time range can aid us in anticipating and avoiding unnecessary delays. We will have less or no hurry to complete even the simplest activities if we do not have such a feeling of timing.

As a result, our devotion will wane, and we may even become accustomed to postponing work. As a result, we must constantly remind ourselves of the projected progression in the schedule we have established for realizing our dreams.

TIMELINE

When you set a goal set a sub goal of when you want to achieve it. Goals should not be open ended. Remember *"a goal without a plan, is nothing more than a wish."*

We must not forget to write down our objectives and create reminders now that we have grasped all of the S.M.A.R.T. goal-setting concepts.

To make these reminders more effective, we can put them on our phones or attach them to locations like our work desks, refrigerators with magnets, or even our televisions.

Ability is what you're capable of doing. Motivation determines what you do. Attitude determines how well you do it".

—Lou Holtz

CHAPTER 14

Keys to success
Winning Starts Now

Conquering Difficulties

There once was a king who decided to do a little experiment. He had a giant boulder put right in the middle of the street. He then hid near the boulder to see who, if anyone, would try to move it out of the way. First, some wealthy merchants walked by. They walked around the boulder, complaining that the king hasn't been maintaining the roads very well.

Next, a peasant walked by, heading home with his arms full of food for his family. When he noticed the boulder, he put his groceries down and attempted to move it out of everyone's way. It took him a while to move it, **but he eventually succeeded.**

After the peasant gathered up his groceries to carry on home, he noticed a bag lying in the middle of the road, just where the boulder once was. He opened the bag to find that it was stuffed **full of gold coins**, along with a letter from the king saying that the bag's gold was a reward for the peasant to keep because he had taken the time and energy to move the boulder out of the road for the convenience of others who would be travelling the road in the future.

What's the moral? The peasant in this story was taught by the king that **every obstacle you face offers an opportunity to improve**. If you're able to push through moments that are challenging, you may end up being much better off than you were before you started trying.

This story also offers a lesson of personal responsibility. If you see a job ahead of you, don't leave it for the next person to do. Rather, step up and get the job done to help the people who come after you.

We will undoubtedly encounter barriers and problems along the way, whether they are difficult to overcome or not. If the issue is one that we have previously encountered, it will be easier to resolve if we have noted it in our reviews, as we will be more likely to recognize better alternatives. However, the most important aspect of dealing with any problem is comprehending the root reasons and our options for resolving them.

We must remain calm and composed, whether as a group or as individuals, in order to assess the possibilities presented by the situation. It is not humiliating to ask for help, even if it comes at a cost. If we cannot solve a problem in a particular manner, it is preferable to try another solution or modify the one we have chosen to better the outcome. A backup plan comes in handy in this situation. Our determination to choose the best answer sometimes results in setbacks rather than the desired outcome. Despite the setback, we should be optimistic that we will be able to recover and develop. At the very least, it would be advantageous if we saw it as a priceless lesson.

However, some factors are beyond our control in our work, such as natural catastrophes, diseases, and accidents. These are the unfortunate circumstances from which we must recover. Furthermore, we must concentrate on what we can influence.

When developing a '**Can't Stop Me**" attitude, passion, commitment, sense of urgency, enthusiasm, creativity and many other positive traits are products of goals which motivate us. Most humans are social creatures who cannot live without a single relationship with others. As such, every human is socially dependent on one another to survive right from our birth. It all started with our relationship with our mothers who give birth to us, and then expands to our other family members, and then friends and lovers and so on. But how important is our social life? Sometimes sharing your goals with friends and family will motivate you to capture your goals. Throughout my life every time someone told me I couldn't do something I set a goal to be able to prove them wrong. Sometimes we set goals for our family members. Telling your child to get A's on their report card is asking them to set a goal to achieve that grade A.

COACH KAPLAN'S CORNER

Learn from Failures

Whether successful or not, many people struggle to learn from their failures, let alone face their failures, as it is easier said than done.

To begin with, we must acknowledge that our failure does not preclude us from improving and progressing as a result of it. As a result, we must be physically and intellectually adaptable to accept defeat and move forward.

According to the truth of success, examining our failures can help us adjust to new situations, evaluate improvised solutions, and move forward from our setbacks.

To begin with, we might look into the reasons for our failures by going through each phase of our preparations. If a flaw was discovered, we could correct the problem and assure that such an error would never happen again.

Success Mindset Conditioning

Our lives are influenced by the words we use. We may begin by altering the language we use in our daily interactions, debates, and writing. We can surely change our impression of our lives by changing particular words or rearranging our phrases. Rather than telling ourselves, *"I can do it,"* we should urge ourselves to believe, *"I will accomplish it."* This motivates us to begin completing the task at hand rather than focusing solely on our strengths and underestimating the task at hand.

Talking to Your Own Mind

The ability to comprehend, accept, and act is not as straightforward for everyone as this line suggests. The mind is not always capable of determining what is best for the individual. As a result, we should increase our awareness of new information, abilities, knowledge, and any sensation that can help us live better lives.

Since awareness is the doorway to understanding, acceptance, and action, we should constantly increase it by assessing our knowledge and perceptions and studying and researching new material. This constantly encourages awareness of how we think about specific topics in life, and we can adjust our thinking habits to be more helpful.

Associating Pain with Our Beliefs

We should maintain ourselves mentally healthy by knowing our emotions and our reactions to changes. Challenging and ultimately shattering old beliefs might cause discomfort or even pain, but we should keep ourselves mentally healthy by understanding our emotions and reactions to changes.

Anticipating such reactions will make it easier for us to adjust to the changes in our life. In another instance, shifting our mentality will require us to leave our comfort zone. Moving out of our comfort zones brings inevitable challenges that we must overcome and nurture to become our best selves.

Shaping and Empowering our New Beliefs

Once we've established that we're aware of how we believe and what we need to change, we must constantly justify our ideas with results. If the results are favorable, our transformation will be successful, and our new beliefs will be reinforced.

Self-doubts, worries, anxieties, and fears are continual emotions that we can't ignore in our efforts to change, but only the results of our actions can conquer them. Otherwise, we'll have to bounce back from setbacks and create a fresh change that will catapult us to new heights.

Conditioning Until Success Becomes Second Nature

It's impossible to avoid change. But why alter when you've already achieved success? We can look at success from a variety of views most of the time. For example, if you're in good financial shape, you can begin to concentrate on other elements of your life.

While it is true that no one can be successful in every way, living a balanced and successful life with our family, friends, business, society, and future generations remains a challenge. So why stop when you can achieve achievement in multiple areas of your life?

Sharing Your Goals

In the last chapter we talked about the importance of goals. Passion, dedication, sense of urgency, enthusiasm, originality, and many other positive attributes are outcomes of goals that motivate us when establishing a *"can't stop me"* mentality. Humans are primarily sociable beings who cannot exist without at least one other relationship. As a result, from the moment we are born, we are socially dependent on one another to survive. It all began with our mothers, who gave birth to us, and then grew to include our other family members, friends, and lovers, and so on.

But what role does our social life have in our lives?

Sharing your goals with friends and family can help drive you to achieve them. Every time someone told me I couldn't do something in my life, I made a goal to prove them wrong. We create goals for our family members from time to time. When you tell your child that they need to receive an A on their report card, you're telling them to establish a goal to get that grade.

Reasons of Failure

Allowing others to judge our shortcomings may never be as useful as evaluating our efforts and analyzing the outcomes. This is due to the fact that we learn more about ourselves than anyone else. Developing these self-learning habits, on the other hand, does not have to be all about ourselves.

In order to fully live our lives, we must constantly challenge ourselves, not only intellectually, but physically as well. I was impressed by a television interview in which former Chicago Bears' coach Mike Ditka discussed a professional athlete who has reached a level so far among his peers that he must prove himself every day and never rest on his laurels. This kind of attitude can keep us from every experiencing "declining years," for we will be using each day to grow rather than simply age.

- *I'm having a bad day*
- *I'm having a frustrating month*
- *I'm having a terrible year*
- *I have been guilty of saying all of these and so has Albert Einstein.*

After Einstein graduated from college, he spent two frustrating years looking for and failing to get a job as a teaching assistant. During this time, he had a child out-of-wedlock and a girlfriend his family disapproved of greatly. For all his efforts during this time, he was only able to secure the lowest position at the patent office, which was really attained by help from his friend's father.

I'm sure Einstein wasn't too thrilled about his life during that period, but this setback is one of the main reasons why Einstein's image has become synonymous with genius. His job as an assistant patent examiner gave Einstein real world training on visualizing the ideas in the patent proposals he examined and at the same time nurtured his skepticism which is inherent to deciding the feasibility of the patents being proposed and a skill necessary to challenge the accepted scientific theories of his day. Both these skills and the free time Einstein had due to the easy workload at the patent office allowed Einstein to conduct thought experiments that led to his four groundbreaking papers which included his theory of relativity and $E = mc2$.

If Einstein had been successful in landing a teaching assistant's position right out of college, he would not have had the time or mindset to create the foundation to modern physics that he is famous for today.

Self-discipline boils down to empowering yourself and taking control of your life. It's really about committing to what you want. Don't fall into the trap of justifying yourself or making excuses when you slip up. Take responsibility and get right back on track.

In the words of Plato, *"The first and best victory is to conquer self."*

Do you do what you're supposed to do even when you don't feel like it? Setbacks create opportunities ... (if you don't believe me, just look into the lives of most successful people)

The key is to focus on the positive and to be aware of opportunities created by the situation. It really doesn't help to ask yourself: *"Why me? What If I had? Why didn't I?"*

Instead, it is better to ask yourself: *"What did I learn? What's next? What can I do now?"*

If you really want to look at true success, and overcoming adversity just look at Abraham Lincoln,

Lincoln:

1816 Forced from home
1818 His mother died
1831 Failed in business
1832 Defeated for State Legislature
1833 Failed in business again
1834 Elected to State Legislature
1835 His sweetheart died
1836 Suffered a nervous breakdown
1838 Defeated for Speaker of State Legislature
1840 Defeated for Elector
1843 Defeated for Congress
1846 Elected to Congress
1848 Lost reelection
1854 Rejected for job of Land Officer
1855 Defeated for Senate
1856 Defeated for Vice President
1858 Defeated for Senate
1860 Elected President of the United States of America

Here was a person with a dream so strong, no failure could dampen it. We were all taught about his greatness. Now I understand that Lincoln's greatness stemmed from his perseverance. In 28 years of politics, he had four times as many defeats as victories. Most men would have decided that life was unfair and given up. Because Lincoln remained true to his goals, he eventually won the most important race of all. In 1860, not only was he elected as President of the United States, but he went on to become one of the greatest presidents our country has ever known.

Still think your failures are of great significance? Don't dwell on the times you failed in life. Concentrate on your dreams and goals instead.

There are millions of people who believe they are fated to suffer from conditions ranging from obesity to poverty by forces beyond their control. Nothing could be further from the truth. God created men and women in his own image, and that image is not one of failure and lack. God created us to succeed, but it is up to us to follow his plan.

"God's gift to man is life, and man's gift to God is what he does with his life."

There are no shortcuts to success. You must **"Never Give Up"** and always do **"Whatever it takes"**.

We should take lessons from the past, not regrets. Donald J. Trump, in his book The Art Of The Deal, says, *"I try to learn from the past, but I plan for the future by focusing exclusively on the present. That's where the fun is, and if it can't be fun, what's the point?"*

Given Trump's ability to turn apparent failures into spectacular successes (as seen in his book, The Art Of The Comeback), I think it is safe to take his advice on this point as it led him to be President of the United States. And, if he runs and wins in 2024, it will be the greatest comeback of all time.

Listen this book is not about politics. I worked with the Trump family for many years. Like him or hate him, he gives 100%, 100% of the time. When patients used to come to my office I never asked if they were Republican or democrat. I asked if they wanted to pay "**cash or check**"

It's been said there are three kinds of people in the world:

1. *Those who make things happen,*
2. *Those who let things happen,*
3. *Those who wondered what happened.*

WHICH ARE YOU?

Abraham Lincoln once said: *"Most folks are as happy as they make up their minds to be."*

You could just as easily substitute "successful" for "happy" in this sentence. If you don't feel successful, maybe it's because you don't know what success is. Many of us were given our ideas on this subject from our parents, teachers, rabbis/ministers/priests, or —worst of all – from television.

Some of us confuse success with wealth.

In 1923, some of the most "successful" financiers in the country met at the Edgewater Beach Hotel in Chicago. The eminent guests included:

Charles Schwab – *president of the largest steel company in America*
Samuel Insull – *president of the largest utility company in America*
Howard Hopson – *president of the largest gas company in America*
Arthur Cutten – *the great wheat speculator*
Richard Whitney – *president of the New York stock exchange*

Albert Fall – *secretary of the Interior in President Harding's cabinet*
Jesse Livermore – *the greatest "bear" on Wall Street*
Ivar Kreuger – *head of the world's greatest monopoly*
Leon Fraser – *president of the Bank of International Settlements*

If money could buy happiness, these men would have been in a constant state of ecstasy. But this is where they were 25 years after the famous meeting:

Charles Schwab – *went bankrupt and lived the last five years of his life on borrowed money.*
Samuel Insull – *died in a foreign land, a penniless fugitive from justice.*
Howard Hopson – *went insane.*
Arthur Cutten – *died insolvent in another country.*
Richard Whitney – *had just been released from Sing Sing prison.*
Albert Fall – *having been pardoned from prison, died at home, broke.*
Jesse Livermore – *committed suicide.*
Ivan Kreuger – *committed suicide.*
Leon Fraser – *committed suicide.*

Still think you'd be willing to trade places with any one of these men? In society's terms, they had it all, but they lived unsuccessfully. People may listen to their opinions, but the ultimate decision must be yours. When I was young I wanted to be an entertainer, but my mother said, *"Young Jewish boys don't become entertainers. You must go to college. You must become a doctor."*

I can just imagine where some of the famous Jewish entertainers would be today if they had come from my home. Would Barbra Streisand, Barry Manilow, Jerry Seinfeld, Seth Rogan, Mel Brooks, Larry David, Jack Black, Paul Rudd, Joey Bishop, Michael Douglas, Tony Curtis, Joan Rivers, Scarlet Johansson, Dustin Hoffman, Daniel Day Lewis, Harrison Ford, Adam Sandler, Jennifer Connolly, Woody Allen, Ben Stiller, and Steven Spielberg to name just a few all be doctors?

What do you want in life?
What price are you willing to pay?

If you're willing to do "**Whatever it Takes**" nobody will be able to Stop You.

Success is based on attitude, and attitude can be altered by time. We are all born with an equal inheritance of approximately 700,000 hours. One of the great differences between life and death is that life offers us a choice, while death offers a mystery. We have a choice of how we live these 700,000 hours and we can choose the quality of our existence on this journey of life. Many people live their lives in a whirlpool, marred by confusion, and absent of direction on their quest to succeed. Man and woman were born to succeed. It's the goal of this book to continually activate endorphins by turning your basic attitude into a success attitude.

To win or lose, to survive or fail is choice. Failure is your choice, not your destiny. Within each and every one of us lies all the answers. Successes, health, happiness, all are within our grasp. Reach for them, fight for them. Today, let's take responsibility for our yesterday, and from this let us plan for our tomorrow. If it is to be, it is up to me. Take control of your life and your destiny, or your destiny will control you. Most often, we have only one boundary and one obstacle: ourselves. Oliver Wendell Holmes said, *"A mind stretched by a new idea will never return to its original dimension."*

Expand your vision; it's time to grow. today, dreaming of the person you want to be. Set a plan to be that person. Affirm the choice that you have made and take an actual step to become the person of your dreams.

Throughout my life I've often been most dissatisfied when I expected someone else to make me feel better, only to be left frustrated and unfulfilled. And even if we could get everyone to do exactly what we wanted them to do, we still wouldn't be happy. Why not? Because the keys to a satisfied life and the power to change lie within us.

It reminds me of the story of a Zen master who was visiting New York City and stopped by a hot dog vendor for what was, to him, a rare treat. He handed the vendor a $ 20 bill for his hot dog, expecting change. When the vendor put the $ 20 into his cash box and closed it up, the Zen master sharply challenged him: *"What about my change?"*

The vendor smiled, and in what seemed to be a reversal in roles, philosophically retorted, *"You know better than I, O great master—that change must come from WITHIN!"*

Yet why do we so often feel that improving our lives is an insurmountable challenge? We tell ourselves: "I'm too old. It's too late. I don't have the background or resources, the right education or experience." Our excuses and rationalizations, combined with the vain hope that others might change, are all stumbling blocks that hold us back. Yet, every January so many of us start the New Year with a list of well-intentioned resolutions. We vow to exercise and lose weight, to be a better spouse, to turn over a new leaf in one way or another, only to find ourselves right back to our old habits in no time.

My travels and education taught me success happens for those people who understand that "**success leaves clues**" from the people that came before us and all we have to do is to be smart enough to look for them. That said, you must also understand that "failure leaves clues", which is why it is important to study history. Most people do not realize that General Patton was a historian, and it was his knowledge of history that helped him win many battles during World War II.

Here is the first of the two ancient laws:

The law of use. *You might have heard the saying if you don't use it, you lose it. Or the way I like to say it, that the lack of use causes loss. If you take your arm and tie it to your body and leave it there long enough, you'll never use it again. It's over for the arm. The only way to keep the use of the arm is to use it. You lose automatically when you quit. They aren't going to ask you for your opinion or talk about how you feel about it. You lose automatically when you quit. Now the same principle that applies to the body holds true for our brain, mentality and all other of our virtues.*

The second law that you need to understand is,
The law of sowing and reaping. How I learned this law isn't as important as what I learned about it. For a long time in my life I was confused on how this applies. I wasn't reaping that well and I was blaming other things for my problems. I'd blame my teachers, I'd blame my schooling, I'd blame my coaches, once I learned that when you point one finger at somebody you have three fingers pointing back at yourself, I realized the power of I.M. The difference between possible and impossible is two letters I.M.

Once I began to understand these two ancient laws, brings us back to the reason why goal setting is important. It's important not just for sports, but it's also important to life after sports. I learned much from my coaches in sports. In sports you set goals to score, to win, to stop or beat your opponent. Is business or life any different.

Paul Lizzo was my coach at Fairleigh Dickinson University, he used to always say your mind controls your body. If you don't think you can do it, you can't do it. If you believe you can do it, you can do it. We often talk about all the benefits of being involved in athletics, and goal setting is no different. So you have to practice the ability to set and achieve goals every day in order to keep that ability in your life. In order to set goals you have to have faith.

Faith to me, is the ability to see things as they *could* be. Now there is a fine line between having faith and being a fool. In college I began having faith in myself. Faith requires you to work, being a fool requires you to hope. You cannot just hope things will change. You cannot just hope things will work out. You cannot hope that success will just happen, that success is your destiny. Life doesn't work like that. You have to understand that the only way life will change for you, is when you change. The way things change for you is when you have a clear image in your mind of what you could be like in the future. The path to that future you, is determined on the goals you set for yourself.

You have to make sure that the greatest pull on your life is the pull of the future. You have to review the past, but you cannot live in the past. It's fine to look at the past and learn the lessons from it, but it can be like gravity, always pulling you back. You see goals can be like magnets, pulling you towards them. When your goals are well thought out and developed in your mind and on paper, they become stronger, pulling you towards them constantly. That pull gets you through the good days, and through the bad days. All the ups and downs.

Goals are the reason we can believe things will be better than what they already are. When we allow our goals to pull us into the future, it unleashes a creative force that lets up overcome anything in our way. When you have a well thought out goal, it starts a chain of events that lets us accomplish that goal. When you don't have a well thought out goal, or without any goal, it starts that same chain of events. You see a year from now, five years from now, or ten years from now you are going to arrive. You are going to arrive at either a designed or un-designed destination. Here is how the trip is going to unfold.

Within all of us is unlimited potential. Think about it for a second. We are living in the most wondrous time in human existence. Food and water are abundant. Medicine is helping people live longer than they ever have before. All the knowledge in the world is at our fingertips on the computer or waiting for us in our local library. We are surrounded by abundance. All of the abundance is found within the freedom given to us. This freedom is not what most people think of, but the freedom I'm talking about is time. We are given the freedom to decide how much of our potential and our time we are going to spend on any specific task.

Making the choice on how much of your potential you are going to spend, might be the most important part of the upcoming chain of events. I say it's the most important part because when we make this choice it dictates the amount of action we decide to take.

It is the amount of action that we take that controls our results. If someone puts a little action into reaching their goal, then they receive a little success in reaching their goal. But when someone puts massive action into reaching their goal, then they receive a massive success in reaching their goal.

Deep down we are programed to understand the direct link between physical work and the changes in our body that happens when we are training. If you need even more proof, look at all the *Rocky* movies. Movies like Rocky, Rudy, Invincible, all Motivate me.

I watched every Rocky movie five times. In all of Stallone's movies the story lines are basically the same. There is always some terribly mean, tough and big bad guy who no one thinks Rocky can beat. Rocky goes to train, he chases chickens, he runs, he eats raw eggs. Then Rocky amazingly wins after getting the crap beaten out of him. We all know that story, and we know what to expect but the movie has to keep with the same plan. We have to see Rocky suffering through all the training scenes. We have to see those scenes because the directors know that we the audience can only relate to the transformation that Rocky is going through, as long as we see part of the work that is happening. Watching that is much more satisfying to the audience than watching Einstein poor over his equations again and again, working the math until he finally has his Theory of Relativity. Both of those examples have everything to do with goal setting, but reaching the physical goals is something more exciting to watch and easier for us to understand.

That is how we start learning how to set up and use goals. We have a mental picture of what we want to do, and then we put in the work to make it happen. Once athletes can start managing how to set realistic goals with their training, they are building their body and physical skills, but they are also working on their mental muscles. Goal setting is a mental talent and, if you remember from past chapters, when talent isn't used then we lose it. But when we do use it, over time it grows stronger and stronger. The more we use our talents; we become more confident and certain in our ability.

Imagine what it would be like to have a team of people that walk around with a swagger because they just know that they will accomplish anything that they set their mind on. How great would that be? That is why we have to be able to teach athletes how to set goals. It is possible to get people started on the path of absolute certainty in their life, just by planting the seed of confidence. That seed does not get planted in the ground, but in their mind.

Once the seed of confidence gets planted in their minds, then they simply don't just reap what they planted. The athletes reap much more that what they planted. That level of unshakable confidence in their own ability to set and achieve goals is, in my mind, the most important thing that we can ever teach an athlete. Goals also help align your focus and promote a sense of self-mastery. In the end, you can't manage what you don't measure, and you can't improve upon something that you don't properly manage. Setting goals can help you do all of that and more. Setting goals not only motivates us, but can also improve our mental health and our level of personal and professional success. Setting goals with my wife is a major part of our lives even today. We set health goals, family goals, future goals. It's a goal to educate myself with a goal to raise a happy family with circles to build a successful practice. Even now as grandparents we set goals on a regular basis.

Goal setting does not have to be boring. Like knowing the ending at the beginning of the movie. If you want a happy ending, you don't give up at anytime until you achieve the ending you desire.

Goals will help align your focus and promote a sense of inner confidence. Remember if you can't measure it, you can't manage it. You can't manage what you don't measure and you can't approve something that you don't properly manage, setting goals can help you do all that and more.

The Dalai Lama wrote, *"Pain is inevitable. Suffering is optional."* Successful people often struggle and feel pain, but don't suffer because they are living their lives and pursuing goals that are in line with who they are, what they value, and what they believe to be their purpose or mission. To them, it is worth it. Most want to be wealthy. So why don't we ever end up getting there? Although most of us face detours to our big dreams, it's typically not external factors keeping us from achieving our dreams. It's internal barriers that stop us. What's stopping you? If you want to build wealth and be successful, you first need to have the right mentality.

CAOCH KAPLAN'S CORNER

1. Goals are golden.

It's no secret there's a positive correlation between setting goals and success professionals who have a measurable goal to work for are far more productive than those who are just "winging it." But being goal-oriented and treating goals as "golden" is about more than just setting them in the first place. You have to treat them as a major priority, making heavy sacrifices to achieve them and breaking them down into smaller chunks when necessary. Creating your goals is just the first step of the process—you also need to have the follow-through to make them count.

2. The future is more important than the present.

This concept, from a subjective standpoint, is debatable. You could easily argue that living "in the moment" is more important than worrying about the future, but People who are goal oriented, who, plan for the future are people who make decisions based on future payoffs, are far more likely to be successful. Future-oriented people aren't afraid to make short-term sacrifices if it means a long-term gain, and they aren't tempted to engage in momentary pleasures that would rob them of some future payoff. Their future selves are the main priority.

3. Failure isn't a bad thing.

The fear of failure permeates our society and it leads millions to live their lives in complacency. For example, you're working in a job you hate with a pay and advancement ceiling. You have the option to quit and start your own business, but you're so afraid of failing that you never give it a real shot. Failure is always a possibility and as a society we need to stop decrying it. Successful people see failure as a necessary step of the process and a valuable learning opportunity. Moreover, few plans are executed smoothly—how you handle them when they go wrong is more important than when they go right. But I also think failure is a good thing. Failure will get us out of bed in the morning and make us go to work for the fear of not paying our bills.

4. Opportunities exist everywhere.

Opportunities arise when you least expect them. I never expected to be President, Chief Operating officer. That was not my training, yet I was trying to be successful when opportunity knocked, I opened the door. When you adopt the mindset that Opportunities exist everywhere, in every moment of every day, you'll be on the lookout for them. By that virtue alone, you'll discover more opportunities for yourself, and you'll end up earning far more value in your life.

5. Calculated risks are important.

Risks are scary, but without them, there's substantially less room to grow. I've open seven offices throughout my lifetime, it's time I had to sign papers with Banks, take great risks, but the great ones always take risks.

Studies suggest that the wealthiest, most successful professionals of our time are ones who One afraid to take a risk—they went against the grain, gambled on an idea they thought was worth the investment and weren't afraid to stake possible sacrifices. If you aren't taking any risks, you aren't making the move toward possible rewards, and, of course, without the rewards, you'll never get anywhere.

6. Consistency is good, until it becomes prohibitive.

This is a complicated mental state to try and achieve, but it's an important one. For the most part, consistency is incredibly important. For example, if one of your goals is to accrue wealth through investments, you have to invest a certain amount of money every month or you'll lose momentum. However, there's a point at which consistency does more harm than good—when it starts to lead you down the wrong path, such as when you've developed a bad habit or an unproductive routine. It's hard to spot when these "bad" kinds of consistency crop up, but you'll need to closely watch for them.

7. Nothing is ever perfect.

Accepting the reality that nothing is perfect helps you in countless areas. You won't be as worried about taking risks. You won't be as hesitant about starting a new project. You won't be as deterred when something goes wrong, or when you overlooked a major flaw. You won't find yourself perpetually waiting for the "perfect" time to launch a product, and you won't abandon your goals just because you didn't achieve them in the way you first expected.

It's not easy to achieve these mentalities. Don't expect to adopt them instantaneously. You'll most likely have a hard time accepting some of them, especially if they conflict with your inherent and learned views of the world. But if you can slowly integrate them into your ongoing mental state and accept their maxims as truth, you'll Start making better decisions and forming habits that will one day lead you to the success you've always dreamed of. Remain patient and never stop moving forward.

In his book, "Grinding it Out" Ray Kroc the father of McDonald's was asked the secret of success. He said I'm forever green, for if I am always green, I am always growing.

Regardless of your situation or upbringing, you should never put limits on your life and what you can do; by placing a limit on your life, you give yourself a reason not even to try. Those who believe their life has no limit will take chances, try new things, and push themselves, enabling them to achieve great things inevitably.

Do not spend years trying to behave appropriately so that other people will accept you; do not even waste a second doing this. You do this because underneath, you feel like your true self is unworthy and undeserving. But once you realize this and unravel this truth, you recognize that you are just as worthy and deserving as anyone else, and you should start being yourself—your true self.

Everything in life involves making a choice. Choose to believe that regardless of how you begin life, the way you live and the person you become is determined by you. Make a choice to seek out new opportunities and surround yourself with good people. Anything and everything is possible if you want it enough and believe in yourself. I am a prime example of this.

Winning Starts Today

Now that you know that goal setters get results by opting for SMART GOALS, *Specific, Measurable, Attainable, Realistic, and Timed.* Applying the same methodology will help you win and transform yourself from ordinary to extraordinary. Requesting assistance or even building a team with experts in various areas and assigning tasks and goals that match the difficulties of their specialty may seem like a better idea.

However, it's just as crucial to be socially healthy as it is to be cognitively and physically fit. One of the social demands of an ordinary individual of any age is to spend quality time with family and friends. Don't just turn on the TV, your phone, or whatever electronic device you have after a long day of business or job. Make an effort to connect with others and pay attention to what is going on in their life.

Increase your communication with your family. Make a date with your significant other. Take the kids on vacation. With your fellow aficionados, discuss a topic. Get together with old friends for a drink. At the park, make new pals. Volunteering or donating to the elderly is a good idea. Send orphans Christmas presents. The concept of a good social life benefits us because it protects us from depression and social isolation, both of which can have significant health consequences.

Being active in meaningful relationships meets our emotional requirements in addition to our social needs. We acquire social support to help us heal from our losses in life when we surround ourselves with people who understand our needs to love and be loved and understand our needs to love and be loved.

Giving and taking are a constant in relationships and social networks. As a result, receiving such assistance is a privilege we enjoy due to devoting as much time and effort as possible to maintaining great relationships with those around us.

To sum up, we should encircle ourselves with people who understand, encourage, and support us in our life, while simultaneously working to share our strengths and inspirations with others.

While most successful people are so dedicated to their profession that their time has become their work time, many people enjoy a variety of interests in their spare time—the amount of time you spend by yourself. You need to de-stress and recover from the stresses of your passion so that you can perform at your best when you return to pursue your goals.

Now is your chance to shine. I set a goal for myself today while I wrote this chapter. The goal is to make this book a "Number One" bestseller; it would be my fifth # 1, best-seller, which will be an incredible achievement. Now that the goal has been established, I must put in the necessary effort. I'll take you from mediocre to amazing by helping you set goals.

"What do you hope to achieve in life"?

Now write it down, and you'll be on your way to making your goals a reality.

"Success is not final; failure is not fatal: It is the courage to continue that counts."

—Sir Winston S. Churchill

CHAPTER 15

The Art of Winning

"Some people believe holding on and hanging in there are signs of great strength. However, there are times when it takes much more strength to know when to let go and then do it."

—Ann Landers

I vividly recall that after my first month of chiropractic school, we had a class on x-ray diagnostics. Truth be told, I did not understand a single word in that class. When the teacher pointed towards something and asked me if I could see it, I could literally see nothing at all.

It was that day, as I remember, that I called my father to confess, *"Dad, this is really tough for me. I'm not sure if I'm meant to be doing this or if I can at all. I feel completely lost."*

He replied, *"Son, you made a commitment to take this up. Now that you've committed to it, stay strong and hold onto it. I am certain that you will find your way."*

I remember hanging up the phone and my roommate Gary Spencer said, *"what wrong?"*

I replied, *"In class today doing x-rays I didn't understand one damn thing, yet everyone was nodding their heads like they knew what the teacher was talking about"*

Gary smiled and said, *"I shook my head because everyone else was, I didn't understand a thing either."*

The moral of the story is, don't underestimate yourself by overestimating others.

During my lectures, there is this one question that I ask all my doctors without fail; *"What do you want from your life, and what is the price that are you willing to pay for it?"*

The law of the universe states: *"You can only become what you think you are."*

This quite a bit different than the work ethic with which most of us have been raised, which tells us only: *"You can be better than you are."*

People who follow the work ethic equate striving with happiness and are too often disappointed when all their hard work does not bring them joy. Remember, happiness starts from the inside out, not the outside in. Perhaps Ben Franklin said it best, "*content makes poor men rich; discontent makes rich men poor.*"

No person worked harder than my dad. I believe my work ethic came from watching him get up at 6 o'clock every morning and not come home till 10 o'clock every night after working two jobs. Jobs that he did not enjoy. He never complained to how hard he worked, how tired he was. He just did what he had to do. My father gave everything he had for his family.

My uncle Herb Punyon was another great influence in my life, like my dad he had tremendous work ethic. He would talk to me about attitude, doing things you have to do even when you don't want to do them. Herb Punyon was a great man; he was my second father. His wife my Aunt Gloria Punyon, maintained the best attitude and had the most energy. They were a dream couple, my aunt Gloria reminded me of Donna Reed, they lived in Teaneck New Jersey. Often on Sunday we would drive to their house. This was my introduction to the suburbs. I loved the suburbs. I dreamed of the suburbs. There was something about the smell of grass that excited my senses. Sitting in a yard with the wind blowing in my hair, playing catch with my uncle, playing board games with my aunt and cousins in their backyard was just so simply magical. Quite the opposite from living in an apartment house in the city you don't have any of those advantages that's why the city is often called the concrete jungle. Going to the Punyon's house on Sundays with cousins Ellen and Amy, helped me develop the dream that I would do **"whatever it takes"** to live this type of life, this was the type of lifestyle I wanted. It was so much more than what I had in Jersey City. That's why my mother was smart, I would say "*I'm gonna have a house like this one day, mom*"

And she would reply, "*well you better work hard in school, and become a lawyer or a doctor that's the only way to afford it*"

Although growing up in Jersey City we didn't have a lot, we did have a lot of family. This is one of the reasons why I admire my wife Bonnie so much because she did not have the advantage of family. What I was able to see, she was able to read about. Yes, I was truly blessed with having a family of significant role models. Early on we used to enjoy our summers in Belmar New Jersey, at my grandmother's house that was willed to her by her brother. It must've had six small bedrooms, and every bedroom housed a different family.

All four Kaplan's in one room, the Punyon's in another room, the Adler's in another room.

Weekly I looked forward to meeting my father coming down by train with my Uncle Herb on Friday evenings because they both worked all week. From ages zero to nine as a youth I spent my summers there and was spoiled by my grandmother Birdie Adler and my Aunt Honey Kramer.

To this day, I still don't know why they called her Honey, maybe because she was so sweet. She was a Worker Bee, always in the kitchen, always preparing food for the family. Food was her love, her passion.

My early years in Belmar were very exciting being surrounded by so much family. This was the German side of my family and they all had a strong work ethic. Always cooking, cleaning or just fussing. My days were spent at the beach, my evenings at the arcade. Where did I get the money?

When I asked my father for an allowance, he said "I'll *allow you to get a job.*"

With my dad there were no handouts, if you wanted money, you worked for it. So, my first job was picking up bottles on the beach. In those days you would get a nickel for every bottle that you returned. I didn't even know I was taking care of nature by recycling and making money at the same time. In my teens I graduated to working evenings on the boardwalk in Asbury Park, New Jersey. There I worked at the basketball shoot, my foul shooting ability in basketball started to pay dividends. The balls were larger and the rims were smaller, so you had to be good and have the right spin. This job actually made me a better shooter.

The key to work is, find something that you like to do so much you would do it for free, but then become so good at it that people will pay you anyway. Work does not bring happiness, but happiness can make work a more enjoyable part of our lives. And please don't lose faith if your goals don't immediately materialize, this is why commitment is so important.

There are a few in the lot who choose to argue with a power of commitment. However, there are very few who have consciously given thought to that power in a deeper sense. Unfortunately, even lesser people than those who give any thought at all actually use this power as consistently as they can, and they should. This is not the first time I am bringing this concern to the table; I have documented this concern before and urge leaders to build and establish the commitment within their teams. However, today, I have taken a step back to explore the great power of commitment for each one of you as sole individuals.

The renowned Scottish mountaineer, W. H. Murray wrote the most powerful words about the idea of commitment in his book *The Scottish Himalayan Expedition*, published in 1951:

"Until one is committed, reluctancy remains, and inefficiency prevails. Concerning innovation, there is one foundational truth, and if that truth is ignored, it destroys phenomenal goals and the innumerable ideas you have in your mind. The moment commitment is manifested, wisdom automatically starts pouring in its contribution. Different things happen to facilitate something that would only occur as a consequence of those. A cascade of occurrences arises from decision-making, allowing an individual favors for all sorts of unpredictable incidents and rendezvous along with monetary assistance, which no man could possibly have dreamt of obtaining the way it would end up coming to him."

As a team member who is about to climb Mount Everest, it is clear as daylight that you need commitment. Nevertheless, Murray's statement about commitment transcends big ambitions, aims, and challenges such as climbing a mountain. In fact, it is very much applicable on both, you and I. Murray's point about commitment is pertinent to:

☆ Goals aligned for your future
☆ Your habits that mandate change
☆ The outcome of your vision
☆ Living your life to the fullest
☆ Landing your dream profession
☆ End up being the impeccable leader that you desire to

It is innate to us to dedicate ourselves to people, things and careers a little too much. The more you tend to invest yourself into something or even an ideology, the harder it gets for us to move on and consider better options. Once you offer your commitment to an entity, thing, or mindset, you feel guilty at the slightest thought of letting go of that belief. It is not the act of letting go, which is hard; it is the psychological bondage that elevates the stress associated with that act.

People daily talk about stress. *"I'm under so much stress they say."*

What stress? Stress about the feeling of fear taking over your existence, a fear that you are in the wrong to abandon a person or a thing that you so heavily rely on. In reality, you initially struggle with abandonment from the same person or thing because you no longer seem to be of use in either situation. However, by denying that we are of no use, we convince ourselves that letting go isn't the best option and that there is still hope for change. In this case, you continue to harbor a belief that there is a possibility for or that a miracle could transform the dynamics between you and the things or ideologies that do not serve your purpose any longer.

Change is fearful, and it makes you anxious. You refuse to change because you feel safe and unharmed in a place where constancy prevails. Change can sometimes come off as a reflection of unreliability and unpredictable circumstances, and the human mind is naturally prepared to defend itself against such a threat. Now, most of you continue to hold on to this ordinary or average identity because you feel comfortable in finding yourself among the ordinary. The moment you surpass the average and step into the extraordinary realm, you feel alienated, despised, or unable to fit with those around you.

Not everybody who surrounds you or forms your social circle is bound to be similar to you. Neither are you bound to be mimicking them, their behavioral patterns, or their perspectives in any way whatsoever. Each of you is a unique personality in your existence. However, because you have lived with this whole concept of trying to fit in even when you can't for years, you become restricted to a certain expected way and nothing more than that.

As a matter of fact, no one should be ordinary. No one should hold onto a monotonous, black and white, polar binary-based life. There's a lot of grey area in between the polarities of life, a lot of free space to canvas whatever you want, to be whoever you desire to be, and so break the curse of the ordinary. To be able to break that curse means you are capable enough of eradicating this life-long cultivation and yearning for a mediocre yet normal life in you. When that happens, you know for a fact that if you break that barrier and adopt change, then you can certainly master the art of letting go of anything.

Let me share a story with you,

One day, a girl came upon a cocoon, and she could tell that a butterfly was trying to hatch. She waited and watched the butterfly struggle for hours to release itself from the tiny hole. All of a sudden, the butterfly stopped moving–it seemed to be stuck.

The girl then decided to help get the butterfly out. She went home to get a pair of scissors to cut open the cocoon. The butterfly was then easily able to escape, **however, its body was swollen and its wings were underdeveloped.**

The girl still thought she had done the butterfly a favor as she sat there waiting for its wings to grow in order to support its body. However, that wasn't happening. The butterfly was unable to fly, and for the rest of its life, it could only move by crawling around with little wings and a large body.

Despite the girl's good intentions, she didn't understand that **the restriction of the butterfly's cocoon and the struggle the butterfly had to go through in order to escape served an important purpose.** As butterflies emerge from tight cocoons, it forces fluid from their body into their wings to prepare them to be able to fly.

The Moral:

The struggles that you face in life help you grow and get stronger. There is often a reason behind the requirement of doing hard work and being persistent. When enduring difficult times, you will develop the necessary strength that you'll need in the future. Without having any struggles, you won't grow–which means it's very important to take on personal challenges for yourself rather than relying on other people to always help you.

Transformation is an important element of growth; mental, emotional, physical, spiritual, and financial growth depends on how well you embrace change. If you continue to keep yourselves locked within the cage of your thoughts, you will never be able to outdo yourself and reach your maximum potential. Your weaknesses somehow always overpower your strengths. This may happen because you haven't learned to use your ability to maneuver through your negative and positive thoughts. This prevents you from growing with what you do best and not succumb to your flaws. Therefore, it would be safe to conclude that change or transformation is essential to allow yourself to grow into the person you're inhibiting yourself from being.

What is inhibiting you? – You are the obstruction in your path to transformation and growth. There is no power or human entity in this world that can stop you from living your best life. The question really is;

do you not want better for yourself? I'm sure you do. Each of you reading this will want to achieve and be better in every way possible. However, if you continue to convince yourself of the hard reality of being stuck in a restricted and unhealthy mindset, how do you propose to make things better in any way?

You manifest whatever you believe. Therefore, a constant reminder that your life is miserable, that the place where you emotionally and mentally find yourself sucks, and that things are always going to be the same is not going to allow you to transform your life. The moment you learn to invest in your constructive thoughts, you will begin experiencing change. When you become invested in something, you tend to attach your identity with that sense of investment or its idea. Hence, it makes complete sense to invest your will and desire to manifest an empowered, successful, and vibrant version of yourself. It is true that in its developing or formational phase, your new identity will clash against your former identity because it will certainly try to suppress the new one. But the process is similar to Darwin's *survival of the fittest*. However, in this case, it isn't nature, but your internal traits that will decide whether or not you allow your improved version to add to your life.

It is hard to let go of your past because you have lived that time for way too long. You have continued to dwell in the past and in a rotting self for a time well overdue. Even though you may be receptive to change, and the idea of transformation resonates with you, it is certainly understandable why it is hard for you to look beyond a time, an identity, and a set of characteristics that defined you. When you continue to live your life below par for way too long, you forget the taste of success. In fact, you do not even know the taste of being *larger than life* without being heroic by simply living up to your maximum potential. You won't know it until you try living your life that way.

As much as I can empathize with you, I also know that sympathizing alongside will do you no good. It is tough, and it is challenging to step out of your past. I am also sure that you feel like a silly person running into monotonous cycles of the ordinary every new day of your life, without obtaining any purpose out of it. Therefore, I know for a fact that you are way beyond sympathies and pity. You are strong, and all you need to do is **recognize**. You must recognize that there is nothing in this world that can stop you from becoming the best version of yourself, and know where you stand in your life while reading this book. You simply need to adhere to an attitude that reiterates your transformation and echoes loud within you, *'You can't stop me!'*

Shakespeare asserts that nothing can really be completely right or completely wrong. However as Shakespeare advises, there is nothing either good or bad but thinking makes it so. If we can refrain from making negative judgments about our daily life events, we can liberate ourselves from a lot of unnecessary suffering. Shakespeare asserts that nothing can really be completely right or completely wrong. The definition of either of them depends on your parameters our outlook at what things are wrong or right. Hence, you are in control of what you wish your mind to think and believe. In all likelihood, it's not the big events in life that are going to make us happy or sad in a lasting way. It's the daily events, situations, and interactions in which we can chose to find joy or suffering. It's easy to find fault or be the critic but thinking about things in this way can really grind us down. If we can remember Shakespeare advice and make it a mantra, it can help us reduce a lot of unnecessary, self-induced suffering. I realize that this is easier said than done (and that, of course, there is REAL suffering in life). But, with practice, we can learn to think about our situations in ways that put a lid on our suffering and, sometimes, help us to find joy in unexpected places.

Each of you has a beast inside, which only needs a triggering factor to be set free. Unfortunately, this beast has been confined by the shackles of your mind, the disbelief that you have in yourself, and the insignificant effort that you make to look beyond your past self. You are full of life; a living, breathing, manifesting beast who need not set his limits. The sky is the limit for people who are bound to grow. However, this beast is usually portrayed in a negative light. Franz Kafka subtly but remarkably explained metamorphosis in his book by showing that when you supersede your capacities and physical and mental restrictions, you become unfit for surviving in a society that is not like you and is rather ordinary.

What you need to understand is that it isn't you who is wrong in that situation. It has been too long since the world has been feeding onto false beliefs and promoting archetypical expectations of a successful person. In essence, a successful person does not confine themself to the boundaries set by society, who does not care if they appear outlandish for wanting to stand out in the crowd. It is someone who exalts in embracing change and who distinctively forms an identity that threatens other people.

In order to that, they had to let go of their past and their former and decayed mindset, which the people around them had inculcated. In doing so, they also had to adopt a *'You Can't Stop ME'* approach and convinced their psychological being that the people around them were bound to pull their legs while they climbed the ladder of success, simply because others couldn't try and reach what they were reaching for. In that case, what seems like the easiest thing to do is to create obstacles, whether physical or psychological, for the one who wants to embrace constructive change.

Even as you read, I so wish that you could interpret the mesh inside my mind. I believe in you and your capacity to achieve nothing but the best for yourself. As a matter of fact, if the same people or world that surrounds you and pulls you down, could uplift you, you have no idea what that could do. Whether you consider yourself to be less talented than others, to have a lower IQ, or to be unable to connect with others, you need to understand that none of those thoughts would have existed in your mind if the same people that affect your aura, could boost you to reach your full potential. Imagine! If the world could encourage each other, be each other's source of motivation, and could somehow maximize their full potential on an individual level, and then on a utilitarian level; the world would be a utopian haven. I can't be sure if that would ever happen because people are so self-centered that they can only destroy other people's thriving souls instead of feeding them positivity.

Change, however, is never immediate. Change is progressive, it is gradual, and it happens over its own course of time. Baby steps are the key to change; one step that you take with the right determination to bring about change that you desire will go a long way. The moment you start believing, you also start manifesting; as you continue to act on your belief and sow the seeds of change, you will gradually feel a shift in your identity. It will feel like you are moving from the decayed to a renewed and blooming version of yourself. The moment you can set foot into your new realm, your success story will automatically begin knitting itself. Confidence breeds more confidence. Hence, if you are confident about your journey and believe in what you're doing while trusting its outcome to be in your favor, then there is a sure shot for success to come your way.

Quick Reflection:

🏹 Imagine all the times when you achieved immense success. Did you initially commit to those results?

Now think - Did your commitment, dedication, and healthy addiction to your goal play an active role in your success?

Well, I believe it did contribute a great deal.

Quick Reflection:

🏹 Each time you could not live up to your expectation of achieving a set goal, was it because you were not wholly committed?

Thus, any task, goal, or feat that you are knitting in your mind at this point; the only question you need to ask yourself for being successful at achieving them should be:

🏹 **How committed are you?**

Commitment is initiated with a decision that is eventually purpose-driven. Lots of decisions can be made, but that alone doesn't promise commitment. The moment you commit to a decision, you allow power to come into existence. Upon wholesome commitment, you will attain a starting a cascade of events and decisions that are bound to increase your probabilities of success. Yes, success leaves clues. Follow those clues and you solve the riddle of success. Even though your commitment isn't a sure-shot promise of you achieving all that you desire. However, it is sure to improve your chances of achieving those things.

The key to never give up.

Once there was a girl who was complaining to her dad that her life was so hard and that she didn't know how she would get through all of her struggles. She was tired, and she felt like as soon as one problem was solved, another would arise.

Being a chef, the girl's father took her into his kitchen. He boiled three pots of water that were equal in size. He placed potatoes in one pot, eggs in another, and ground coffee beans in the final pot.

He let the pots sit and boil for a while, not saying anything to his daughter.

He turned the burners off after twenty minutes and removed the potatoes from the pot and put them in a bowl. He did the same with the boiled eggs. He then used a ladle to scoop out the boiled coffee and poured it in a mug. He asked his daughter, "*What do you see?*"

She responded, "*Potatoes, eggs, and coffee.*"

Her father told her to take a closer look and touch the potatoes. After doing so, she noticed they were soft. Her father then told her to break open an egg. She acknowledged the hard-boiled egg. Finally, he told her to take a sip of the coffee. It was rich and delicious.

After asking her father what all of this meant, he explained that each of the three food items had just undergone the exact same hardship—twenty minutes inside of boiling water.

However, each item had a different reaction.

The potato went into the water as a strong, hard item, but after being boiled, it turned soft and weak.

The egg was fragile when it entered the water, with a thin outer shell protecting a liquid interior. However, after it was left to boil, the inside of the egg became firm and strong.

Finally, the ground coffee beans were different. Upon being exposed to boiling water, they changed the water to create something new altogether.

He then asked his daughter, "*Which are you?*"

"When you face adversity, do you respond by becoming soft and weak? Do you build strength? Or do you change the situation?"

Life is full of ups and downs, wins and losses, and big shifts in momentum, and adversity is a big part of this experience. And while many of us would rather not face adversity, it doesn't have to always be a negative thing. In fact, handling adversity can be a positive experience that can lead to personal development.

You choose how you respond to adversity, whether you let it break you down or you stand up in the face of it and learn from it. In many instances, facing adversity gives you a chance to learn important lessons that can help you grow as a person.

When facing adversity, it's important to recognize your freedom to choose how you respond. You can respond in a way that ultimately limits you, or you can choose to have a more productive response that could potentially open windows of opportunity that we didn't know existed.

You have to continue to remind yourself that you are not done with who you are; there is always room for improvement. You are a work in progress, and your self-improvement is an endless process that should never stop.

Being extraordinary, in essence, is simply exceeding the parameters of being ordinary. Once you realize the thin yet extremely extensive difference between the two, you will also understand that being extraordinary only requires you to improve your existing self. Whatever you already are, whatever you possess within yourself since the beginning of time, you can improve it to make the most of it and bring out the best in yourself. No matter how intense your insecurities are or how pathetic you think you are, there will always be a version of you that you had constantly refused to see earlier in your life when you lived in your past identity. When you think positive all the time you have finally transcended into the new self of yours, that vision of yours will no longer be a myth but a reality that you will experience wholeheartedly.

COACH KAPLAN'S CORNER

Remember,

- *It's negative. If you sow bad, you reap bad. If you plant apple seeds, you don't get tomatoes.*
- *It's positive. If you sow good, you reap good. If you plant peppers seeds, you don't get thistles.*
- *Do not reap what you sow, you reap much MORE than you sow. You get out much more than you put in and it works both for the negative and positive.*
- *You could lose. There are times that even when you do everything right, everything to the best of your ability, and then...you lose. That is just the way this world works, so you better prepare for that. But that takes us to the final point.*
- *If you don't sow, you don't reap. You don't even have a chance. You better look at where you are heading and if you don't like it get some sowing going.*

"We can't be afraid of change. You may feel very secure in the pond that you are in, but if you never venture out of it, you will never know that there is such a thing as an ocean, a sea. Holding onto something that is good for you now, may be the very reason why you don't have something better."

—C. JoyBell.

CHAPTER 16

The "Can't Stop Me" Mentality

"If you see the invisible, you can do the impossible"

—Dr. Eric Kaplan

Narrating my story through this book was not only to share the events of my life but also to motivate the readers of this book to learn from my example. I want you to move forward in your life with no excuses within your will. Your drive should be strong enough so that whatever comes your way has no power over you.

Hopefully, as we have progressed through this book, you were able to develop a *"can't stop me"* mentality. Remember, you are the only one who can stop yourself; now, some may look at my narrative, or the tale of my wife, and say, *"You are the exception, not the rule,"* which may be correct. However, I am often inspired by other people who have risen from obscurity to prominence; from ordinary to spectacular.

You, too, can do it. I'm going to say that no matter where you stand in life, there's always room for improvement.

"The road to success is always under construction."

Say this repeatedly. You will begin to witness improvements in your life beyond your wildest expectations after accepting this statement and dedicate yourself daily to better each and every day.

I have compiled some of the most inspiring stories that exist on the face of the Earth in today's era for you to learn from. I hope that through acquiring these, you will be able to build your true drive in its full form.

Richard Branson

"If your dreams don't scare you, they are too small."

Do you know that Richard Branson established the Virgin Group business from the ground up and seemed to be having the time of his life while doing it?

His father was a lawyer, and his mother was a flight attendant, but the two instilled in the young tycoon enough confidence and desire for him to become one of the world's wealthiest men.

Despite his family's backing, they were never able to provide him with a significant financial advantage. Instead, he negotiated, set his own rules, and figured out how to establish a tiny, multi-media conglomerate while maintaining an optimistic attitude and an open mind.

Joy Gendusa

"I believe in showing empathy, understanding, and compassion for employees because during my own career, I've worked in enough places where those values were not encouraged — and they were not happy places."

Your gender doesn't determine success; it's determined by the monster inside of you that yearns for more. Consider what you want out of life and how much you're willing to spend for it. Does this ring a bell? My father's comments to me as well.

Here's a story you might not be aware of. Joy Gendusa revolutionized direct mailings in a digital environment. However, she may not be as widely recognized as some of her colleagues. Her business, PostcardMania, took advantage of the untapped potential of direct mailing campaigns and converted it into a multi-million-dollar enterprise.

It grew into a corporation that earns more than $50 million each year under her supervision. Her poor beginnings stemmed from trying to market graphic creations while overworked and underpaid. She was so enraged by a horrible customer service encounter that she felt she needed to do something differently. She had an epiphany and realized a market want that she could obviously satisfy, and she did everything she could to make that vision a reality.

Elon Musk

*"When something is important enough, you do it
even if the odds are not in your favor."*

There are several narratives of people and businesses that began as nothing
and grew into something.

"Your imagination creates your reality," Disney stated. Hopefully, you
learn from this book that it's good to dream, establish goals, and state
affirmations on a daily basis.

Despite the fact that I do not own a Tesla, Elon Musk is one of my
heroes since he is a visionary and a dreamer. All eyes are on the Tesla car-
creating entrepreneur following his history-making SpaceX Falcon Heavy
launch. Musk, unlike many of his multi-millionaire friends, did not come
from a wealthy family.

His father was an electromechanical engineer, and his mother was a
nutritionist. His childhood was far from perfect, as he frequently mentions
how many difficulties he suffered throughout his life.

Do Won Chang

*"Forever 21 gives hope and inspiration to people
who come here with almost nothing."*

The charm of successful individuals is that they can be born anywhere
in the globe; success is determined by their attitude, not their geography
location or heredity.

Do Won Chang, the creator of the major fast-fashion retailer, Forever
21, wants his success story to inspire others. Born in a little town outside of
Seoul, in South Korea, he was just 21 years old when he decided to travel
to the United States,

He worked three jobs to make ends meet, never giving up on his dream
of owning his own company. Finally, he and his wife were able to open their
first Forever 21 outlet. They worked patiently and diligently while waiting
for their business to flourish, and their patience paid off handsomely in
the long run.

Will Smith

*"Wealth can also be that attitude of gratitude with which
we remind ourselves every day to count our blessings."*

Will Smith has long been one of my favorite actors, and I had the opportunity
to meet him and spend time with him when I was picked to be an extra
in the film, Ali. Being on set was a blast, but seeing this man's attention to
detail was incredible. What an actor he was; he stayed in character all day,
and by the end of the day, he had cloned Ali in his head and projected him
onto the screen. It has a remarkable ability to peer into other people's minds
and recreate them.

Most people don't have the opportunity to meet Will Smith, let alone
watch him act in a major Hollywood film, as I did. And yes, he was a
great guy. Most individuals, though, aren't Chris Gardner. And the fact
that a movie star depicted him is one of the least noteworthy aspects of the
outstanding man. He was admittedly a less-than-perfect citizen growing up
in a problematic atmosphere. During his early years, he was subjected to a
great deal of violence and cruelty. Despite numerous setbacks, he became
an expert at maintaining an optimistic outlook.

Much of his career challenges, including his homelessness and tenacity in
the face of enormous adversity, are depicted in his book and subsequent film.
Years after climbing to the top as a stockbroker and founded Gardner Rich
& Company, he now travels the world motivating people and discussing
how his optimistic attitude has helped him achieve success. Will Smith
or Denzel Washington could have only portrayed this part. Will Smith
is known for selecting his roles with care, and he frequently uses them to
send a message.

Mark Zuckerberg

*"The biggest risk is not taking any risk... In a world
that is changing really quickly, the only strategy that
is guaranteed to fail is not taking risks."*

Let's face it; Facebook isn't going away anytime soon. Personally, I don't like
his politics as I am big on our constitution's first amendment, but sometimes

we can learn even from those we don't like. My father used to say *"Even a clock that doesn't work is right twice a day"*

Mark Zuckerberg was just another college student honing his art before he revolutionized the face of the internet and our social interactions with Facebook. He was able to educate himself on a plethora of abilities that would help build what would become the digital beast that is Facebook through his zeal and a relentless interest in side projects and developing his own skillset.

Employees that share and demonstrate this similar passion in pursuing projects outside of their necessary duties continue to pique Facebook's interest. This is a nice reminder that just because you aren't doing what you want with your life doesn't mean you can't pursue your passions in your spare time.

Larry Ellison

"When you live your life in different ways, it makes people around you become uncomfortable. So deal with it. They don't know what you are going to do."

It's amazing, I've dined with President Trump, as well as many other Senator's, Congressmen, people whose names are household names like Presidents Donald Trump, George Bush Jr & George Bush Sr., Congressman Thomas McMillan, Surgeon General Everett Koop, but one name I never heard of was Larry Ellison.

Larry Ellison is one of the richest men in the world, with an estimated net worth of $35 billion. And, despite having a loving stepmother, his birth father was absent from his life, and his unwed mother gave him up for adoption when he was just nine months old due to pneumonia. Despite his intelligence, he struggled with school structure. He didn't start influencing the world until he found computer programming and moved to Northern California's developing digital metropolis. Because of the Oracle Database's huge success, he started investing in other initiatives and ventures.

George Bush Junior

"It doesn't matter how many times you have failed, you only have to be right once."

Many people are unaware that George Bush Junior was formerly one of the Dallas Mavericks' owners. It was there I met him and actually dined with him and his wife Barbara. He was actually an engaging man with a strong personality. He was polite and interested in what I do, I didn't think as much of it at the time as I do now. Who knew he'd become the President of the United States one day?

His dreams led him to become President even though his father preferred his brother for that role. Some say he wasn't smart; however, you can't become President of the US if you're stupid. He paid his dues and did what he had to do, and he was not only elected, he was re-elected, which his father couldn't accomplish.

Mark Cuban

Many people are unaware of this, but most people associate Mark Cuban with the Dallas Mavericks. Cuban really took one of my favorite players, Kristaps Porzingis, from the New York Knicks. Yet now many are saying he did the Knicks a favor. Only time will tell.

Cuban's ability to be astute in business may be applied to any aspect of your life. Though his presence on Shark Tank has made him a face of entrepreneurship and investment, Mark Cuban's path to financial success hasn't always been straightforward.

His life wasn't exactly glamorous as a door-to-door waste bag salesperson who ate ketchup and mustard sandwiches to make ends meet.

He worked odd jobs throughout college to get his bills paid. But he finally started a computer consulting firm, which he was able to develop into an online broadcasting empire, which he was able to turn into his first billion. He's notoriously hard-working and always on the lookout to continue to make more and more money.

John Paul DeJoria

*"Success is how well you do what you do
when nobody else is looking."*

John Paul DeJoria, like a handful of the other tremendously successful people on our list, struggled with poverty and homelessness as he built his firm. He started selling small items at a young age, but he lived out of his car even when he began selling shampoo door to door – the business that would go on to become the legendary John Paul Mitchell hair care system.

His positive attitude and work ethic never failed him, and he began diversifying his income almost as soon as he began earning it. Slowly but steadily, he would build on every small gain to amass a vast fortune.

Mohed Altrad

Mohed Altrad, the president of the Montpellier Rugby Club and Entrepreneur of the Year, once lived on one meal a day. The entrepreneur with a $1 billion in net worth, was born into a nomadic tribe in the Syrian desert to a destitute mother who was raped by his father and died when he was young. His grandmother raised him in Raqqa, the city that is now the capital of ISIS, who forbade him from attending school. Altrad attended school anyway, and when he moved to France to attend university, he knew no French and lived off of one meal a day.

Still, he earned a PhD in computer science, worked for some leading French companies, and eventually bought a failing scaffolding company. He transformed it into one of the world's leading manufacturers of scaffolding and cement mixers, Altrad Group. He has previously been named French Entrepreneur of the Year and World Entrepreneur of the Year.

Howard Schultz

Howard Schultz, the founder of Starbucks, grew up in a low-income housing complex.

His estimated net worth is $2.9 billion. Schultz claims in an interview with the British tabloid Mirror:

"Growing up, I always felt like I was living on the other side of the tracks. I knew the people on the other side had more resources, more money, happier families. And for some reason, I don't know why or how, I wanted to climb over that fence and achieve something beyond what people were saying was possible. I may have a suit and tie on now, but I know where I'm from, and I know what it's like."

Schultz was awarded a football scholarship to the University of Northern Michigan, and following graduation, he went to work for Xerox. He subsequently took over a Starbucks coffee store, which had only 60 locations at the time. Schultz took over as CEO of the company in 1987 and grew it to more than 16,000 locations worldwide.

Snoop Dogg

Snoop Dogg is considered a West Coast King and is one of the most renowned rappers in the world, but it wasn't an easily won title. Cordozar Calvin Broadus, Jr. was born in California's Long Beach neighborhood. During a time when the hood was overrun with gang wars, young Snoop had to pick a side. Broadus joined the Rollin' 20 Crips as a teenager and was frequently arrested for selling drugs during his high school years. It wasn't until he found the outlet of hip hop and rapping along with his friends Warren G and Nate Dogg that Snoop was able to get off the streets.

In my mind it shows you don't have to be the most talented to succeed. He believed in himself and he maintained a positive personality. He is now worth hundreds of millions and his brand continues to grow.

Arnold Schwarzenegger

Arnold Schwarzenegger lived in a house without running water or a telephone. A seven-time winner of Mr. Olympia with a net worth of $400 million and filmography that has grossed $4.73 billion worldwide, he is now one of the wealthiest action actors of all time. He also holds the position of California's 38th governor. However, his homeland of Austria had been ravaged by World War II when he was born in 1947, and the future "Governator" grew up in a house without running water or a telephone. Outside his door, riots fueled by hunger were raging. Despite all of this, he was able to grow and become one of the most recognizable stars in the world.

Now imagine I got to lecture for him at the **Arnold Classic** in Columbus Ohio. He was even nice enough to take a picture of me with my book. At lunch that day I sat with him, Barry Larkin, (Hall of Famer, for Cincinnati Reds) and the legendary Jack LaLanne. Jack looks at me and said,

"Doc, I exercise for three hours every day and I hate it."

I replied *"why do you do it then?*

He said, *"because I'm Jack Lalanne."*

To this day as I force myself to exercise, I repeat his words, I do it because **I'm Dr Eric Kaplan**.

Celine Dion

I had the pleasure of meeting backstage Celine Dion with Prince in Vegas in a makeshift adjustment room. I was there to treat her dancers after a performance. What a beautiful individual. She was there that night with Prince. I was stunned how short he really was, which shows you "size doesn't matter". This was an exciting night for me as I treated many of the dancers. Who would have thought they actually have an adjusting table on the premises? I guess you never know till you get backstage.

Celine Dion was born into a low-income family. The youngest of 14 children, Celine Dion grew up in extreme poverty because her parents couldn't make ends meet to provide for all of their children equally.

Despite this, her passion for music remained a constant in her life. She began her career as a young star with an angelic singing voice, participating at local events and gradually gaining renown as a teen star with an angelic singing voice. She strived to win several honors at an early age and more as she grew up to be a hit singer with the help of her loving family. She had to mortgage her home simply to release her debut album. Her current net worth of $800 million speaks much about what she has accomplished in her life. It also emphasizes Dion's unwavering commitment to her love for music.

Walt Disney paved the way for so many people, his ability to see the future is truly amazing, how we took Disneyland from California to the orange groves of Florida and create a Disney world is truly a miracle of business nature. Sometimes just working for a brilliant person, can give you that can do attitude, that **can't stop me** attitude. One such person is Sarah Blakely. After failing to become a lawyer and quitting a job at Disney that she hated, Sara Blakely was stuck at the bottom of the sales food chain, trying to turn cold calls into fax machine clients. She used the resilience those difficult years taught her as she created Spanx and began to build her company and, eventually, her incredible estimated $1.1 billion net worth.

A Favorite Quote of hers:

"Don't be intimidated by what you don't know."

One of my dearest friends **Joe Littenberg,** is a patent attorney, and I love the stories he shares with us, Joe is a true genius because he has the ability to not only see but believe in other people's ideas. Joe became one of the most successful patent attorneys in America and abroad, with clients like Sony, Google, Harvard. However, he was raised without a father and his mother worked in the bakery. He worked his way through school, and even went to Law School at Seton Hall University at night, Joe truly embraced the **"can't stop me"** attitude he dreamed of making other people's dreams a reality. He's recognized nationally and internationally as one of the top patent attorneys in the world.

There are so many rags to riches stories, I don't know where to stop. So I won't. While playing college football, **Kevin Plank** saw the spark for the idea that would eventually become Under Armor. Without any investors, he saved $20,000 of his own money and went into $40,000 of credit card debt to first form and fund the company in 1996. The first year, the business only made $17,000 of sales. Despite seemingly insurmountable odds, growing credit card interest, and a market that didn't yet understand the product, Plank continued eventually contracting directly with 12 NFL teams and picking up demand from there. Thanks to that perseverance, the company now has an annual revenue just under $2 billion, and doesn't seem to be slowing down its massive growth anytime soon. Though it took a little while for his product to catch on, Plank didn't give up on his dream or his vision for what it could become. And that gamble has paid off handsomely for him.

A Favorite Quote of his:

*"I never knew exactly what [Under Armor]
was going to look like, but more important, I got up every
single day and never believed it couldn't happen."*

One of my favorite stories is that of **Ray Kroc**, I read his book "**Grinding It Out**." Then I watched the movie "**Founder**". He was a man 52 years old, a blender salesman with a "**can't stop me**" attitude. Ray Kroc may not have created the first McDonald's company, but he is the wind beneath its incredibly successful wings. His story has become somewhat of folklore amongst entrepreneurial hopefuls who hope to strike idea gold like Kroc. And, given the fact that the self-made millionaire was a high school dropout who found himself driving ambulances during World War I and eventually dabbling in all sorts of odd jobs, it's not like his path to success was a clear one. But when he met the McDonald's brothers and saw an opportunity in the growing fast food restaurant business that he decided to capitalize on, he certainly became incredibly successful.

Imagine it all began in 1955 Kroc then a 52-year-old milkshake machine salesman amazingly out of heart and determination acquired franchising rights to the small California based hamburger restaurant chain. In 1961, he bought out the McDonald brothers for $2.7 million. His story is a great reminder that opportunities may be all around you if you keep your eyes and mind open to them.

A Favorite Quote of his:

"Look after the customers and the business will take care of itself."

It's amazing how things catch on, how technology, has changed the world how people of great vision and imagination have transformed the technology business. When **Jan Koum** signed the $19 billion deal to sell his company, WhatsApp to Facebook, he chose location extremely close to where he used to wait in line to get food stamps. But if you had told the young boy who was born to a housewife and construction worker in Kiev, Ukraine that he'd someday be worth several billion dollars, he understandably might not believe you. Koum migrated to the United States with his mother, who packed basic Soviet-issued school supplies rather than buying them. She babysat and he worked to sweep floors in order to make ends meet. After years of dabbling and adjusting to American culture, he eventually found a knack in computer sciences and eventually landed a job at Yahoo that he credits for causing him to drop out of school. Despite investing in the early '90s dotcom boom, he lost tons of money. But he didn't **GIVE UP**, eventually started carefully crafting and creating WhatsApp, which would go on to revolutionize digital communication.

A Favorite Quote of his:

"I want to do one thing and do it well."

Are you feeling inspired yet? There are so many more that most people don't know of or may have heard of. Let's take a further look.

*****Kenny Troutt,** the founder of Excel Communications, paid his way through college by selling life insurance.

Net worth: $1.5 billion Troutt grew up with a bartender dad and paid for his own tuition at Southern Illinois University by selling life insurance. He made most of his money from phone company Excel Communications, which he founded in 1988 and took public in 1996. Two years later, Troutt merged his company with Teleglobe in a $3.5 billion deal.

He's now retired and invests heavily in racehorses.

*Investor **Ken Langone**'s parents worked as a plumber and cafeteria worker. To help pay for Langone's school at Bucknell University, he worked odd jobs and his parents mortgaged their home.

In 1968, Langone worked with Ross Perot to take Electronic Data Systems public. (It was later acquired by HP.) Just two years later, he partnered with Bernard Marcus to start Home Depot, which also went public, in 1981. Net worth: $2.8 billion.

The founder of Cirque du Soleil worked on the street: The Canadian-born **Guy Laliberté** began his circus career busking on the streets: playing accordion, walking on stilts and eating fire. He gambled by bringing a successful troupe from Quebec to the Los Angeles Arts Festival in 1987, with no return fare. The bet paid off, and the circus group was eventually brought to Las Vegas, where they became the world-famous Cirque du Soleil we know today.

***Mark Wahlberg** used to sell drugs: The Ted actor dropped out of school at the age of 14 to become a street thug, who sold drugs and indulged in gang wars. Wahlberg also had to serve a 50-day sentence in prison for a violent assault on two men. His current estimated worth is around US$ 165 mm.

***Eminem** had a rough childhood: By ninth grade, he dropped out of high school and decided to pursue music full time. It took performing and local rap battles, working dead-end jobs and creating a crazy alter ego, the famous "Slim Shady," to get noticed by the likes of Dr. Dre.

***Selena Gomez** couldn't afford gas: Her mother was just 16 years old when she gave birth to Selena and had to work several jobs just to keep a roof over their heads and put food on the table. She also revealed, "I remember my mom would run out of gas all of the time and we'd sit there and have to go through the car and get quarters and help her get gas."

***Sarah Jessica Parker** was on welfare: The 49-year-old actress may be an old timer in the movie industry but long before she found stardom in the TV series Sex and The City, Sarah Jessica Parker and her family lived on welfare for many years. Growing up in Nelsonville, Ohio, Parker said in an interview that her family seldom celebrated Christmas, birthdays, and other family occasions. She vividly remembers living with no electricity and their phone lines cut because they couldn't pay the bill. Today, Parker's net worth has risen to $90 million.

***Daniel Craig** used to sleep outside: The Bond actor Daniel has many critically acclaimed films in his kitty, but according to Hollyscoop, the actor used to sleep on park benches during his struggling days. He is worth an estimated US $65 million.

***Leighton Meester's** Leighton Meester's mother gave birth in prison: Leighton Meester may portray the rich spoiled brat Blair Waldorf without any difficulty, but Waldorf's fictional life is nothing compared to Meester's actual upbringing. Meester's mother gave birth to her while serving time in prison and was raised by her grandmother for most of her childhood in Mango Island, Florida. When Meester mother got out, the two went to live in New York, where Leighton started a career as a model. In 2007, they relocated again, this time to Los Angeles, where she eventually managed to get a break in the show business. She is best known for her starring role as the devious socialite *Blair Waldorf* on *Gossip Girl* on *The CW* (2007–2012). She has also appeared in films such as *Killer Movie* (2008), *Country*

Strong (2010), *The Roommate* (2011), *Monte Carlo* (2011), *The Oranges* (2011) and *The Judge* (2014). Meester made her Broadway debut in Of Mice and Men(2014). She portrayed Angie D›Amato on the ABC sitcom *Single Parents* (2018–2020).

In addition to acting, Meester has ventured into music. After featuring in the top ten *Billboard* Hot 100 with single Cobra Starship›s «Good Girls Go Bad», she released her solo singles under Universal Republic label «Somebody to Love» in 2009 and «Your Love›a Drug» in 2010. Meester has also recorded songs for various soundtracks. Her debut album, *Heartstrings*, was independently released in 2014. She has also modeled, having been the face of the Jimmy Choo, Herbal Essences, and Vera Wang brands.

* **Chris Pratt** lived in a van: After cutting his teeth playing sidekicks and funnymen, the character actor was immediately promoted to the A-list when he was named the MCU's Star-Lord, going on to secure gigs fronting 2015's Jurassic World (and the sequel) as well as sci-fi tentpole Passengers and a Magnificent Seven remake. Turn back the clock to the late '90s, however, and there were no red carpets and caviar, only shag piles and fleas—he was living in the back of a van with a friend.

***Tyler Perry** was physically abused: He was a victim of physical abuse, courtesy of his father, to the point of him even attempting suicide. Inspired from 'The Oprah Winfrey Show', he started immortalizing his life on paper, only to discover the joy of writing and eventually the desire to be a professional story-writer. He then began to create musicals and stage plays on sentimental themes, slowly building himself up to be one of the most successful playwright of modern times. His current net worth stands at $400 million, exemplifying how perseverance can always end up on top.

***Leonardo DiCaprio** lived in a dangerous town: The actor used to live in a seedy LA neighborhood where he saw drugs, poverty, prostitution, and violence at a very tender age. He told The Times, "It goes back to that neighborhood. It came from the fact that I grew up very poor, and I got to see the other side of the spectrum." Now DiCaprio's net worth is estimated at $245 million.

***Mila Kunis** acted her way out of poverty: Kunis may be worth $55 million now, but she hasn't forgotten her roots. She's even publicly vowed that her and Ashton Kutcher won't raise entitled children. And we guess the reason for that is pretty clear. It's because she knows how it feels to be poor.

*__Halle Berry__ lived in a homeless shelter: The Oscar winning actress ran out of money when she moved to US to become an actress. She even stayed in a homeless shelter. During an interview to Star Pules, Berry said, "It taught me how to take care of myself and that I could live through any situation, even if it meant going to a shelter for a small stint."

*__Hilary Swank__ lived in a trailer park: Long before she became the Million Dollar Baby, Hilary Swank had to endure the hardships of poverty. Growing up, Swank lived in a trailer park back in Washington with only her mother to care for her and her two siblings. Swank's father left the family when she was young. When her mother lost her job, the family decided to take a chance at life and moved to California. Living in their car, Swank and her family worked on several jobs before they could afford an apartment. Swank's break came when she got a lead role in Boys Don't Cry. The award-winning actress now lives well and beyond her former state, with $40 million stashed in the bank.

*__Steve Jobs__ could not afford college: Jobs was given away for adoption by his biological parents and he became interested in electronics after his foster dad showed him the joys of technical tinkering in their garage. He had to drop out of college, because his education was costing his foster parents a lot. He used to return Coke bottles for money and live on free meals at the Hare Krishna temple. A hippie who used to trip on LSD, Jobs went from a technician in Atari, Inc. to becoming the CEO of Apple Inc.

*__J.K. Rowling__ dealt with poverty: Born in a lowly English family, Rowling battled depression, suicidal tendencies and poverty to become one of the most loved British authors in the world for her hugely popular Harry Potter series. Highly imaginative as a kid who thrived on stories, she drew from her surroundings and the people in her life as inspirations for the books which have now become one of the biggest movie franchises. From her humble beginnings, she has gone on to become one of the most powerful women in the United Kingdom.

*The manufacturer of Ray-Ban and Oakley lived in an orphanage: __Del Vecchio__ was one of five children who could not be supported by his widowed mother. After growing up in an orphanage, he went to work in a factory making molds for auto parts and eyeglass frames, where he lost part of his finger. At 23, he opened his own molding shop. That eyeglass frame shop expanded to the world's largest maker of sunglasses and prescription eyewear. Luxottica makes brands like Ray-Ban and Oakley, with 6,000 retail shops like Sunglass Hut and LensCrafters. His estimated net worth is now above $10 billion dollars.

*Jim Carrey lived in a van: Comedian-turned-actor Jim Carrey boasts a net worth of $150 million and a resume of movies that have grossed nearly $4.9 billion worldwide. But before a role on "In Living Color" launched the Canadian comic's career in 1990, things weren't so smooth. At 12 years old, the actor was homeless and living in a van after his father lost his job.

What do all these people have in common. To me it's a "**Can't Stop Me**" attitude. As you can see, we live in the greatest country in the world, opportunities are everywhere perseverance is not. So many people in the chapter rose from nothing to something they went from being ordinary to extraordinary. We all have the ability to change, we all have the ability to work, with positive goals, work ethic, desire, perseverance, there is nothing that can stop you. Where are you today is not where you have to be tomorrow. Planning tomorrow's, plan your future. Whether you like or not like any of these people is not the point. The point is, nothing can stop you but you. The reason I share with you all these stories is so you can clearly see that all of these people had a "**can't stop me**" attitude these people that took their ordinary lives and created extraordinary things. What are your dreams? What are your passions, imagine that greatness is a seed deep inside of you and you must cultivate the seed to become the person that you want to be?

It does not matter whether you like these people or not, we can learn from all of them. They all had the same mentality of *"Can't Stop Me."* I was astounded by the challenges that so many of these people faced. There were no silver spoons in their mouths when they were born. I'm sharing these with you because each of these individuals has a *"can't stop me"* mindset; these are people who took ordinary lives and turned them into exceptional achievements.

What are your aspirations?
What are your passions?
Imagine that greatness is a seed inside you that you must nurture to grow into the person you want to be. What is the lowest price you are willing to pay? Nothing can stop you if you are willing to pay the price and have a *"can't stop me,"* mindset. Except for you. And this is what is the key determinant of your success.

The rationale of including these stories is as simple as it can get; I want you to look at them and understand that there were no excuses in their life. If you truly want to be unstoppable, you have to minimize all the excuses revolving around your unwillingness to do things. Once you overcome that, you will be truly on your way to success.

"Even if you are on the right
track, you'll get run
over if you just sit there."

—Will Rogers

CHAPTER 17

Phases of Life

When you see the invisible, you can do the impossible

As I look back, I can see that there were numerous stages in my life, and each one shaped me in some way or another. I consider myself fortunate. I've learnt a lot of lessons along the way, and I'll share them with you at the end of this book.

Let's start at the beginning, with **AWARENESS.**

We are helpless from the moment we are born. We can't move, communicate, or feed ourselves in any capacity; we're completely reliant on the people around us to fulfil our basic wants and needs. This is a crucial stage in life; it is from here that our learning begins.

As youngsters, we are wired to learn by seeing and imitating others. We begin by learning about our motor functions, such as walking and talking. Then we practice our social skills by observing and imitating our peers. Finally, throughout late childhood, we learn to adapt to our culture by adhering to the laws and conventions surrounding us and attempting to behave in a manner that society considers acceptable.

The purpose of our mentors, our teachers, in the beginning, in Stage One, is to teach us how to function within society so that we can become autonomous, self-sufficient adults. The notion is that the adults in our community assist us in reaching this point by assisting us in making decisions and taking action on our own. This can be challenging if you don't have the correct professors, coaches, or mindset.

However, I realized that if you are an independent thinker, many professors and community members will dislike you and will not support you. These self-proclaimed leaders frequently try to penalize us for our freedom. They disagree with our choices. As a result, we are unable to develop complete autonomy. Instead, we become locked in Stage One, continuously imitating those around us and seeking to please everyone to avoid being evaluated.

There were numerous teachers from whom I learned and those teachers who attempted to hold me back. I had no desire to be ordinary, the best of the worst and the worst of the best. When they decide what you want to do with your life, you must remain focused and never give up on your goal.

Last month at one of my seminars speaking in Myrtle Beach South Carolina I began a seminar by showing an audience of 150 people a crisp $100 bill.

I asked, *"Who wants this $100 bill?"*

All 150 people nodded.

I said, *"I am going to give this money to someone, but first…."*

I then proceeded to crumple the bill up.

I then asked the crowd again if anyone wanted it.

All 150 hands went up in the air.

I then dropped the money on the floor and stomped all over it.

I then raised it in the air to show the crowd. The money was filthy.

"Does anyone want it now?"

Every hand went up.

I proceeded to tell the crowd that no matter what I did to ruin the money, people still wanted it because **its value remained the same**. It was still worth $100.

The moral to this story is life often beats us up to the point where we feel inadequate. We deal with bad circumstances and make bad choices that we have to deal with later. However, no matter what you go through, **your value will remain the same**. You have something special to offer that no one can take away from you.

I wanted to please everyone when I was younger, but I quickly understood that this was impossible. Because I was outspoken in elementary school, many teachers disliked me. The truth is that I was gregarious, and I liked people. Once we accept who we are, we can move forward. Accepting who you are is a form of self-discovery.

Self-Discovery

As we enter the next years in our life, we enter into self-discovery. For me, I believe this began when I entered college at Fairleigh Dickinson University. As we enter this important phase of life, we begin to make decisions for ourselves, test ourselves, and understand ourselves and what makes us unique. Here is when I knew what I wanted and was willing to pay the price.

Self-discovery is a process. We try things. Some of them go well. Some of them don't. The goal is to stick with the ones that go well and move on.

This lasts until we begin to run up against our own limitations. Naturally, this doesn't sit well with many people. But despite what Oprah and Deepak Chopra may tell you, discovering your own limitations is a good and healthy thing. It is only through recognizing our weaknesses that we learn how to develop strength. Abraham Lincoln once said, *"the ability to recognize ignorance is the first step towards knowledge"*.

You're just going to be bad at some things, no matter how hard you try. For me, that's golf. I put in my 10,000 hours; I enjoy the game and wanted to be great. I'm not. However, I learned it was a great way to meet people, a great way to make friends, and build my practice. Through my failures at golf came more success.

Your limitations are important because you must eventually realize that your time on this planet is limited and, therefore, you should spend it on things that matter most. That means learning that just because you can do something doesn't mean you should do it. That also means realizing that just because you like certain people doesn't mean you should be with them. Finally, that means recognizing that there are opportunity costs to everything and that you can't have it all.

Some people never allow themselves to feel limitations either because they refuse to admit their failures or because they delude themselves into believing that their limitations don't exist. These people get stuck in Stage Two.

At some point, we all must admit the inevitable: life is short, not all of our dreams can come true. So, we should carefully pick and choose what we have the best shot at and commit to it.

But many people spend most of their time convincing themselves of the opposite that they are limitless and can overcome all. As a result, they believe that their life is that of non-stop growth and ascendance in the world, while everyone else can clearly see that they are merely running in place.

A mother camel and her baby were lying down, soaking up the sun. The baby camel asked his mom, *"Why do we have these big bumps on our back?"*

The mom stopped to think and then said, *"We live in the desert where there is not much water available. Our humps store water to help us survive on long journeys."*

The baby camel then stopped to think and said, *"Well, why do we have long legs with rounded feet?"*

His mother replied, *"They are meant to help us walk through sand."*

The baby asked a third question, *"Why are my eyelashes so long?"*

The mother replied, *"Your long eyelashes offer you protection from sand when it blows in the wind."*

Finally, the baby said, **"If we have all of these natural abilities given to us to walk through the desert, why are we camels stuck in the Zoo?"**

The moral of this story is skills and abilities that you possess won't be useful if you're not in the right environment. Part of self-discovery is accepting where you are and what you must do to succeed. I knew I wasn't the best student, so I worked harder. We all have gifts unique to us. Know who you are and do the best you can.

If you're stuck in a career that isn't the right fit, you have to do some self-reflection to realize where your strengths lie that are going to waste. **Turn to people that you know the best as well as professionals in any given market so you can start thinking about what may be better for you.** Think big and remain open to new ideas.

In healthy individuals, self-discovery begins in mid-to late adolescence and lasts into a person's mid-20s to mid-30s. After that, we all must grow up. If not, it is referred to as the *"Peter Pan Syndrome"*, eternal adolescents, always discovering themselves but finding nothing.

Commitment

After self-discovery comes commitment. We used to always say at Nutrisystem that people commit to go on a diet, but are they really committed? Like the person who makes a New Year's resolution and says, *"I'm going to go on a diet"*, and then the next day when the birthday cake is served, they say, *"One piece won't hurt."* They made a commitment but weren't committed. To be successful, you have to make a commitment and be dedicated and commit to sticking with it.

Commitment is all about maximizing your potential in this life. It's all about building your legacy.

What will you leave behind when you're gone?

What will people remember you by?

Whether that's a breakthrough study or an amazing new product, or an adoring family, this phase of life I call commitment is about leaving the world a little bit different than the way you found it.

It's about knowing what you want and being willing to pay the price. I wanted to be a doctor. Who would've thought during my first two years of professional school my days consisted of class from eight till three, and then off to the library from 3 to 11? Each and every day, day in day out. Weekends were spent in the library from 9 to 5. Not me, that's for sure, but I was committed, which was far stronger than my commitment.

In 'normal' individuals, the phase I call commitment generally lasts from around 30-ish-years-old until one reaches legacy age. Do you see in Florida where I live with some of the most successful people in the world, retirement is something true entrepreneurs never do?

You will never see someone like the President of United states fully retire. Even Joe Biden, at 78 years old, aspired to become President and did that at his age. He might not have had the strength, but he had the desire to continue. Now Trump on the other hand is 74 and he is far from done whether it be in politics, business or both. Successful people are committed to building a legacy. George Bush Sr., worked till the end of his life, in politics, mentoring his two sons, etc., and let's not forget the great comedians Bob Hope and George Burns who both lived to 100. Others like Jerry Lewis, Frank Sinatra like so many celebrities never quit working. Clint Eastward is still acting and directing at 91 years young. You have to admire Bob Newhart 92, William Shatner 90 and still going strong, Harry Bellafonte 94, Gene Hackman 91, James Earl Jones 92, Sidney Poitier 94, Bob Barker 97, Barbara Walters 91, Angela Lansbury 95, Betty White one of my all-time favorites 90, Mel Brooks whose movies I still laugh out loud at 95. The great Tony Bennett still singing his heart out at 95. The amazing Dr. Ruth Westheimer to name just a few greats that give, give, give and never even thought of retiring.

Legacy

People arrive at the legacy phase of life, having spent somewhere around half a century investing in what they believed was meaningful and important. They did great things, worked hard, earned everything they have, maybe started a family, wrote a book, or seven.

I am 69 years old. I've sat with three Presidents of the United States of America, two Surgeon General's, been appointed as an advisor to the President's Council on Sports and Physical Fitness, and I was featured in the USA Today newspaper. I've appeared on Good Morning America, Dr Oz, Montel Williams, and almost every television network. I've written six books, all bestsellers, and reached an author's pinnacle with **four "# 1" bestsellers.**

As a doctor, I've owned seven clinics, lectured all over the country and have written 25 manuals for my profession. I am married to the same woman for 41 years and would marry her again tomorrow; she is my best friend. I've been the President, Chief Operating Officer and board member of a public company that was losing $1 million a month when I started. I turned them profitable inside of one year and more than doubled our stock price.

Even today, I am honored to be the board of one of President Donald Trump's businesses, Trump National Golf Club in Jupiter, Florida. I have two sons, one of whom attended medical school and the other attended chiropractic school, both of whom have wonderful wives, and I have two grandchildren.

It was not an easy voyage to get here; I was frequently greeted with hurdles and obstacles, and had to take numerous detours along the way to success. However, many of the lessons that I've learned I will share with you at the end of this book hopefully to help guide you on your personal journey to success.

After commitment, to family, to career, the goal is to create a legacy and making sure that it lasts beyond one's death. My brother Steven Kaplan died of lung cancer at the age of 65 years old. When I came to Florida after graduating from chiropractic school (which I paid for 100% on student loans) and getting my D.C., license I drove to Florida with only $500 in a broken-down Pontiac Catalina. Five hundred dollars was all I had to eat, to live. I was so determined that I was too naive to know it's not feasible or obtainable, or was it? How did I get the $500 dollars? I had overdraft checking from the bank. I figured since I left the state, I'd find a job and have the money to pay them back by the time they found me. I went from office to office looking for a job.

No one wanted to hire me, and no one wanted to offer me a job. If I wanted to start my own business, I needed $12,500. My then-partner, Dr.

Julian Hirsch, told me that his father would contribute $12,500, so I went to my father, who simply didn't have the funds. Although my father loved me, and I believe saying no to me was the hardest thing he ever had to do, I didn't know where to turn, so I went to my older brother.

Steven was four years older, and I asked him to cosign a loan because the bank would not loan me the money on my signature alone; not on my diploma or my potential. My brother and his lovely wife Gloria agreed to do this for me. I am proud to say that I paid my brother back within the first nine months. After that, I had them released from the loan. I would do whatever it takes to succeed; I was going to develop a legacy, and I was committed to my commitment to be successful.

I hope that my commitment to being the best person I could be a lesson that my children and grandchildren will always remember me by. My family is part of the reason for writing this book, and my books are a part of my legacy. When my brother died of lung cancer at 65 years old, I said his eulogy,

"A person dies two times; once when they stop breathing, and once when we stop thinking of them."

My brother's children, Beth and Richard and his four grandchildren will carry on his legacy. Steven was a loving father, brother, and husband who left a wonderful legacy of dedication to his family through his hard work and commitment to family. Dad would have been proud. Our father taught us to be committed, follow our dreams, do whatever it takes to be successful, and **"NEVER GIVE UP"**.

Steven and I both passed on this quality to our children, and now I desire to impart it to my Disc Centers of America doctors. Dr. Perry Bard, my partner but, first and foremost, my inspiration, a phenomenal family man. He's a wonderful companion, friend, spouse, and father to his two boys. I am always grateful that he believed in me as much as I did him.

Earlier I discussed I started with my partner Dr. Perry Bard one of the most successful companies for disc injuries, Disc Centers of America. With over 167 clinics throughout the United States, we set the standard for treating disc injuries using non-surgical procedures and technologies. It was through this journey I met Carlos Becerra and his family.

Carlos, Chello, Larry and Gidgette Rubin, taught me a lot about the science of Non-Surgical Spinal Decompression. Carlos remains a genius in his own right. He worked with all the pioneers, especially both Dr. Norman

Shealy and Dr. Alan Dyer. He connected me with both these legends. And for months on end I would drive to Marietta, and he would patiently sit with me and show me the insides of each and every machine. He not only taught me the fundamentals but the nuts and bolts literally of Non-Surgical Spinal Decompression. Carlos and his wife lovely wife Chello are leaving a great legacy for future generations of doctors. His equipment proudly sits today in the Museum for Surgical Sciences, in Chicago Illinois.

Dr. Bard and I have continued to talk, research and study with Dr. Norman Shealy, this neurosurgeon and former Harvard professor, bestselling author took a liking to us. The hours he's spent with us is priceless. Dr. Shealy gladly and freely gave the torch to us as DDD, Degenerative Disc Disease educators and authorities in the United States. We were both honored by this man's confidence and endorsement of the two of us. He also endorsed Disc Centers of America, saying they set the standard in disc care. We thank him for his confidence and are working on a book which will be considered one of the definitive manuals.

I told you earlier my mom was not impressed when I first informed her I was going to be a chiropractor. She wanted me to be a dentist; she wanted me to be a podiatrist, but I wanted to be a chiropractor. Sometimes, we have to take the road that is obvious to us, even if it isn't obvious to others.

People become stuck in life because they always feel imperfect and different from others, so they devote all of their efforts to conforming to what those around them want to see.

Some people get stuck because they feel they should always be doing more, doing something better, new and exciting, or should have been improving at something. But no matter how much they do, they feel as though it is never enough.

Some people get stuck because they feel as though they have not generated enough meaningful influence in the world to make a greater impact in the specific areas they have committed themselves to. But no matter how much they do, they feel as though it is never enough. Remember this, sometimes; all you can do is all you can do. However, in whatever you do, strive to be the best version of yourself.

One could even argue that some people feel stuck because they feel insecure that their legacy will not last or significantly impact future generations. So, they cling to it and hold onto it and promote it with every last gasping breath. But they never feel as though it is enough.

The solution is then reversed at each phase. To get past the early stages of our lives, we must understand that we will never be enough for everyone all of the time and that we must make our own decisions. Second, you must recognize that you will never be able to achieve all you desire, so you must focus on what matters most and commit to it. Third, you must recognize that your time and energy are limited, and you must redirect your efforts to assisting others in continuing the important initiatives you started.

Remember everything you think, say or do, may influence all the people around you. This my friends is your legacy. Make a special life, accomplish things that people will always remember. Like a burning candle, if you use it to continue to light other candles, your flame, your legacy will live infinitely. My mother used to say, **"Live your life like a field covered with snow, for wherever you walk your steps will show"**.

There was once a boy who became angry so frequently with his friends at school that he was constantly getting sent home. His temper was disruptive to the class and hurtful to other students.

His father came up with a strategy to try to deter the boy from getting angry so easily. He gave his son a hammer and some nails and told him to hammer a nail into the family's fence every time the boy got angry in the future.

The following day, the boy got angry 37 times, and had to hammer as many nails into the fence. Over the next few weeks, the boy got tired of hammering nails into the fence and he gradually started to control his temper. Slowly, the number of nails he was hammering into the fence started to decrease. The boy realized that it was easier to remain calm when he started to feel angry than to gather the tools, go outside, and start hammering.

Eventually, the boy stopped losing his temper altogether. His dad noticed and told the boy to remove a nail from the fence every day that he was able to keep his temper under control.

Eventually, as the weeks went by, all of the nails had been taken out of the fence. The father and son then stood in front of the broken fence, which was completely scattered with holes.

The father turned to his son and said, *"You have done well, but look at the holes in the fence. They cannot be repaired. When you get angry at other people, it leaves a scar just like the holes you see in front of you. It doesn't matter if you say I'm sorry one hundred times, the injury is still there."*

The moral of this story is simple. Be patient with people. In today's world there is so much anger. Throughout your life what has angered you? Where did it get you? Through all the phases of life look at what you've done and what you're leaving behind.

Whether it be anger, or loss of discipline, remember people see in you, what you see in them. The key to inner happiness is to try to always control your negative feelings toward other people while you remove any anger, any hostility and lack of patience from your life. While you may not see the damage that it does, it can leave irreparable wounds that can eventually break them. Be kind to others and think before you let your emotions get the best of you. Remember as you go through the phases of life you leave a trail. Make your trail one that your family, your children your grandchildren or simply or front want to follow you on.

Once you accept yourself for who you are, (self-discovery), and move into the phases of your life remember that change is unavoidable and that one person's impact, no matter how strong, powerful, or significant, may fade with time.

And life will go on. And your legacy will live on.

"The road to success is dotted with many tempting parking spaces.

—Will Rogers

CHAPTER 18

3D's Discipline Desire & Dedication

"People often say that motivation doesn't last. Well, neither
does bathing—that's why we recommend it daily."

—Zig Ziglar

I hope you have been enjoying my book. There are so many lessons to learn
and implement, but the 3' Ds are germane to mastering your success.

Once you decide to take on the mindset that no one person or thing
can stop you from reaching your goals, you take on a "CAN STOP ME"
attitude and your road to success and happiness lay in front of you. I
assure you; you can do anything you dedicate and discipline yourself to be.
Throughout this book my wife and I shared parts of our life with stories and
philosophies to not only motivate but to hopefully enhance other people's
lives, our stories and philosophies to enhance others. To pay it forward. We
wanted to share our stories to help you reach your dreams So you can go
from ordinary to extraordinary.

Let me share a story with you. The great king of the jungle, the lion,
was proud of his mastery over the entire animal kingdom. One day the lion
decided to make sure all the other animals knew he was the king of the
jungle. In fact, he was so supremely confident that he bypassed the smaller
animals, who weren't even worth his time, and instead went straight to the
great bear.

"*Who is the king of the jungle?*" the lion demanded, baring his teeth.

The bear quickly replied, "*Why, you are, of course, Mr. Lion!*" The lion
gave a mighty roar of approval and moved on.

Next, he asked the tiger,

"*Who is the king of the jungle?*"

And the tiger was equally agreeable, answering,

"*Everyone knows that you are, mighty lion.*"

Next on the list was the elephant, who stood still, towering over the
lion, ignoring his question altogether. Then, the six-ton giant grabbed the
lion with his trunk, whirled him around in the air six times, and slammed

him into a tree! When the lion attempted to get up, the elephant pounded him onto the ground several times with his trunk, dunked him underwater in a nearby lake, and finally dumped him out onto the shore.

The lion—bruised, bloody, battered, and seemingly beaten— struggled to his feet, looked the elephant straight in the eye, and, without hesitation, said:

"Look, just because you don't know the answer doesn't mean you have to get nasty about it!"

Friends, that lion knew who he was. And so must you. You must know your true worth, your values, strengths, and weaknesses. You must know what matters to you and what you believe in. And even when you're disappointed, rejected, or seemingly beaten by life, you will live to fight another day, solid in your conviction that you can conquer any challenge. Every day is a new day and each day we all face challenges. Be the King of your universe, love yourself and live life with passion and confidence. If you do this neither a lion, an elephant or any naysayer around you can steal your dreams or deflate your passion.

I've learned that the secret to a satisfied life and true empowerment is, first and foremost, understanding who you really are—from the inside out—and not letting others define it for you. The key is to like yourself regardless of any limitations. I never listened to what people said I couldn't do; I did what I believed in, and I did it with passion.

I often think that with literally a world of knowledge at our fingertips, knowing ourselves is actually more difficult than ever. Why?

The answer to this quest is so simple. But before I share it to you, allow me to make you a promise. When you come to know yourself, your strengths, your weaknesses you will become invincible, just like the mighty lion. Develop a **"CANT STOP ME ATTITUDE"** and no one can stop you, but you.

I've spent my life creating that kind of unwavering spirit, one that cannot be defeated or beaten. If you're willing to do **"Whatever It Takes"** you will become unshakable, invincible, indomitable, and incapable of being conquered or overcome by anyone or anything.

Does the idea of becoming this powerful seem too far-fetched, or too good to be true? It isn't. Believe me, if I can do it, you can. I have no superpowers, just a super attitude. I don't have an exaggerated sense of my own power to change you, or to put something in you that you don't already have. My job is much easier than that. I'm not interested in talking about what you need, or what you don't have, or where you can go to get what you "ain't got"! I'm here to uncover what you already do have, about what is already true, and about who you already are.

Many of the great artists and sculptors of the world have stated that they didn't so much "create" something, as uncover it. As Rocky Balboa said in his latest movie, *"You, me, or nobody is gonna hit as hard as life. But it ain't about how hard you hit; it's about how hard you can get hit and keep moving forward."*

With passion for yourself, for life whatever hits you, you will get up again just as that lion did. Why? It's because you are truly invincible. It's really not that difficult to live an extraordinary life. Most people look at those who are having success around them, and desire the same thing, but end up tossing their dreams in the too-hard-basket. They don't understand that going from ordinary to extraordinary involves doing just a little bit extra.

To reach your goals in life, no matter what the situation you must maintain positive thoughts. Let me ask you how many times have you sabotaged yourself with negative thoughts or destructive feelings like guilt or shame? If the answer is more than once, that's already too many times. Doing this for most of us isn't uncommon. Many of us struggle with recurring negative thoughts that undermine our confidence, outlook, mood, and self-esteem. However, the problem with this is that they often become self-fulfilling prophecies.

We must first and foremost believe that what we think about ourselves becomes our reality: our thoughts shape the way we act, and the way we act shapes our destiny. So, at some point, our negative beliefs become firmer, and we begin to retreat from the valuable things in life and drag our ambitions, relationships, careers, or friendships down that hole. But doesn't have to be this way? The secret is to just let go.

A wise man once faced a group of people who were complaining about the same issues over and over again. One day, instead of listening to the complaints, he told them a joke and everyone cracked up laughing.

Then, the man repeated the joke. A few people smiled.

Finally, the man repeated the joke a third time—but no one reacted.

The man smiled and said, "You won't laugh at the same joke more than once. So, what are you getting from continuing to complain about the same problem?"

The goal of this book is to teach you about positive thoughts, goals and affirmations to get you through the day. Positive thoughts triggered by affirmations help you turn those self-doubts and negative thoughts into inspiring daily affirmations.

What are Positive Affirmations? Although there's a broad body of scientific research about positive affirmations, there's not an official definition of what they are. The name says it all: they are positive statements that help you confront the negative, destructive thoughts that sometimes inhabit your mind.

We use them to motivate ourselves to make positive changes in our lives or to enhance our confidence and self-esteem. If you often struggle with negative thoughts, perhaps daily affirmations are the best way to replace these destructive patterns with more adaptive ones! Self-affirmations help us cope with events that threaten our integrity, performance, and personal growth. They are most often all about rethinking our core personal values. Timely affirmations can help improve education, health, relationship outcomes. The benefits can persist for months or even years.

Louise Hay was one of the most famous American motivational writers, whose books empowered and helped millions of people across the globe. She dedicated her life to helping others achieve a positive mindset trough practicing self-affirmations, and her inner and outer beauty, as well as the long life she lived (she died at the age of 90), were proof that self-affirmative thinking and behavior do represent a path to longevity, as well as mental and physical health.

In Louise Hay's words: Affirmations are like seeds planted in soil. Poor soil, poor growth. Rich soil, abundant growth. If you want to become a more positive person, you need to change your overall perspective on life. It's not enough to just generically repeat positive statements, you need to instill new habits, values, and behaviors.

I affirm daily, "You can't stop me."

I never stop, I never give up, I never discourage myself! My head is always up, and I feel encouraged! My motivation never stops, and I try again and again! My passion never leaves-me! My goals are in front of me all the time! I see my dreams, and I myself fulfilling them! Daily, I do my best, and I achieve my best!

Enough about me, let's talk about you. What's stopping you from living your dreams, what is stopping you from living life on your own terms, and what is stopping you from taking action. The answer is nothing, you have no excuse to make, the only reason you are not living the way you want to live is because you're not serious about success.

A lack of action stems from a lack of dedication, no one is stopping you from sacrificing your entertainment time to make time for success, it's you who is in charge of your time, you are the one who decides to spend your days engaging in meaningless activities that don't move your life towards living it on a new level, you are the one who chooses to sit around doing nothing. If you want to make progress in life, get rid of the nonsense and focus on success and align all of your activities towards the achievement of your goals.

People have a tendency to let their thoughts about becoming an entrepreneur deter them from getting started, people give up before they have even tried, amazing. Every single day you need to be doing more, you need to be growing your life day after day, do more each day, push harder, the more you do the more you become, the more you push your limits the further out they will expand, get up and push yourself towards greatness, don't just wish for it, get up and work for it, success is earned by what you do.

From this day forward do away with your excuses, excuses don't help you make progress in life, I have never seen anyone complain their way to success, success comes from what we do on a consistent basis. Become an action taker, not an excuse maker, losers make excuses, which is why they don't get anywhere in life.

The journey of success is actually not that difficult, so it seems, it seems to be one in which that is dependent on hard work and persistence. In the beginning don't think anything, just focus on creating something of value to society that is aligned to who you are and how you want to live. I urge you to take action, it does not have to be perfect, just start creating, every single day keep adding, one brick at a time, one step at time, in one year's times you will have built yourself something great if you stay consistent on this journey.

Nothing is stopping you but yourself, your negative mindset must change to a positive mindset, your excuses must be replaced with action, and your talk must turn to silence so that you can turn your dreams into a reality. Your ability to develop the habit of self-discipline will contribute more to your success than any other quality of character.

Napoleon Hill, after interviewing 500 of the richest people in America, concluded that **"Self-discipline is the master key to riches."**

You must ask yourself, what do you want and what price are you willing to pay? Dr. Edward Banfield from Harvard University concluded that *"Long time perspective"* was the key to upward social and economic mobility in America or anywhere else in the world. He discovered in fifty years of research, that people who succeeded greatly had the ability to think long term, to delay gratification in the short term so that they could enjoy even greater rewards in the long term. They thought ten and twenty years into the future while making decisions for their current actions.

My father used to say, ***"Success takes tons of sacrifice and discipline."*** Dr. Bard says, ***"Discipline weighs ounces, but regret weights tons."***

The key word is *"sacrifice."* It is the ability for you to sacrifice immediate pleasure or gratification in the present so that you can enjoy greater rewards down the road. That is where desire and dedication fit in. You have to desire something and have the discipline and dedication to complete your task. Goals in essence are desires and goal setters are goal getters.

Albert Einstein once said, *"Compound interest is the most powerful force in the universe."*

This is why saving and investing in the present is the first key to becoming financially successful in the future. Self-discipline means self-control, self-mastery, and the ability to have *"dinner before dessert."*

This doesn't mean that you don't have pleasurable experiences in life, but it means that you have them after you have done the hard and necessary work and completed your key tasks. The payoff for practicing self-discipline is immediate. Whenever you discipline yourself, and force yourself to do the right thing, whether you feel like it or not, you will like and respect yourself more. Your self-esteem increases. Your self-image improves. Your brain releases endorphins which made you happy and proud. You actually get a payoff every time you hold your own feet to the fire.

The most important point is that self-discipline is a habit that you can learn with practice and repetition. It takes approximately twenty-one days of repetition, without exception, to develop a habit of medium complexity. Sometimes you can develop a habit faster, and sometimes it will take longer. It is up to you, and how determined you are.

Some years ago, a businessman, Herbert Grey, began searching for what he called ***"The common denominator of success."*** He researched and interviewed successful people for eleven years and finally concluded that successful people are those who **"Make a habit of doing what unsuccessful people don't like to do."**

Rich Devos, founder of Amway, once said, **"There are lots of things in life that you don't like to do, like prospecting, selling and building your business in the evenings and weekends, but you do them anyway so that you can do the things that you really enjoy later on."**

There are disciplines you can develop that will improve every area of your life. It turns out that every exercise of self-discipline strengthens every other discipline at the same time, just as every weakness in self-discipline weakens you in other disciplines as well.

Let me share with you my top ten.

KAPLAN'S CORNER
MY TOP 10,

1. The Discipline of Clear Thinking:

Thomas Edison once said, *"Thinking is the hardest discipline of all."*

It has been said that there are three types of people. There are those who think (The small minority); there are those that think they think, then there are those who would rather die than think. Take time to think though the critical issues and problems in your life. Put aside long, unbroken chunks of time, thirty, sixty and then ninety minutes.

a. **Peter Drucker** said, "Fast people decisions are usually wrong people decisions." In addition, fast decisions with regard to your family, career, money or any other major issue are usually wrong decisions.

b. Sit quietly for 30-60 minutes to think. Practice solitude on a regular basis. "Go into the silence."

c. Whenever you practice solitude for more than thirty minutes you activate your super conscious mind and trigger your intuition. You get it right from the "still, small, silent voice within."

d. To think better, take a pad of paper and write down every detail of the problem situation you are facing. Sometimes, the right thing to do immerges as you write down the details.

e. **Aristotle** once said that wisdom *"The ability to make good decisions is a combination of experience plus reflection. The more time that you take to think about your experiences, the more vital lessons you will gain from them."*

f. Go for a walk or exercise for 30-60 minutes. Very often when you are exercising, you will get insights or ideas that help you to think better and make better decisions.

g. Talk your situation over with someone else who you like and trust, and who is not emotionally involved. Very often, a different perspective can totally change your viewpoint.

h. Always ask, *"What are my assumptions?"* What is it that you are assuming to be true about the situation?

i. What if your assumptions were wrong? What if you were preceded on the basis of false information?

Always be open to the possibility that you could be completely wrong in your current course of action. Be open to doing something completely different.

2. The discipline of daily Goal-Setting:

Focus and concentration are the essential qualities for success.

a. Start by asking, *"What do I really want to do with my life?"* Ask this question over and over again until you get a clear answer.

b. Imagine that you had ten million dollars cash, but only ten years to live. What would you immediately do differently in your life?

c. Imagine that you have no limitations. That you could wave a magic wand and have all the time and money, all the education and experience, all the contacts you needed to achieve any goal. What would you do then?

d. Buy a notebook and write in it every day. Begin by writing out ten goals in the present, positive and personal tense. Begin each goal with the word "I" followed by an action verb.

For example, you could write, "I earn $xx,xxx by December 31, 2022."

e. Every day before you start your day, rewrite your top ten goals in the present tense, as though you had already achieved them and you were reporting on this success to someone else. Rewrite your goals without looking back to the previous page. Rewrite them from memory. Watch how they grow, develop and change over time as you rewrite them each day. Many people have said that the discipline of daily goal setting has transformed their life and far faster than they had ever imagined. The discipline of Daily Time Management:

Rule: *"Every minute spent in planning
saves ten minutes in execution."*

The more you plan, the better you use your time, and the more you accomplish. Plan your life and live your plan. Begin by making a list of everything that you have to do. The best time to write your daily list is the night before so that your subconscious can work on it while you sleep.

Organize the list by priority before starting work.

Practice the 80/20 rule, which says that 80% of your results come from 20% of your activities. What are they? For more on this go to my fourth book www.5minutemotivator.com, page 80 😬

Use my ABCDE method to set priorities. This is based on considering the consequences of doing or not doing a particular task.

A = Must do - serious consequences for non-completion

B = Should do – mild consequences for non-completion

C = Nice to do – no consequences for non-completion

D = Delegate – everything possible

E = Eliminate – everything you can to free up more time- or as Jiminy Cricket said, "accentuate the positive, eliminate the negative"

3. Organize your list daily:

Start on your tasks first thing in the morning, this is where the 5-minute discipline comes handy. Discipline yourself to concentrate single-mindedly on your most important task. Stay on it until it is 100% complete. The discipline of good time management spreads to all your other disciplines. It has immediate payoff in improved results, and long-term payoff in terms of the quality of your life work.

4. The Discipline of Courage:

Courage requires that you make yourself do what you should do, that you deal with your fears rather than avoiding them.

a. The biggest obstacle to success in life is fear of failure, expressed in the feeling that, *"I can't! I can't! I can't!"*
b. Courage is a habit, developed by practicing courage whenever it is required.
c. As **Emerson** said, ***"Do the thing you fear and the death of fear is certain."***
d. Make a habit of confronting your fears rather than avoiding them. When you confront the fear and move toward it, especially if it is another person or people or situation, the fear gets smaller and you become braver.
e. Repeat the words to cancel fear, **"I can do it!"** over and over, to build up your courage and confidence.

5. The Discipline of Excellent Health Habits:

Your goal should be to live to 100 in superb physical health.

a. Design and imagine your ideal body. What would your body look like if it was perfect in your own estimation? This is your goal.
b. The key to health and life can be summarized in five words, "Eat less and exercise more."

c. Develop the discipline of exercising every day, even if all you do is go for a walk. Exercise is best done in the morning, immediately after you get up, before you have time to think about it. If you do this for 21 days, it will become part of your regular routine for the rest of your life.

d. Eliminate the three white poisons: flour, sugar and salt.

e. Eat more salads and lighter foods; eat before 6pm and eat half portions.

f. Get regular medical and dental check-ups. They can add years to your life.

g. Use the Michael Jordon method: ***"Just do it!"***

6. The Discipline of Regular Saving and Investing:

Resolve today to get out of debt, stay out of debt and become financially independent.

Your goal, and everyone's goal is to achieve financial independence as soon as possible in life. This requires continuous financial discipline with every dollar you earn. The key is for you to save 10%, 15% and even 20% of your income throughout your life.

a. Because you are probably in debt already, begin by saving 1% of your income and discipline yourself to live on the other 99% until this becomes a habit.

b. Increase the amount of monthly savings to 2%, 3% and eventually 10% and 15%. Discipline yourself to live on the balance.

c. Rewire your thinking from *"I enjoy spending"* to *"I enjoy saving."*

d. Delay; defer major purchases for 30 days.

e. Investigate before you invest. Two thirds of investment success comes from avoiding mistakes. Invest as much time in studying the investment as you invested to earn the money in the first place.

f. Pay cash for as many things as possible. Get rid of your credit cards. When you pay cash, the amount you are spending is far more visible and painful.

g. ***"If you cannot save money, the seeds of greatness are not in you."*** (W. Clement Stone)

7. The Discipline of Hard Work:

Goal: Develop a reputation for being a hard, hard worker.
"The harder you work, the luckier you get." (Thomas Jefferson)

The average work week in America is 40 hours but many work only 32 hours.

The average person wastes 50% of the workday in idle chit-chatting with co-workers, extended coffee breaks and luncheons, personal business, reading the newspaper and surfing the internet.

Rule: *"Work all the time you work!"*

Start one hour earlier, and immediately get to work.

Work harder, through your lunch hour, all day long; don't waste time. Work one hour later; be the last to leave. Use this time to wrap up all your work and plan your next day. Three extra hours of work will translate into 6-8 hours of productivity.

Ask; what is the most valuable use of my time right now? Whatever your answer, work on that every hour of every day. If you get distracted, or interrupted, repeat over and over, *"Back to work! Back to work! Back to work!"*

8. The Discipline of Continuous Learning:

"To earn more you must learn more."
Jim Rowan: *"Work at least as hard on yourself as you do on your work."*

a. Read books in your field 30-60 each day. This will translate into one book per week, 50 books per year.
b. Listen to motivational material or books in your car as you drive from place to place. This will amount to 500-1000 hours per year.
c. Attend seminars and take courses given by experts in your field. One idea from one course can save you years of hard work.
d. The average income in America increases at 3% per annum. With compound interest, the average person doubles their income every 22 years.
e. With the additional knowledge and skill, you can apply to get better results, you increase your income at 10%, 15% and even 25% per year.

- 10% per annum increase means that you double your income in 7.2 years.
- 25% increase per annum means that you double your income in 2 years and 8 months.

f. Work on yourself as if your future depends on it, because it does.

9. The Discipline of Persistence:

The greatest test of self-discipline is when you persist in the face of adversity, and you drive yourself forward to complete your tasks 100%, no matter how you feel.

Courage has two parts:

The first part is the courage to begin, to start, to launch forward with no guarantees of success.

The second part is the courage to endure, to persist, when you feel discouraged and want to quit.

a. Your persistence is the measure of your belief in yourself, and in what you are doing.
b. The more you believe in the goodness and rightness of what you are doing, the more you will persist.
c. The more you persist, the more you will tend to believe in yourself and what you are doing. The principles are reversible!
d. Persistence is actually self-discipline in action.
e. Self-discipline leads to self-esteem, a greater sense of personal power, which leads to greater persistence, which leads to even greater self-discipline in an upward spiral.
f. *"Persistence is to the character of man or woman as carbon is to steel."* (Napoleon Hill)
g. You take complete control over the development of your own character. Eventually, you become **unstoppable**.

10. The benefits of practicing self-discipline in every area of your life are many:

1. The habit of self-discipline virtually guarantees your success in life, both with others and with yourself. It will make you a better, stronger person by persisting when you feel like quitting.
2. You will get more done, faster and of higher quality with discipline than with any other skill.
3. You will be paid more and promoted faster.
4. You will experience a greater sense of self-control, self-reliance and personal power.
5. Self-discipline is the key to self-esteem, self-respect and personal pride.
6. The greater your self-discipline, the greater your self-confidence and the lower will be your fear of failure and rejection. Nothing will stop you.
7. With self-discipline, you will have the strength of character to persist over all obstacles until you eventually succeed.

Begin today to practice self-discipline in every area of your life. Persist in this practice until self-discipline comes to you as automatically and as easily as breathing in and breathing out. Your future will be guaranteed. Begin by Identifying one fear in your life and then discipline yourself to deal with it, to confront it, to do whatever it involves, as quickly as you possibly can. The payoff for identifying a fear and confronting it is tremendous, it gives you the courage and confidence to go through your life and deal with every fear-inducing situation. Begin today to practice self-discipline in every area of your life. Persist in this practice until self-discipline comes to you as automatically and as easily as breathing in and breathing out. Your future will be guaranteed.

Remember, the past is history, what's done is done. The future is a mystery, but, this moment of life, right here, right now is the PRESENT. So, unwrap your PRESENT, your gift, which is the GIFT of life. So say goodbye to ordinary, it's time to give it the extra and become extraordinary. If you develop a **"Can't Stop Me"** attitude, no one or nothing will hold you back. If I could do it, so can you. Now it's your time, your turn. Thinking Successfully is the beginning to developing a **"Can't Stop Me"** attitude.

Always remember the way that we think has the same effect on our outlook as the way that we speak, and positive thinking has long been heralded as a factor that can influence the odds of success. That's partly because taking the optimistic view can reduce stress, declutter our thought process and actually allow us to focus more on the job in hand - making it a self-fulfilling prophecy.

First stop thinking that life is some game to be won. No, it isn't. The richest man on earth, the most successful man, your colleague who you are jealous about for getting a promotion, the girl who rejected you— everyone is eventually going to Die. Who's the winner? No one.

How can you make the best out of this ride? Just do your best that you can in life. Be the best you, you can be. I am proud to say although I'm far from perfect," I can honestly say, *I'm the best me I can be."*

The one thing I will promise you out of life is you won't get out of it alive. So if you only have one life to live, live it. Go for it, do it now.

COACH KAPLAN'S LESSONS FOR LIFE

- **Failure**—can often be an eye opener, it will wake you up — and teach you how to eventually win. Success teaches you to enjoy life and fires you up to do things that you love and to see your purpose and what you should do to get there.
- Be open to learning encourage yourself to learning. Never stop learning.
- Be curious. Curious about everything.

Ask questions - Why? What? How? Where? When? Who?

- Any problem in life—Identify the solutions and distractions and eliminate the distractions. Remember you can always do something about the problems life gives you. Learn how to grow as a person while creating healthy, happy relationships. The best way to do this is to create a fulfilling lifestyle filled with love and positivity.
- **Make mistakes**. Ask questions. How can you do better? Start over. Try again.

- **Learn skills.** As many as you can. Easy skills. Difficult skills. Different skills. Lecturing, golf, carpentry, cooking, even learning another language. Just anything. But keep learning.
- **Participate.** Participate in everything whenever you get an opportunity. It doesn't matter if you lose and if you're bad at it. keep at it, practice with persistence leads to perfect.
- **Experience Failure.** Fail. Fail. It's okay to fail. You will learn a lot more than a person who passed the first time in doing things. It's how you respond to the failure determines your ability to be successful in life.
- **Create.** Create anything. Whatever the idea. Go out there and try and create. Even at a smaller scale. Make time and space and create.
- **Time is ticking.** So much to do in such little time. Feel that. Feel that you are running out of time.
- **Push yourself.** Don't just sit in a comfort and safe zone. Take risks. These experiences will help you gain confidence and the resources to deal with uncertainties of life.
- **What are you doing for the community?** What are you giving? Think about that. Be a part of your community.
- **Don't hurt others.** There is no need for that. Live and let live.
- **Appreciate the beauty around you.** Practice mindfulness. Be present. If you stop for a second there is so much to see. Notice them. This helps to reduce your stress, anxiety, improves focus.
- **Learn to be self-sufficient.** You are not boring person. Learn to love yourself, enjoy your own company.
- **Learn to forgive.** Know that forgiveness and trust are important.
- **Learn to take accountability.** The consequences of your choices. Take Responsibility of the choices you make. How you react to something is in your hands.
- **Your attitude towards life shapes how you experience things.** Accept life as it comes to you. This will empower and equip to whatever comes your way.
- **Be Grateful.** Gratitude helps you to lead a content and Fulfilled life.

Every moment of evert day you should focus on what you want to happen and work towards it, reminding yourself that, like Wayne Gretzky said, *"You miss 100% of the shots you don't take"*

Can't Stop Me

Only you can decide what success looks like, but ultimately it doesn't matter - hopefully these tips will still apply whether you want to become a competitive gamer, the country's leading expert on science or the best dad in the universe. With enough passion, talent and commitment, and a **"Can't Stop Me"** attitude you can be a success at anything. Good luck.

"Nothing is impossible, the word itself says "I'm possible!"

—Audrey Hepburn

CHAPTER 19

Kaplan's Life Lessons

"The best way to get started is to quit talking and begin doing."

—Walt Disney

So now you know the only difference between possible and impossible is two letters—I.M. So in conclusion, I wish to share with all of you the practical constructs of life which I have learned, realized, and implemented throughout my life. I have penned down 75 life lessons that have stuck by me either as maxims taught by my dad or lessons that I practically embraced and implemented in my life over the years.

"When you truly know what makes you happy and when you really follow your joy, that's what increases your chances of success."

Aunt Gloria Punyon

"What is the point of success if we're not enjoying it?"

Elsie Kaplan

The words above were some of my mother's last words. On this winter day, I saw 249 patients, yes 249 in one day. Mom had to be put in the hospital as she had pneumonia caused by the flu. Now remember this some 30 years ago. As I entered the hospital she knew I was upset about something, she said "what the matter son"

I said, *"Mom today I set a record I saw 249 patients, I really wanted 250, so I missed it by one"*

Her reply was, *"son be grateful for the 249 that trusted you, came to see you, not the one stupid person that didn't"*

My mother passed on that night, that was her last lesson to me, one I will never forget.

For the first part of my life, I really thought work was just about making money, buying stuff, and increasing your net assets. Now work is about expressing yourself and being creative. It's about making a contribution, showing the world who you are. Why? Because I wanted everything, my father never had. I wanted the American dream. So now I ask you, what is success? What does success look like?

Success comes in all shapes and sizes. My CEO when I was the President of Nutrisystem was Thomas McMillan, 6'11". From Tom, a former NBA veteran and three term Congressman, I learned the power of a positive mindset. To understand why mindset is everything (especially when it comes to your success, fulfillment, and happiness), it's important to understand what success looks like. Because it's not just about wealth, accomplishments, or external approval…it includes being happy.

Many of us overachievers face a dilemma that I call **THE OVERACHIEVERS DILEMMA.**

There's a vicious cycle that many overachievers fall into. First, you work hard to succeed…only to find that success doesn't bring the happiness and fulfillment you imagined. And so, you double down on what you do best (work harder, push more).

Rinse and repeat.

Before you know it, you're on the edge of burnout and craving something more in life (only to feel guilty about that because…shouldn't you feel grateful for all that you have?). This is why I will leave you with my 75 rules for a successful life.

The problem isn't just that you're working too hard; it's that you're working to meet the expectations, values, and priorities of society and other people. So, **FROM THIS DAY FORWARD, PUT YOURSELF FIRST AND FOREMOST.**

This is not always easy to do and is not a unique problem for us overachievers because we're gold star collectors. However, earning respect from others and being seen as a leader is important – and so we often adopt a definition of success that's based primarily on what other people want of us.

When working towards a definition of success, not entirely your own, it's easy to push your own priorities aside. That's because success brings with it new responsibilities and obligations. And so, something has to give. . . which is usually your own priorities (it's the easiest thing to push down your list).

But because your list of obligations continues to grow, your values and priorities have been pushed aside entirely before you know it. That's when you end up:

- *losing self-confidence,*
- *uncertain about what you want,*
- *questioning your decisions,*
- *feeling bitter (even resentful), and*
- *ruining once strong relationships.*

That's not exactly a formula for a successful, happy life. And it's why mindset is everything when it comes to succeeding in life. . . because your mindset is the foundation for how you feel about yourself and your place within the world.

Here's the deal...success starts from within. It's not just about achievement or wealth. You must also feel content with who you are and your decisions.

Nor is success one-size-fits-all. Your success definition should be based on your specific strengths, values, needs, and priorities. Because they are what make you uniquely you (and what bring you purpose, meaning, and happiness).

That's why it's so important to redefine success on your terms (from the inside out) so that you can include your strengths, values, and needs within that definition. I've covered my secrets in my COACH KAPLAN'S RULES FOR A SUCCESSFUL LIFE

As my valuable confidantes on my life's journey are shared in this book, I wish to share the practical constructs of life with all of you that I have learned, realized, and implemented throughout my life. I have penned down 75 life lessons that have stuck by me either as maxims taught by my dad or lessons that I practically embraced and implemented in my life over the years.

My only wish for all those who have accompanied me so far on this word tour through my life is that they will be sure to cherish the lessons imparted through these quotes, maxims, or valuable morals as listed here.

COACH KAPLAN'S LIFE RULES

1. Life isn't fair, but it is still better than the worst.
2. Your road to success is always under construction.
3. Even a clock that doesn't work is still correct twice a day a day – It is all a matter of how you use the situation to your convenience.
4. You do not necessarily have to be a millionaire to live like one.
5. If you want to lead the band, you have to face the music.
6. Even if you fall flat on your face, you're still moving forward.
7. There are no mistakes in life; you only learn lessons, which create scope for improvement in you.
8. If you're in a poker game and you're not aware of who the Mark is in the first five minutes of the game, then *you're the Mark*!
9. A fish can only get caught if it opens its mouth. Remember - Don't be a fish.
10. The difference between possible and impossible is two letters – I'M.
11. When life puts you in a doubtful dilemma, just take the next small step.
12. The one outcome of life that I can promise you would face is not getting out of it alive.
13. The reality is, life is too short – Enjoy it while it lasts.
14. The vitamin of friendship is *B1*; if you want a friend, then *Be One*.
15. Your best friends in life are those who bring the best out of you.
16. Your job will not take care of you when you are sick - It is your friends and family who will.
17. Clear off your credit card debts every month.
18. You don't have to win every argument. Staying true to yourself is contentment and arguing in the face of ignorance is foolishness.
19. In life, you have two choices: you can always be happy, or you can always be right.
20. It is okay to cry with someone. However, crying alone imparts a level of healing beyond our comprehension.
21. When it comes to chocolate, resistance is futile.
22. Make peace with your past so that it doesn't screw up your present.
23. It is only fair and completely acceptable to let your children see you cry.

24. Don't compare your life to others; you have no idea what their journey is all about.
25. The grass is not always greener on the other side; the grass is greener where you water it the most.
26. If a relationship you share with someone needs to be a secret, you shouldn't be in it.
27. Everything can change in the blink of an eye. However, God doesn't blink, so you do not need to worry.
28. When in doubt, take a deep breath; it calms the mind.
29. Get rid of anything that isn't useful - Clutter weighs you down in many ways.
30. Whatever doesn't kill you essentially makes you stronger.
31. It is never too late to be happy, but it's all up to you and no one else to manifest that happiness.
32. When it comes to chasing what you love in life, you must never take *no* for an answer.
33. Burn those scented candles, spread the exquisite bedsheets, wear clothes that make you feel handsome, beautiful and confident – you deserve all the pampering every single day of your life, for all the hard work you do.
34. Don't save it for a special occasion – Realize that today is special.
35. It is good to over-prepare, but once that happens, you must go with the flow.
36. Be eccentric now – Stop waiting for old age to wear purple.
37. The most important sex organ is the brain.
38. No one but you are in charge of your happiness.
39. Frame every so-called emotional, mental, internal, and external catastrophe with these words, *'In five years, will this matter?'*
40. Always choose life.
41. Forgive, forget and foster measures for betterment, avoiding any regrets.
42. What other people think of you is none of your business.
43. Time heals almost everything. Learn to give time.
44. However good or bad a situation is, it is bound to change - Change is an imperative process in life.
45. Don't take yourself so seriously - No one else does!
46. Believe in miracles.

47. Don't try to audit life through and through. Show up and make the most of it now.

48. Growing old beats the idea of dying young.

49. Your children have only one childhood; let them live, let them cherish it, and be a part of their ecstatic childhood memories that will go a long way.

50. All that truly matters, in the end, is that you loved.

51. When you harbor bitterness, happiness will dock elsewhere.

52. Everyone is gifted – You must remember to open your package.

53. Average is the best of the worst and the worst of the best.

54. When you point a finger at someone, you have three fingers pointing back at yourself.

55. Step outside your literal and figurative boundaries every single day, for miracles are awaiting your presence in places unknown and almost everywhere.

56. If you were to throw and stack up your problems alongside others', trust me, you would willingly and immediately grab yours' back.

57. Envy is a waste of time. Accept what you already have and stop looking for what you think you need.

58. The best is yet to come – Be patient and hopeful.

59. If you cannot see the bright side of life, polish the dull side.

60. A genius is a person who aims at something that no one else can see, and he eventually hits the right spot.

61. No matter how you feel, even on a bad day of your life - Get up, dress up, and show up. You stop looking for an excuse, and life will stop making excuses and delays in the path of your success.

62. There are no speed limits on the road to excellence.

63. You have to do what others fail to do to achieve what others failed to achieve, believing that you can.

64. Ignoring the facts does not change the facts.

65. Life is about choices; choose wisely.

66. Follow the path of your heart, and you will know you have made the right decision.

67. Only humans have free will - the will to be free.

68. There is no right way to do the wrong thing.

69. Build a reputation of delivering more than you initially promised, but never compromise that reputation by delivering less.

70. No one can stop you from reaching your goals unless you give them the power and allow them to do so.
71. Life is for living, loving, laughing, and learning; not just whining, worrying, and working.
72. No matter what your state of health, wealth, or happiness may be, you can always strive to become healthier, wealthier, and happier.
73. If you see the invisible, you can do the impossible.
74. Life isn't tied with a bow, but it's still a present – Learn to live in the present, for it is indeed a gift.

What a ride my life has been. Everything has a backstory; a past that it carries with it. The chair you're sitting in was most likely a tall tree from some unknown wilderness. Years ago, the feather pillow you sleep on was part of a duck or a goose's body. When you sit in your chair, you probably don't think about the tree, and when you fall asleep, you probably don't think about the duck or goose. But have you ever considered how each of them came to be the way they are today?

Wow, it was fun looking back, but now I'm looking forward. And from here on in, so should you. There's still more work to be done.

My life has been a wonderful adventure. Who would have guessed that this prematurely born baby from Jersey City would dine with three US Presidents, be honored by his university, get featured in USA Today Newspaper, including this book write 7 books, with four and now hopefully five #1 Bestsellers? This former athlete, whose career was ended by knee surgery went on not only to become a doctor, but to specialize in sports and disc injuries. I'm proud to have worked with dozens of professional athletes and numerous Hall of Famers from virtually every sport 69 years ago? And now my youngest son's walls are adorned with all the professional athletes he's treated. This is a legacy I am proud of.

Not only that, but I became a father a grandfather, the Temple's President and was subsequently honored to become Chairman of the Board. I ran a public company on Wall Street that was losing roughly a million dollars every month and turned it around and made it profitable inside of one year. I was blessed to be featured on practically every network television Good Morning show and talk show. Today, I've been married to the girl of my dreams for 41 years and counting. I been blessed with a partner of which we have worked together 34 years. I started from scratch and owned six clinics, wrote six best-selling books, four of which were #1 bestsellers, and I am now serving as the CEO of Disc Centers of America, one of the country's largest disc treatment companies, with over 167 clinics. Imagine I came to Florida in 1978 in a broken-down Pontiac Catalina and only $500 which I borrowed from the bank with an overdraft check. I came with a dream and a positive mindset. I live the American dream and so can you if you can master 3 words; **"NEVER GIVE UP."**

The truth of life is that there are seven billion of us, and who we are is due to our life experiences. Only we know our journeys; only we know what we've faced, encountered, and what has shaped us into the people, we are now. Everyone has an explanation for their actions, their loves, and their lives. That is what distinguishes each person from the next, like each raindrop stands out in a sea of similarity.

We are, after all, raised in a society that is solely concerned with the ultimate product. Therefore, the trip, the difficulties, and the *'life'* are simply not acknowledged, and in many cases, forgotten. The judgmental glasses that society has implanted in our eyes often distort our perspective, and we fail to perceive things for what they are. As a result, we overlook the trip, which is the most important aspect of life because it was the voyage, the trials, and the stumbling blocks that brought us to present-day heaven.

Every action, every decision, and every thought have a purpose. We must accept that, just as someone else will never entirely comprehend our situation, we will never fully comprehend their situation from their perspective. For us, a minor stumbling block could be a dream come true for someone else. A friend's odd habit could be the result of a former ailment. So rather than passing judgment on anything or anyone, we should endeavor to comprehend their backstories, their unique and fascinating adventures.

Perhaps then we will realize that the world is a wonderful place and that life is truly a gift.

The journey known as life is a lovely one. The journey begins when you decide where you want to go and what you want to accomplish. Tell them the external environment is swaying you. Many examples of people around us who aspired to succeed can be found in this book, and their efforts led to their achievement. Each of them undoubtedly had their own definition of success.

Even if you haven't thought about your destination yet on your life's journey, it's never too late, and there's always tomorrow. Perhaps today now is the time for you to look within yourself for the places you've always dreamed of. That destination lies in every one of us, waiting for you to find the key to unlock it so you can experience it.

My friends know you have all the power and resources you need to take the journey you want to take. Your own intrinsic wisdom will push you to remain firm and not be affected by the external environment. It's your life, your trip, and you're the only one who can decide where you want to go.

So, today, let us put down our judgmental glasses and try to understand the rationale behind everything that happens to us. Let us strive to comprehend and acknowledge why something is the way it is. Let us embrace the adventure that is life. "There are no mistakes in life, only lessons," I've often remarked. In closing I'd like to share some final thoughts and philosophies I've learned and embraced along the way that hopefully may be useful to you, as they were to me as you embark on your own journey.

> *"It's not whether you get knocked down,*
> *it's whether you get up."*

—Vince Lombardi

"There are no mistakes in life, only lessons."

Life is like a complex puzzle however when all these pieces come together, not only does your work move toward greatness, but so does your life. For, in the end, it is impossible to have a great life unless it is a meaningful life. And it is very difficult to have a meaningful life without meaningful work. Perhaps, then, you might gain that rare tranquility that comes from knowing that you've had a hand in creating something of intrinsic excellence that makes a contribution. Indeed, you might even gain that deepest of all satisfactions: knowing that your short time here on this earth has been well spent, and that it mattered.

So in conclusion, I challenge you to improve your life. The world is full of opportunities waiting to be seized and as you've seen, new ones turn up every day. The key to most of these opportunities is taking action—action fueled by desire and complemented by energy. I challenge you to take action now.

I love to finish all my books with a challenge to you the reader; I challenge you to decide every day to be the best you can be. Remember, the key is to not change the world, but to change yourself.

Imagine that in the **Game Of Life**, you own a bank account that credits your account each morning with $86,400. However, it carries over no balance from day to day.

Every evening the bank deletes whatever part of the balance you failed to use during that day. What would you do? Draw out every cent, of course!

Each of us within us has such a bank account—it's called TIME.

Every morning, we receive 86,400 seconds for the day. Every night it writes off as lost whatever TIME you have failed to invest.

Life carries over no balance of TIME. It allows no overdraft. Each day it opens a fresh new account for you. Each evening it burns the remains of the day. If you fail to utilize your daily deposits of TIME, the loss is yours. There is no going back. There is no drawing against the 'tomorrow'.

You must live in the present on today's deposits. Invest it wisely so you derive the utmost in health, happiness, and success. The clock of life is running. Make the most of today, every day. Invest your 86,400 seconds wisely and deliberately. In life you can always get more money, but time spent is lost forever.

- *To realize the value of ONE YEAR, ask a student who failed a grade and was held back*
- *To realize the value of ONE MONTH, ask a mother who gave birth to a premature baby.*
- *To realize the value of ONE WEEK, ask the editor of a weekly newspaper.*
- *To realize the value of ONE HOUR, ask the person holding on for his or her life.*
- *To realize the value of ONE MINUTE, ask a person who missed their plane.*
- *To realize the value of ONE SECOND, ask a person who just avoided an accident.*

Treasure every second, every minute and every hour, of every day, for the rest of your life. Live each day as it is your last. My wife and I were as close to death as you can come, we appreciate the little things and realize life is for living.

At the end of your life you only have three things that matter: your friends, your family, and your memories. During my coma, it was these three things that I held on to, that I cherished, that brought me back to life.

If you were told you were going to die, how much would you pay for one more hour with your family? It is at these moments that we realize that time, not money, is life's most valuable commodity. Live a life with no regrets and give thanks to your friends and family because they shared their time and their life with you. They believed you were someone special enough to spend their lives with you.

Remember that time waits for no one.

The past is history.

The future is a mystery.

But this moment of life, right here, right now is the gift.

*That is why we call it the **PRESENT**.*

I challenge you now to appreciate your gift and make use of your present. The future is right here, right now. Take the time to write down your goals and create a personal plan of action to get what you want out of life. Invest your 86,400 seconds a day wisely. To change yourself, to change your life. Don't spend another second, minute, hour, day, month, or year of your life settling for less than you deserve. Give life all you've got. Life is not only a challenge, but an opportunity. Life is complex with its paradoxes of pain and pleasure, success and failure. You just need to search within yourself.

I challenge you to get excited about life. You have 86,400 seconds every day to make a difference. Use them wisely. Remember each day is a new day. The only one that can stop you is you.

The most valuable thing is life is time. You can spend money, lose money, and you can earn it back. But time, once you spend it, it is gone. My final lesson is spend your time on this planet wisely. Enjoy each day, each moment, every second of every day.

The clock is ticking—go to work.

Good luck!

 *E*pilogue

The key to happiness and success is simple: simplify your life. Give thanks for all you have.

It's the implementation part that is hard, but here are the rules to live by to help you with that:

Coach Kaplan's Guide to Happiness.

1. Believe in Yourself, but Be Aware of Your Limitations

The first step to accomplishing all your goals and making your dreams come true starts with this simple realization that you are human:

You are not perfect and you can't do everything alone.

Always keep things realistic. Don't put so much pressure on yourself that you find it hard to move; trust yourself to deliver what you need to, but also be prepared to cut yourself some slack.

Own up when you make a mistake. Set goals and enjoy the journey.

2. De-clutter and Simplify

You have a thousand different things screaming for attention:

You have to tidy up the kids' room again; you have to do the dishes and laundry; and the never-ending household chores are waiting. You have to organize your calendar and make room for more appointments; make time to socialize; help the kids with homework; and make a gazillion school runs.

Don't even get started on what needs to be done at the office.

Let's get one thing straight—you cannot accomplish anything unless you get yourself some of the clarity that comes from creating space in your life, in your relationships and your environment.

You need to reduce, cut back, simplify—Only then will you stop the feeling of being overwhelmed and rushed.

Give anything you haven't used for the past 3 years to charity. Get organized

Enjoy the concept of enjoying without owing and appreciating without acquiring.

3. Use Everything in Moderation

This is something I live by, be it work, socializing, family commitments, overeating, shopping, or watching too much TV—it helps with every single thing.

Embrace the philosophy of "having enough":

There's no need to go to extremes, so exercise common sense and learn to curb any obsessive behavior.

Spend less money than you make. watch your diet and watch less TV.

4. Keep Things in Perspective

I admit there will be times when nothing will go your way, and you will find yourself fighting battles, fixing problems and minimizing damage all day long.

We all have those days, and it is too easy to get caught up in the drama. Get a handle on things: this, too, shall pass.

Your child will get better soon, the noisy neighborhood parties will end, your backstabbing colleague will get transferred (we can hope, can't we?), and there will be actual days where you tick off all the items on your to-do list.

Don't sweat the small stuff. Have an open mind.

5. Treat Others How They Want to Be Treated

You might end up getting in trouble if you try treating others how you want to be treated, instead of how they would like you to treat them.

For instance, if you are not a phone person, you might not call your friend because you assume that they feel the same way you do, which may not be the case.

Try to be sensitive to the needs of others, and occasionally going out of your way to do something for them.

Try not to judge. Be generous; try to do something nice for somebody on a regular basis.

6. Family First

My priority has always been my family, and when I left Wall Street to start my own coaching career for the flexible hours it has provided me. Running a Public Company was a 24/7 job. However, even then I was always there for my sons and even while working on Wall Street, I never missed a game of theirs. Some days I'd fly from Washington D.C., back to Florida for a game and back to D.C. in the morning.

That doesn't mean that my work is not important—it just means that I have to operate in a way that works for me and my family.

How important is it to you that you spend time with your family? Are you making sure that your work doesn't prevent you from doing just that? What sort of arrangements have you made to make it happen?

You don't have to stop living your life for your family members, but you'll feel far less guilt if you prioritize and make time for them.

7. Pay Attention to the Moment

Stop thinking about what happened in the past or worry about what might happen in the future.

Live in the moment and learn to savor each one.

8. Have a Positive Mindset

You are what you think all day long.

If you have nothing but negative thoughts racing through your ahead, then that's what you are going to get, so try shifting to a more positive outlook on life.

You will be surprised to see that whatever you wished for will start to manifest itself around you.

"Whether you think you can, or you think you can't—you're right."— Henry Ford

9. Educate Yourself

The most interesting people are the ones who take an interest in life and never let go of the "beginner's mind". They discover learning opportunities and continue to grow, both personally and professionally.

Be a life-long learner. You don't have to get old to become wise.

Read good books. Try to learn something new every day. Take courses in subjects you enjoy.

10. Be Passionate About Something

There are some people who are so bursting with energy and vitality that others feel compelled to listen to them and feel drawn to them.

Passionate home cooks, budding interior designers, gourmet chocolate lovers, antique collectors—just try asking them a question about their interest and they will talk your ears off.

You want to be that person:

Someone who's full of love for something significant.

Have one meaningful hobby that encourages you to follow your passion, and you'll begin each day looking forward to something special.

11. Always Be Reflective

Do you ever think about yourself in moments of solitude?

What makes you, you? What makes you tick? What bores you to death? What sort of things do you dream of? What can't you get over? What regrets do you have of your past?

Take some time to think about those things and you'll understand yourself more clearly and deeply. You'd be surprised at the life-changing impact such reflection can bring.

12. Surround Yourself with Supportive People

Three things can change your life: friends, books and your thoughts.

Choose them wisely.

Avoid naysayers and party-poopers.

13. Banish the Word "Perfection"

Listen to what you tell your children: always do your best and forget about the rest.

You are expert enough. Strive for excellence, not for perfection.

14. Fix It or Deal With It, Stop Whining About It

Nobody likes a person who complains all the time.

If you look around, you'll see many people who have been dealt a bad hand but are making the best of things.

Don't blame others for your problems. Don't make excuses. Don't be overly sensitive. Don't be a drama queen.

15. Remember Things That You Are Grateful For

Try this exercise:

Whenever you are feeling low, make a list of all the things that make you happy, joyous, and grateful.

A beautiful family, adoring kids, kind friends, health, happy home, a job that pays the bills, surprise dinner prepared by a loving spouse, a blog, favorite books and keepsakes, unexpected twenty-dollar bill in your jeans pocket.

Everything counts.

After you've done this, consider what has happened to the feelings of doom and gloom. It is impossible not to be cheered up after remembering all the fantastic things you have in your life.

Be grateful, and always make room for more happiness.

16. You Can Have It All, Just Not at the Same Time

There is no greater truth than this:

You cannot have everything at the same time. You have only 24 hours in a day and need to take care of your relationships, work and spirit.

One any given day, the focus will shift. Some days your children have to go to after-school care because you have an important meeting, while other times work has to take a back seat because of a sick child with a high fever.

Sometimes you just need to chill with your girlfriends because it has been ages since you last took a break.

You don't have to do everything all at once, and life doesn't have to be complicated.

Simple living is mindful living.

Coach Kaplan's Things You Should Be Thankful For

These are crazy times, daily we live in fear of a deadly virus. Craziness in politics. We are a country divided. There is so much that is wrong with the society we live in. There is so much about ourselves that we wish to change. In an attempt to make ourselves better and to change our society, many times we forget to be thankful, yes grateful for the things we do have. We focus so much on the negative that the positive loses its place in our hearts.

Here is a list of little and big things we all should be thankful for.

1. Your Life

No matter how you think it is, it is a gift. So many individuals don't get a chance to make it as far as you did.

Disease, poverty, famines, and droughts claim thousands of lives each year, but you were lucky. You got to live, to survive, to exist and to be able to dream. Be grateful for your life.

2. Your Situation

Wherever you are, if you're reading this you are already in a better situation than the hundreds of millions of individuals who are struggling to have two square meals a day. Be grateful for your situation.

3. Your Friends

They're the family you picked. Think of the crazy inside jokes, the embarrassing memories, the late-night phone calls and the fact that they've always got your back. Be grateful for that priceless relationship.

4. Your Parents

Your biggest fans and most honest critics. The only beings who could possibly love you more than you could ever love them. Not all parents are great, I agree, but they did choose to let you live and gave you life.

Be grateful to your parents for their support, their encouragement, for their strength and undying love. Be grateful for the opportunity of life that they gave you.

5. Your Courage

You've lived so long; you've come so far. You made it despite heartbreaks and pain, though disappointment and failure. Yet here you are, alive, motivated and rearing to go.

Remember to be grateful to whatever is giving you the will to drag yourself out of bed and face the world. Be it your motivation, your goals, your God, whatever, be grateful for the courage.

6. Your Strength

The fact that you didn't break down that once. The time when you supported your friend in despair, that time you smiled for the family photo when all you wanted to do was to cry, but you didn't.

Be grateful for your strength to face your troubles and overcome your sorrows.

7. Your Mind

A complex science, a firm friend. Your mind can wander to destinations unknown and yet be back to the present in a fraction of a second. It keeps you hoping, dreaming, thinking. It is in essence a part of what makes you, you.

Be grateful for your mind's ability to contribute to making you who you are.

8. Your Heart

Scared, wounded, healed, and still up for more of the same, your heart is like the spirit of a three-year-old. No matter how much it bears, it bounces back. If it were to stop even for a second, your life could be in danger.

Be grateful for you heart for its mettle.

9. Your Senses

To touch, to smell, to see, to feel all the beautiful feeling we take for granted. Think of a day when you couldn't feel. Think of the misery if you couldn't taste. Think of the beauty that you would miss out on if you couldn't see.

Be grateful for your senses that make the world so pretty.

10. The Things You Love

Everything you love gives you joy. It becomes a part of you and can easily make you smile or tear up.

Be grateful for its presence and its effect in your life.

11. Your Belongings

Your bag, your clothes, your couch, your table, everything that's yours has a story. Even if it's boring, it's a story. When you got it, why you got it, how you got it, when you used it, every little detail works its way to make your life more complete.

Each story captures a moment in your life that will never come back. Be grateful for those moments hidden in your belongings.

12. Your Tears

Remember that time you cried in joy? That time when you thought you couldn't be happier? Do you also recall that terrible night when you thought your heart couldn't take any more?

13. Your Mistakes

A clouded judgment, a tinted perspective, an unfair remark, that stupid, stupid, phone call. Some mistakes that were forgiven and some that weren't. Some mistakes that warranted an answer and some that didn't.

Every mistake helped you grow, to learn, to understand. Be grateful for the wisdom that your mistakes enabled.

14. Your Life Lessons

A lesson could be anything. Basic etiquette, the touch of a hand, the path back home, the stranger who helped, the little girl you learned to console.

A lesson in life is one that only experience can enable. With every lesson learned, you're one step more experienced than you were yesterday. Be grateful for the experience.

15. Your Mentors

Be it your family, friends, professors, or bosses, be grateful for those individuals who took time out of their lives to help you. To make you feel more competent and give you the cheat sheet of life that they never had. Be grateful for their guidance.

16. Your Happiness

Happiness is a misunderstood, often misquoted commodity. To be loved is to be happy, to be an artist is to be happy, to walk in a park alone with your thoughts is to be happy.

Happiness is how you define it. Many people are robbed of their happiness for they often try to follow someone else's definition of it. It's a rare commodity today, one that the world is scrambling to own. Be grateful for your happiness.

17. Your Disappointments

With every disappointment that you encountered, be it academic, emotional, physical, artistic or mental, you got a little stronger. Your disappointment temporarily saddened you though, taught you to overcome the sadness and be happy again.

Be grateful for the strength your disappointments gave you.

18. Your Job

For all the hard work you put in and for the job that pays your rent or mortgage. It may not be the best yet, but it could help you get the best.

It's one door that will lead to another. It's a door that you had to fight to get to. Be grateful the door opened.

19. Your Enemies

Your enemies taught you about the world the way that no book or reality show could. They taught you how to fight, how to be true to yourself and, most importantly, what not to be like.

Be grateful to your enemies for showing you who you never want to be.

20. Your Teachers

They encouraged you, corrected you, motivated you and applauded you, asking for nothing in return from you. Some you loved, some you didn't, yet they cared for you all the same.

Be grateful for their time and effort that they spent on you.

21. Your Heartbreaks

Each heartbreak made your heart s stronger, wiser, more experienced. It gave you the wisdom to tell between loyal and faithful, a lie and a truth, and eventually between reality and expectations.

Your heartbreaks taught you to bounce back and introduced you to your quieter side and your best friends. Be grateful for that knowledge.

22. Your Laughter

To be able to extract humor from a situation is nothing short of a talent, a gift if you will. To be able to look at something with such an eye that you couldn't help but laugh.

Be grateful for the talent that enables you to laugh.

23. Your Body

It's able, it's healthy. Be grateful that your body is responsive, healthy and yours. Your body is yours alone and for that be grateful.

24. Your Pain

The funny thing about pain is that when you feel it, it hurts so bad; but when it's gone, you can't remember how it felt.

You have an idea that you hurt but not how much. Be grateful that it's over, that the pain you once felt is no more. And the pain you feel will slowly die out.

Be grateful for the pain for it introduced you to a greater joy after it passed.

25. Your Siblings

Your first and last friends, your partners in crime, your shoulders in despair. Your siblings are the best thing that could ever happen to you.

Whether it's an inside joke, an anniversary gift, a heart break or even plotting a plan, they're always there and always on your side. Be grateful for your siblings.

26. The Sun

Every day, it comes and spreads its light over all of us. Unselfish and kind, its warmth spreads in every direction.

Be grateful for the sun, for without it, food wouldn't grow, and your body wouldn't experience its tender warmth.

27. The Trees

Ask any child, they'll tell you why. But if there isn't a child around, let me tell you.

Trees make the world prettier, give us fruits and purify the air. Be grateful for the selfless trees that allow us to live so well.

28. Your Privileges

No matter how few privileges you have, at least you have some. You may work towards a fairer society and that is awe inspiring, but don't forget to be grateful for the knowledge of their existence and the power to utilize your privileges.

Be grateful that you know your privileges.

29. Your Choices

Your choices—good or bad—were yours alone. You were lucky to have an opportunity to make your choice, to do as your heart desires and to be able to pick from among options. You were lucky that it wasn't just one way.

Be grateful for the opportunity to make your own choices.

30. Electricity

If it's hot, we have fans. If it's cold, we have heaters. Imagine those who have nothing.

Be grateful that you have electricity to pamper yourself. It's not a right, it's a luxury.

31. Drinking Water

Every day on the streets on television, I see children begging for mercy, for food, but even more so, for water. Be grateful for the water you drink. For the ease of the availability of that water and the purity of the water.

Be grateful, for millions are dying because they don't have water. For water, too, is a privilege.

32. Your Name

It's an identity you were born with. Your name gave you a place in the world. It doesn't matter whether you changed it, or kept it or hate it, it's your first, not only, identity, but an identity, nonetheless.

Be grateful for an identity.

Here you'll find 60 very solid things to be thankful for in your everyday life. These are great reminders for you to treasure everything you have.

33. Good Health

Even if your health isn't great, it could be worse and you likely still have some working parts to be thankful for.

34. Money in the Bank

Having just a few coins makes you richer than most people on Earth.

35. Good Friends

Often, it's the quality of friendships, not the quantity.

36. Freedom of Religion

Being able to worship whomever and however you want is something many people don't ever experience.

37. Your Parents

Even if they're dysfunctional, they gave you life.

38. Weekends

There's something magical about weekends.

39. Having a Partner

Being in a romantic relationship can teach you so much about the world and yourself.

40. Pets

Pets offer one of the best examples of unconditional love. We love our Golden Doodle Gucci

41. Learning from Mistakes

If we never made mistakes, we wouldn't learn from them, so it is one of those things we should be thankful for.

42. Opportunity to Get an Education

The opportunity to attend school is something many people don't have

43. Having a Home

Whether you live in an apartment, a mansion, or a tent, having a place to call home is something to be thankful for.

44. An Ability to Read

If you're reading this right now, you have a lot to be thankful for. Thanks for reading my book.

45. Breathing Fresh Air

Being able to step outside to breathe in fresh air is a good reminder how many little things we should be thankful for. Trust me after being on a ventilator for 8 plus weeks, breathing fresh air is a gift.

46. A Bed to Sleep

A bed is one of those things that's easy to take for granted, until you don't have one.

47. Laughter

Without laughter, the world would be a sad place.

48. Safety and Security

Being able to wake up without immense fear frees us up to really live life. Yes, fund the police.

49. Cars

Without cars, it would take a lot longer to get our activities done.

50. Sunshine

The sun's warmth can brighten any day. Living in Florida, you can appreciate the warmth of the sun and the impact of vitamin D 3

51. Time

Although we often don't think there's enough of it, time is something we shouldn't take for granted. And every talk I give, in every lecture my goal is to give everybody their times worth. In life you can lose money and get your money back, but once you lose time it's lost forever.

52. Clean Water

Many people on earth lack access to clean water. Who would've thought growing up, that a bottle of water would cost more than a Coca-Cola?

53. Cell Phones

Cell phones make talking to loved ones easy. If right now you're thinking of someone pick up your phone and give them a call, or a text.

54. Love

The world sure would be a different place if we lacked the ability to love. I am blessed to have a woman that loves me more than I love myself, for that I'm forever grateful

55. Books

Books provide an opportunity to enter another world all from the comfort of your own home. This is my seventh book, thank you for reading my books, and hopefully you'll help me become a five time #1, bestselling author.

56. Waking up Today

Simply waking up today means you have things to be thankful for. I want to ask my father what he was thankful for, he said *every day he puts his feet above the ground is thankful*", it took me a lot of years to truly understand that

57. Indoor Plumbing & Electricity

Indoor plumbing & electricity not only provides convenience, but they also power our appliances, and it spares us from disease. Something so simple, that we take for granted many people did not have 100 years ago.

58. Eyesight

Being able to see allows us to view the world's beauty. I have a friend named James, he's 100% blind who is married to a great woman Elza, and he lives every day with such passion, travels all over the country utilizing all of his senses to compensate for his sight, what an amazing man an amazing couple.

59. Your Mind

Being able to think, remember, and solve problems sure makes life easier. Remember the mind of the most powerful man in the world it's right out of life what you think, and helps make you what you become

60. Air Conditioning

Staying cool on a hot day is something people wouldn't have dreamed about in past centuries. Trust me, I couldn't live in Florida without it.

61. Children

Watching children laugh, grow, and dream can keep things in perspective. I am so blessed to have two great sons Michael and Jason to great daughter-in-law's Stephanie and Jessica, and two beautiful grandchildren so far Eleanor and Rory.

62. Oceans, Beaches, Lakes, Water Views

I've always been drawn to the water, living on or near the water is special. I loved my days in Bayville New York while in chiropractic school. Now living in Palm Beach Florida going out on my son's boat breathing that ocean air is amazing. Now if you're feeling stressed find the nearest bed of water and just sit there and meditate, good things will come from it.

63. Music

Music brings out new emotions. Every morning when I exercise, I love listening to music, when I drive I love listening to music, music is a gift that we all get to appreciate daily.

64. An Internet Connection

It's hard to believe how easy it is to take the internet for granted, seeing how none of us had just a couple of decades ago. Where would I be without it, I don't know, but I am so grateful.

65. Armed Forces

Our lives would likely be very different if we didn't have protection from the armed forces. My dad taught me this. Imagine what our life would be like today, if we did not win World War II.

Realizing all the things you should be thankful for is the first step, practicing gratitude is what you should start doing:

Conclusion on finding things to be grateful for

In life we have so many little things to be thankful for. However, it's the little things in life that make a big difference. Friends finding gratitude in your heart shouldn't be hard, and if you struggle, it might mean you should make it a priority. Life is wonderful no matter where you live and what you do. And we all are obligated to enjoy it and appreciate it. There are countless ways to express gratitude: by writing a letter of gratitude, a card, saying it out loud, whispering it in the darkness of the morning, or writing it in an email, a journal, or as I did in a book.

Never measure your gratitude, and never think of how many things you can be grateful for. Just let it flow and notice how easy it becomes to find it in your heart every day. Remember, there is no better time than now and no better day then today.

ONE ...
One tree can start a forest;
One smile can begin a friendship;
One hand can lift a soul;
One word can frame the goal;
One candle can wipe out darkness;
One laugh can conquer gloom;
One hope can raise your spirits;
One touch can show you care;
One life can make the difference,
be that one today.

Made in the USA
Las Vegas, NV
21 October 2021